T0226140

Bitcoin and Lightning Network on Raspberry Pi

Running Nodes on Pi3, Pi4 and Pi Zero

Harris Brakmić

Apress®

Bitcoin and Lightning Network on Raspberry Pi: Running Nodes on Pi3, Pi4 and Pi Zero

Harris Brakmić
Troisdorf, Germany

ISBN-13 (pbk): 978-1-4842-5521-6   ISBN-13 (electronic): 978-1-4842-5522-3
https://doi.org/10.1007/978-1-4842-5522-3

Managing Director, Apress Media LLC: Welmoed Spahr
Acquisitions Editor: Aaron Black
Development Editor: James Markham
Coordinating Editor: Jessica Vakili

Cover designed by eStudioCalamar

Cover image designed by Freepik (www.freepik.com)

Distributed to the book trade worldwide by Springer Science+Business Media New York, 233 Spring Street, 6th Floor, New York, NY 10013. Phone 1-800-SPRINGER, fax (201) 348-4505, e-mail orders-ny@springer-sbm.com, or visit www.springeronline.com. Apress Media, LLC is a California LLC and the sole member (owner) is Springer Science + Business Media Finance Inc (SSBM Finance Inc). SSBM Finance Inc is a **Delaware** corporation.

For information on translations, please e-mail rights@apress.com, or visit http://www.apress.com/rights-permissions.

Apress titles may be purchased in bulk for academic, corporate, or promotional use. eBook versions and licenses are also available for most titles. For more information, reference our Print and eBook Bulk Sales web page at http://www.apress.com/bulk-sales.

Any source code or other supplementary material referenced by the author in this book is available to readers on GitHub via the book's product page, located at www.apress.com/978-1-4842-5521-6. For more detailed information, please visit http://www.apress.com/source-code.

Printed on acid-free paper

For my wife and our daughters.

Table of Contents

About the Author

Harris Brakmić is a senior software engineer from Germany. He has experience working with C#, Java, JavaScript, Angular, React, and NodeJS. Occasionally he has worked on projects targeting Android and iOS platforms. He discovered Bitcoin a few years ago, but decided to approach it differently. While most people working in the cryptocurrency space were looking for quick gains, Harris ignored the whole monetary component and concentrated on learning Ethereum's programming language. Ethereum itself is an alternative blockchain implementation that unlike Bitcoin script offers a turing-complete programming language, Solidity. Gaining a solid understanding of the programming behind cryptocurrency in general, he returned to Bitcoin to see what he could do with the world's most popular cryptocurrency.

About the Technical Reviewer

Sai Yamanoor is an embedded systems engineer working for an industrial gases company in Buffalo, NY. His interests, deeply rooted in DIY and Open Source Hardware, include developing gadgets that aid behavior modification. He has published two books with his brother, and in his spare time, he likes to contribute to build things that improve quality of life. You can find his project portfolio at `http://saiyamanoor.com`

PART I

Enter Bitcoin

CHAPTER 1

What Is Bitcoin?

There are four major factors that make up Bitcoin—money, decentralized network, Proof-of-Work, and time. We'll explore each in this chapter to understand the basics of what we're going to be working with.

Money

Bitcoin is money. In my humble opinion, this is the simplest and, at the same time, most precise definition of Bitcoin. Of course, there is much more beneath it as Bitcoin's fundaments reach very deep into many different areas of science. There is cryptography, information science, computer science, probability, logic, economy, game theory, just to name a few. However, in the end we're still looking at Bitcoin as money. In this book we will learn about Bitcoin mostly from its technological perspective by building concrete examples with Raspberry Pi 3, Pi 4, and Pi Zero, but nevertheless, we will also touch a few bits of its history and theory that underpin it.

At the very beginning, Bitcoin might appear as very complex, hard to grasp, maybe even a chaotic system, that's seemingly trying to "reinvent the wheel". In the end, we not only have money but too much of it, actually.

There are hundreds of different monies out there. And most of them are digital as well. These days we're more and more using credit cards or online payment systems like PayPal than the old-fashioned paper cash. And even companies are now trying to establish their own cash, like

© Harris Brakmić 2019
H. Brakmić, *Bitcoin and Lightning Network on Raspberry Pi*,
https://doi.org/10.1007/978-1-4842-5522-3_1

Facebook with its Libra currency. The road toward a cashless society is nothing exceptional anymore but merely a question of time.[1] Therefore, a legitimate question would be: *Why do we need Bitcoin at all?*

For this question to be answered, we'd have to define money first. However, not being an economist,[2] I must consider myself unable to fulfill this task completely[3] and will therefore give a simplified definition by stating that money is a *concept* rooted in *human practice* that functions as *medium of exchange, store of value,* and *unit of account.* In general, the task of *acting as money* could be fulfilled by any *medium* that's able to fulfill the aforementioned *requirements.* There is no definition of what the nature of this medium should be nor that it has to be a physical thing, but only how it should behave. Therefore, anything that can serve us to

- Pay for something (medium of exchange)

- Save value for future consumption (store of value)

- Calculate price of something (unit of account)

could be considered money. In fact, throughout history human cultures have developed and used various media for these purposes,[4] for example, seashells, beads, necklaces, and even giant stones.[5] But all these different monies have one thing in common: they're scarce. This is what makes them valuable and generally acceptable as money.

The fact that one can't that easily create new money out of thin air assigns each "coin" its value. The scarcity can be achieved by different means, for example, the fact that gold is rare, because there is only so much of it within Earth's crust, or that it's exceptionally hard to create giant stones from Yap. We can say that the harder it gets to produce

---

[1] www.forexbonuses.org/cashless-countries
[2] For the economic fundamentals, see *Economics in One Lesson*, Henry Hazlitt
[3] More about the history of money in *The Ascent of Money*, Niall Ferguson, 2008
[4] https://nakamotoinstitute.org/shelling-out
[5] https://en.wikipedia.org/wiki/Rai_stones

something, it's value would be higher. Our modern paper cash too is very hard to produce. Just try to count all the counterfeit symbols on a single note. Bitcoin in this case is no different, as there will be only 21,000,000 of bitcoins in existence. The single unit, *bitcoin*, written in small caps to differentiate it from the underlying protocol, is limited to this number, and its production is getting smaller every 4 years. In an event called "The Halving", the production of bitcoins drops by 50% thus decreasing their emission. Currently, it's at 12.5 bitcoins per block, but in May 2020, it will drop to 6.25 bitcoins.

However, being practically oriented we instinctively know that today's monies or, more general, *monetary systems*, don't quite exactly fulfill all those requirements. Especially not when it comes to scarcity. The prices rise continuously, in some countries at a staggering rate, which leaves us with the question, why did the value of money drop? According to our previous theory, our money should have been scarce enough to maintain its value. This negative effect is what we call *inflation*, although I'd rather call it *price inflation* to separate it from the *money inflation*, but this is a separate topic that fills whole libraries,[6] and not even economists agree on it.

In any case the result is the same: what we have saved today will be, more often than not, much less worth when our children have inherited it from us. The sad reality is that one of the three properties of money can't be maintained with today's monetary systems. Our money is simply not a very good store of value.[7] Also, every now and then, those who are in power will decide that our money should be used for purposes contrary to our individual plans. Bank bail outs and even bail ins like in Cyprus 2013 are not impossible anymore. The global crisis of 2008[8] is yet another topic that easily fills libraries. I could continue with even more drastic examples, but these few lines alone should be sufficient to recognize that our today's

---

[6]https://mises.org/library/defining-inflation
[7]*The Ethics of Money Production*, Jörg Guido Hülsmann
[8]*Crashed: How a Decade of Financial Crises Changed the World*, Adam Tooze

money doesn't *function* the way we'd expect it to be. It loses its value, and someone else can take it from us against our will. Money that works the same way in practice, as it's been defined in theory, is hard to find. Of course, there is a certain group of people, often called "gold bugs", who are praising the advantages of gold as being non-inflatable and therefore an ideal store of value, but as we will see later, gold itself has certain inherent problems so that it could never compete with let alone outperform Bitcoin. Bitcoin is money that fulfills the three requirements, because

- Its supply is predictable and limited to 21 million bitcoins.

- Its inflation rate is predefined. Currently, it's 12.5 bitcoins per generated block. This rate halves every 4 years, with the next halving that'll happen in May 2020.[9]

- It's not controlled by anyone. That is, *it is decentralized*, as it has no intermediaries like banks or clearance houses. Nobody can change it, or take it from you, because of some political or strategic concerns.

- Everyone can use Bitcoin without permission. You don't even have to be human to participate. Any device could send and receive bitcoins just like its human counterparts, or cats, or dogs, etc.

- Its properties can only be changed when a supermajority of participating nodes agrees on a particular change. And this is an extremely hard process.[10]

---

[9]www.bitcoinblockhalf.com

[10]A good real-world example is UASF from 2017: https://www.weusecoins.com/uasf-guide

Consensus Rules of Bitcoin

These rules with all their technical details are what's being called the *Consensus Rules,*[11] which is what every participating Bitcoin node strictly follows. The Consensus Rules are basically code every participating node executes, which then helps them reach the *Emergent Consensus* on the current state of Bitcoin's blockchain. Although the rules hardwired in code get executed by every single node separately, they'll ultimately reach a Consensus on the current state of the decentralized network. It is important to differentiate between those two: the code inside a node and the finding of the consensus between participating nodes. The fact that nodes execute certain code part doesn't mean they'll blindly reach some predefined consensus, but moreover will have to find it out, for every block to be included in the blockchain.

We say that the Consensus *emerges* as result of the communication between nodes. Every 10 minutes, which is roughly the time needed to generate a new block, all participating nodes will react to data they've received from one another and ultimately find a Consensus that will be applied on this very block. And as soon as they've agreed on it, the game will start anew, because a new block will be generated, thus putting the nodes in the same state as before: they'll have to find consensus again. Such a strategy is needed to solve a decades-old problem called the Byzantine Generals' Problem.[12]

This problem deals with the question how nodes can agree on valid states in decentralized networks, where those can get damaged, behave maliciously, or simply be unreachable at certain points in time. One obvious solution would be to simply install some kind of "coordinating node", where all other nodes would have to register themselves, but in

---

[11]https://bitcoin.org/en/glossary/consensus-rules
[12]https://en.wikipedia.org/wiki/Byzantine_fault

case of Bitcoin, this is impossible, as it explicitly prevents centralization, censorship, and trusted third parties. A solution like a "registry of nodes" would make Bitcoin end up being just another variant of PayPal or Visa. In Bitcoin there are no governing bodies of any kind. Or as one can often hear in Bitcoin circles, there are only *Rules without Rulers*.[13]

With this we mean the encoded Consensus Rules running in every node. This fact makes Bitcoin resistant to external changes, which also makes it mathematically predictable in the future. Unlike our today's money, we exactly know how many bitcoins have been generated so far and how many will be generated in the future. We can easily calculate future *Halvings* and how long it'll take until the last bitcoin has been mined (it'll be in the year 2140).

If we take a medium that is resistant to sudden changes, that is, predictable and not controlled by anyone, that can't be changed because of some "important reasons", we easily recognize that these properties constitute qualities any medium must have to function as money according to our definition from the beginning. Therefore, Bitcoin is money. Or to distinguish it from the money we use today, Bitcoin is *hard* money. Given the fact that Bitcoin can't be found in nature, or touched, or smelled, the attribute *hard* might sound like an exaggeration. However, as the human progress continues, we will not only be continuously updating all the many devices and software around us but also our shared mental models and concepts. One of them is the understanding of *what money is* and what should constitute it. Thinking about it is a necessary prerequisite to understand Bitcoin in general, because taking only the technical perspective will make it look like yet another network or funny *nerd money* with questionable use cases (and sometimes also users).

---

[13]https://youtu.be/2tqo7PX5Pyc

Changing Our Mental Model of Money

Just like our perception of gold, paper money, and credit cards have changed over time, we will change our definitions of monetary systems of the future, switching from centralized networks with banks and other governing bodies, who decide who can participate and on what terms, to more decentralized alternatives, where your money is your money alone and can neither be seized nor its value diminished because of external factors. Censorship resistance will become an integral part of every successful monetary system.

It takes some time to grasp the profound changes and to accept that they affect us all at an individual level, but the earlier we begin to face some of our comfortable truths and start updating our shared concepts, the more likely we will have prepared ourselves to become independent actors in the paradigms to come and not remain mere spectators. Just like today when having a smartphone is considered a necessity, our successors will consider running a Bitcoin Node a necessity.

It will be hard for them to believe that once we had to use banks. Not to mention those funny "pausing of banking activities" on weekends, because banks were closed back then. The transition toward the new monetary system won't be easy or quick, as there never was any profound change without resistance and necessary learning processes, but the change is already there. Currently, it's mostly attracting early adopters, the usual idealists, and also a fair share of speculators. But just like WWW began as a project for specialists working in high-energy physics,[14] Bitcoin is a project that began in an obscure mailing list[15] for cryptographers and idealists from the *Cypherpunk* movement.[16] Who could have imagined back then that it'd become a multibillion industry one day?

---

[14]https://webfoundation.org/about/vision/history-of-the-web
[15]https://satoshi.nakamotoinstitute.org/emails/cryptography/1
[16]https://en.wikipedia.org/wiki/Cypherpunk

Decentralized Network

Bitcoin operates an open-source, permissionless, borderless, decentralized, censorship-resistant peer-to-peer network. Tens of thousands of nodes, many of them so-called *full nodes*, that contain the whole transaction index since its beginning in 2009 participate in validation and dissemination of transactions. Network participants create transactions, which very often simply transfer ownership of bitcoins from one party to another. As every transaction needs to be validated, before it can become part of a block, nodes are busy with sending and receiving them throughout the network. And roughly every 10 minutes, some of those transactions will get included in the next *candidate block* that was generated by nodes who are not only validating transactions but also creating new blocks.

These specialized nodes are what we call miners, because they're continuously generating special numbers, called hashes, at an extremely high rate. Those mining nodes collect incoming transactions and bundle them together in *candidate* blocks. Each time a miner creates a candidate block, it pushes them as fast as it can throughout the network so that other nodes can validate it. The success of validation depends on several factors. One of them is the existence of the aforementioned hash value, which must be of certain form.

This is how a block comes into existence. A node creates a transaction, which gets validated by other nodes. And then there are certain nodes that are creating blocks, which will contain this transaction as well. Bitcoin's network is home to various kinds of nodes, for example, miners, validating nodes (Full Nodes) and mobile nodes (SPV wallets), but all of them obey the same rules, the Consensus, thus making all participants just that: nodes. The Bitcoin protocol only knows nodes. There is no explicit handling of individual specialization of nodes, like the aforementioned mining functionality.

Public Blockchain

Being a decentralized network that serves for value transaction and ownership is opening several questions:

- How does the money, bitcoins, come into existence in such a network?

- If Bitcoin has no governing body, like a bank, then how is anyone supposed to transact money or own it in the first place?

- If nobody is taking care of money supply, how do we prevent the double-spending problem, that is, how do we make sure that money spent once cannot be spent again by the same party?

In our daily experience, we know where the money is coming from and who takes care of preventing double spends. In the beginning, a state and its agencies like central banks are issuing currencies. This money then is being forwarded to local banks, which use them to interact with businesses and individuals. They take care of every single transaction by utilizing *digital ledgers*, which trace all monetary in- and outflows. This method hasn't changed for centuries. The only innovation is that instead of physical ledgers as shown in Figure 1-1, nowadays computerized systems take care of transactions.

Figure 1-1. *Entries in a physical ledger*

Each time an individual or company takes a loan or deposits funds to an account, certain entries will be made or updated by a bank. Therefore, we don't have to do any bookkeeping on our own, as there is an *authority* doing the necessary checks. But Bitcoin, being a permissionless, decentralized system, has no such authority at all.

However, Bitcoin has its own ledger too, also called the *Blockchain*, that gets replicated in every participating node. More precisely, Bitcoin's blockchain is a "public" one, because anyone can participate in the process without asking for permission. Each time a new entry has to be inserted into the blockchain, all participating nodes will include this change into their own copies as well. From this perspective, sending money with Bitcoin looks no different than sending money via bank, or PayPal, or by using a credit card. Someone sent a certain amount of money, that is, created a *transaction*, and our distributed, or better, *replicated*, ledger got updated accordingly. What previously belonged to the sender now belongs to its recipient.

But unlike traditional ledgers, Bitcoin as a network automatically takes care of every transaction, because all participating nodes follow the same set of rules. Not having a central authority doesn't mean that Bitcoin has no rules or can't enforce them. Moreover, the same rules are found in every node and only when all of them have agreed upon a transaction will it be accepted as valid and can become part of a future block. Unlike traditional systems, where the power to decide is concentrated in a particular center, be it a person or a governing body, the rules of Bitcoin are located in every node, thus making any kind of authority or trusted intermediary unnecessary. Bitcoin's authority is decentralized and automatic. The network is its own authority. However, merely agreeing on inclusion of transactions isn't enough to properly answer questions from above. The *double-spend* problem is still with us, and we still don't know how the bitcoins get created in the first place. Spending bitcoins can only happen if we know how to create them. This is the point where we have to introduce another term: *Proof-of-Work.*

Proof-of-Work

Being a decentralized network of nodes who don't care about each other and can join and leave the network at will, there is a problem with introduction of new blocks and bitcoins. Why should a node include any block into its own blockchain copy? The question of validity of blocks goes hand in hand with the question of creation and ownership of bitcoins. Creation and validation of blocks must always lead to global consensus among all participating nodes to keep the network together. However, there is one important difference: while validation is very fast and inexpensive, the creation of blocks is extremely costly and requires vast amounts of energy to be spent for mathematical calculations, that produce hash values which must be included in each block. To check a block for its validity is a matter of milliseconds, but to create it needs minutes and great amounts of electricity. This is due to the mathematical nature of those hash values, which make any shortcuts in calculation impossible. The hash function used in Bitcoin is called SHA-256.[17] Hash functions are often being used to generate tamperproof fingerprints of other data, because it's very easy to generate a hash of data, for example, a book text. Good hashing functions are *collision-free*, that is, they don't produce the same hash for different input data. However, being *currently* collision-free doesn't mean that a hashing function will always return unique hashes. It simply states that until now nobody has found a mathematical method to successfully generate a collision.

We can use such functions to test the integrity of data, for example, to check if a copy of a document sent via e-mail represents the original. A hashing function would process this document as its input data and based on it generate a *digest value*, which functions as the *fingerprint* of data in question. One could later compare the hash of the original document with the hash of the copy. Even a slightly changed input value would lead to a drastically different fingerprint. This property is being used in Bitcoin to create blocks that have their own unique fingerprints, thus making them very easy to validate, because any later change, no matter how small, would immediately generate a completely different hash. This technique renders any manipulation attempts futile. This property is also being used by miners to search for the expected hash value, or *target*. As the contents of the block header comprise of data that can't be changed, like the hash value of the previous block, there must be a way to generate the expected hash values without invalidating already existing data.

To achieve this, miners use so-called Nonce values as shown in Figure 1-2, which can be changed, because they'll later also serve as input values for block validation. As the process of finding expected hashes is following the simple trial-and-error approach, as there are no known optimization techniques, the only option miners have is to keep on changing the Nonce until they've found a hash value that is smaller as the expected target, which is reflected in the number of leading zeroes.

---

[17]https://en.bitcoin.it/wiki/SHA-256

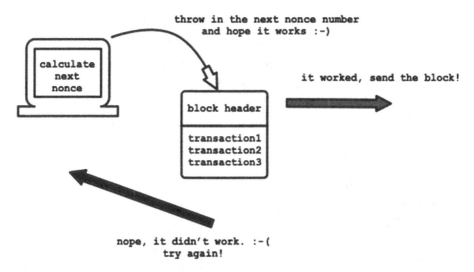

Figure 1-2. *Calculating Nonces to be included in the block header*

Imagine a miner who's continuously increasing the Nonce value, until it finds the target. As soon as this happens, the miner would create a block that contains a certain number of transactions plus the block header together with the Nonce and subsequently send it on its way throughout the network. The receiving nodes would read the block header, get the Nonce, and simply execute the same hashing function but this time without having to go through the ordeal of finding it as they'd only have to recalculate the hash value and compare its structure with the expected target. If the hash starts with the expected number of leading zeroes, the block will be accepted and included in the chain. To understand this operation better, let us examine the contents of a block.

Every Bitcoin block comprises of two parts: a list of transactions and a header. For now, we will focus on the block header and come back later to transactions when we meet Bitcoin's scripting language. As shown in Figure 1-3, a block header comprises of these parts:

- Block version.

- Hash value of the previous block.

- Hash value of the Merkle Tree,[18] which uniquely represents all transactions in this block by combining them into a tree of hashes. Any change in any of the transactions would lead to a different Merkle Tree.

- Block creation timestamp.

- Expected target.

- Nonce.

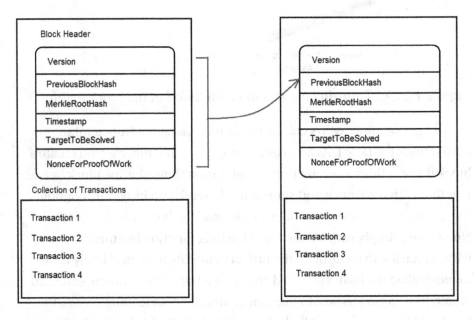

Figure 1-3. *Bitcoin block structure*

---

[18]A Merkle Tree is a special mathematical structure that creates a treelike structure of correlated hashes. https://en.wikipedia.org/wiki/Merkle_tree

These values will be used to produce a hash for the upcoming block. A miner would take all available values to feed the SHA-256 function and check if the result is smaller than given target. If it isn't, it would then increase the Nonce and try again, until either the value reflects the expected target or some other mining device has found a solution in the meantime. In this case, the "losing" miners would accept the new block by updating their own blockchain copies, throw away their own unsuccessful candidate blocks, and the race would start anew.

When we look at the structure from Figure 1-3, we recognize that Bitcoin's blockchain is a *back-linked list of blocks*. The data of a previous block header gets hashed and becomes one of the entries in its succeeding block header and so on. This in turn means that if you change anything in one block, you indirectly change all entries in all of the following blocks.

This is how Bitcoin prevents manipulations, because regardless which of the previous blocks got manipulated, for example, by changing the amounts of bitcoins spent, the immediate reaction would be a drastically changed block header hash value, which would affect its successor's block hash value. Any change would literally provoke a chain reaction. This is how Bitcoin solves the double-spend problem.

By using transactions and block hashes as input values for one-way functions, Bitcoin creates a structure, called the blockchain, that gets replicated over tens of thousands of nodes that validate all transactions and blocks. And just like block headers get hashed, the same happens to transactions as well. By using a mathematical structure called *Merkle Tree* (Figure 1-4), we create pairwise hashes of transactions. Those values then become new pairs in the upper levels of the structure, until there are no more pairs left.

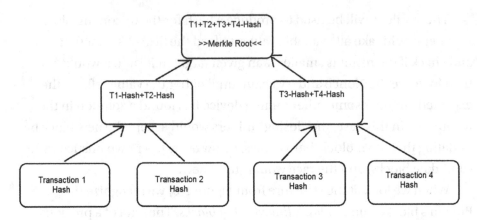

Figure 1-4. *Merkle Tree of hash values*

In case when blocks contain odd numbers of transactions, remaining transaction hashes get duplicated to balance out the structure. The final hash at the top then gets included in the block header, thus making transactions immutable. Any change in the transaction list would affect the Merkle Tree as a whole. This of course would also invalidate the block header and the block as well. Again, this technique makes any subsequent changes practically impossible, because miners that want to include such blocks would have to expend excessive amounts of energy not only for direct block manipulation but also to manipulate their predecessors and ancestors. The fact that it is extremely expensive to change already included data in Bitcoin's blockchain is one of the reasons that make it so valuable. The strength of Bitcoin isn't that it's needed to expend vast amounts of energy to create new blocks, but that one would have to expend even higher amounts of energy to change data already included in the blockchain.

A coin spent once can't be spent again, because changing the past in Bitcoin is not only mathematically challenging but also extremely costly. To change transactions in a single block, the attackers would have to have at least 51% of the overall network hash rate, which means gigawatts of electricity, and even if they were successful, they'd have to maintain the manipulation for at least six more blocks, because in Bitcoin a transaction is only then accepted as settled after six blocks have been generated and included in the blockcain after it. Bitcoin's defense is not only based on mathematics but also deeply rooted in the constraints of the real world. Bitcoin doesn't exist in a vacuum, as there are many participants with very often different goals.

Exchanges, for example, would reject coins coming from manipulated, that is, invalid, blocks, just like most of the individual investors would reject them as well. Trying to manipulate a single entry in Bitcoin's blockchain would provoke an immediate reaction of various participants. And there is no way to force others to accept those blocks and transactions.

Now the question is whether a miner should expend energy for attacking the network, which would fail anyway, or rather participate in the racing game to actually get rewarded by solving puzzles. The incentive structure of Bitcoin renders manipulative acts useless not only by making them costly but also by offering lucrative alternatives.

Figures 1-5 and 1-6 show the difference in the expected difficulty for the very first block and block 500,000.

Summary	
Height	0 (Main chain)
Hash	000000000019d6689c085ae165831e934ff763ae46a2a6c172b3f1b60a8ce26f
Previous Block	0000000000000000000000000000000000000000000000000000000000000000
Next Blocks	00000000839a8e6886ab5951d76f411475428afc90947ee320161bbf18eb6048
Time	2009-01-03 18:15:05
Difficulty	1

Figure 1-5. *Bitcoin's Genesis Block*

Summary	
Height	500000 (Main chain)
Hash	00000000000000000024fb37364cbf81fd49cc2d51c09c75c35433c3a1945d04
Previous Block	00000000000000000007962066dcd6675830883516bcf40047d42740a85eb2919
Next Blocks	000000000000000000005c9959b3216f8640f94ec96edea69fe12ad7dee8b74e92
Time	2017-12-18 18:35:25
Received Time	2017-12-18 18:35:25
Relayed By	BTC.com
Difficulty	1,873,105,475,221.61

Figure 1-6. *Bitcoin block no. 500,000*

Creating blocks in Bitcoin is a *racing game* of highly specialized machines, which do nothing else, but crunching values with the ultimate goal of being the first one, who solved the current puzzle. The more mining nodes join the network, the harder to solve the puzzles it gets as the difficulty algorithm adapts automatically to the hash rate of mining devices. The more hash power in being thrown into the game, the harder to solve the puzzles get. This racing game is ongoing since January 3, 2009, when the anonymous Bitcoin creator, Satoshi Nakamoto, started the first Bitcoin nodes that produced initial blocks.

And as every subsequent block is hardwired to its predecessor, the result is an immutable chain of blocks that is reaching back to its root, the Genesis Block.[19]

As roughly every 10 minutes a new block gets created, this also means that each time a new block got included in the blockchain, the racing game starts anew. To participate in this extremely competitive business means that each time one of your competitors solves the puzzle first, you've expended electricity without having received any reward. However, the more machines participate in the Bitcoin network, the more secure it gets, because the chance of manipulation is getting lower with every additional CPU cycle invested.

---

[19]https://en.bitcoin.it/wiki/Genesis_block

Every mining node is trying to be the first one that solved the puzzle, because it will make them eligible to write a special, and always the first transaction in the upcoming block. This special transaction, also called *coinbase*, contains the amount of newly generated bitcoins and the address of their recipient: the miner's own address. A block can contain many transactions, but the first one created contains the current bitcoin *reward* for the miner of this block. This is how miners get paid in the Bitcoin network and also how bitcoins come into existence in the first place. But block rewards aren't the only way to pay miners for their services. As miners usually don't generate empty blocks, but actually include many transactions, those who send them will have to include a properly calculated fee, which then will be collected by miners. Of course, transactions with higher fees will be likely processed faster, while those including lower fees will have to wait a bit longer.

The combination of Proof-of-Work, block rewards, and transaction fees is how miners get incentivized to participate in this highly expensive racing game without trying to manipulate the blockchain. Without rewards there would be much less mining activity in the network, thus making its security much weaker as the few participating miners could reorganize the network at will. The more expensive the racing game gets, the harder it becomes to take over the network.

Imagine a small network with only a hundred mining nodes based on off-the-shelf computers with standard x64Bit CPUs. Powerful competitors with only a few computers running specialized graphic cards for mathematical calculations could easily become the fastest runners, thus preventing other mining nodes from generating any of the future blocks. If they keep on generating the majority of blocks, they could also become powerful enough to decide *what* can become part of any upcoming block. Such miners could, for example, reject certain transactions, for whatever reason. They could only include transactions that pay a certain fee for example. In short, a network like that would become centralized and not that much different from any other legacy payment system, where regulators can decide which transaction is valid and which is not.

To prevent problems like these, the Bitcoin network reacts to changes in the overall computation power by increasing the hardness of the puzzle itself. Roughly every 2 weeks, which equals 2016 blocks, the *difficulty algorithm*[20] gets readjusted to keep the average time needed to provide a solution at 10 minutes. Therefore, the more miners join the network, the harder it gets to solve the puzzle. Basically, the number of leading zeroes in future hash values increases, that is, the expected target value gets smaller. This in turn increases the demand for new hardware to stay competitive in this vicious race, which in turn has an effect on the price level of Bitcoin.

It's a cycle where the price of Bitcoin is determined by the energy consumed to create bitcoins, which itself increases the incentive to participate and stay as miner in the network in the first place. These of course aren't the only participants in the network, as merely mining blocks would be pretty much useless, if there was no one willing to actually use them. Also, the mining itself isn't enough to keep the network secure as we need other actors who will take care of "reminding" miners to follow the predefined Consensus Rules.

This is the task not only of other mining nodes, who compete against each other anyway, but also of non-mining nodes, who don't participate in mining at all. Every Full Bitcoin Node, that is, a node that contains the whole history of transactions generated since the creation of the Genesis Block, is contributing to the overall security of the Bitcoin network by validating blocks produced by miners. By running a Full Node, like the ones we will be building throughout this book, you don't have to trust or rely on anyone as the Consensus Rules embedded in your node would automatically reject any nonstandard transactions and blocks.

If you are now asking yourself how a small Raspberry Pi Node could ever force a powerful miner to follow the Consensus Rules, imagine a

---

[20]https://bitcoinwisdom.com/bitcoin/difficulty

situation where a miner deliberately creates a block inlcuding a coinbase transaction that assigns him 1000 bitcoins. As we already know, in a decentralized network like Bitcoin's, the newly created block must be validated and accepted by the majority of nodes to become part of the blockchain, which in turn confirms the ownership of bitcoins and transaction fees assigned.

Being incentivized by Proof-of-Work and promised bitcoins from coinbases and transaction fees, all miners have an economic interest that the majority of Full Nodes accepts their blocks. However, there is no way for miners to force other nodes to accept a block, like the one with 1000 bitcoins in its coinbase transaction. Every node executes only its own code, and if the embedded Consensus Rules say that a block is invalid, then there is no way to make it valid by any means. Creating nonstandard blocks ultimately leads to rejection by Full Nodes and also to enormous electricity costs, because such miners would be paying money for mining blocks that nobody wants. This too is one of the security measures embedded in Bitcoin's ecosystem.

Bitcoin maintains a carefully aligned system of rewards, incentives, and punishments, that keeps all parties working together, although every participant actually only works for itself. In Bitcoin, every node can join and leave at will, but if a node wants to continue participating in the network, it must follow the Consensus Rules, because there is nothing else that could be done without other nodes noticing it. Any manipulation by any party would be rejected by the network, which ultimately leads to one or another kind of loss in physical space. This too is what makes Bitcoin so valuable in "real life", because people have to expend money, energy, and time to participate in it. The time factor, however, plays another, very significant role. Although the focus on mining and validating blocks constitutes a valid approach in understanding the complexity and different factors in Bitcoin's network, the time itself is what actually makes the whole ecosystem "tick".

Time

Without time the network would neither be able to create blocks nor to execute transaction scripts. It would simply not be able to come into existence and maintain its structure. As Bitcoin is completely decentralized and doesn't rely on any trusted 3rd parties, and even the most precise atomic clocks would constitute such parties, the question is: How does the network know what happened at which time? To generate a block by finding the needed target is a question of expended energy and processing power. To put transactions and blocks *in order* is but a question of time, because without time there would be no order at all.

And without order Bitcoin wouldn't be able to locate and validate anything. If my node says that it owns 10 bitcoins, then other nodes must somehow be able to validate that indeed *at some point in time,* my node participated in a transaction that gave it 10 bitcoins. Therefore, the most important function and the real reason why Proof-of-Work exists is to associate events with points in time. Receiving bitcoins, sending them, generating blocks, creating transactions, and so on are all *events.* But those must be *ordered* must be associated with some point in time, because without it, there would be no way to prove ownership of coins, not even a way to create them in the first place. The last part of this chapter therefore is dedicated for exploration of the time component in Bitcoin.

Nothing can exist without order, and Bitcoin's blockchain is no exception. In fact, even if Bitcoin didn't have a blockchain, but instead used a NoSQL database like MongoDB, for example, we'd still have to deal with questions like "when did this transaction happen?", or "when did address X receive those Y bitcoins?". Blocks must be ordered in a meaningful way, according to a time factor, to be able to answer such questions. But how are we supposed to create any order in a *decentralized* network that could never ask anyone "what time it is"? When any node can join and leave the network *anytime*, there is a problem of communicating the changes between nodes, and time is one of those changes.

Dealing with a system that's trustless by design, we also encounter the problem that no node is required to trust anything, not even time data. The blockchain, due to its nature as a closed system, can't use external tools like clocks or timestamp servers, which could tell it what time it is. As there is no way to ensure that all participants have received *the same information at the same time*, any clock, no matter how precise, would be simply useless. This would simply go against Bitcoin's design as decentralized network, because it would need some kind of controller that's taking care of delivering the same information to all participants without any delays or changes.

But because a blockchain relies upon a collective of independent entities, there is a problem of having the globally available knowledge of time. Therefore, our main question is, how can we create a notion of time in a decentralized network? Or, more general, is there a way to create a decentralized timestamp server? Surprisingly, the answer is the blockchain itself is a *decentralized, distributed timestamp server* and its Proof-of-Work mechanism is actually the solution for getting a proper notion of time. Simply spoken, a blockchain is a clock.[21] Not a typical clock though, but still, it has its own concept of time. The advantages Proof-of-Work provides, like securing the blockchain, keeping it immutable, keeping it at a 10-minute block creation time, and incentivizing miners are extremely important of course, but these wouldn't be possible if there was no time embedded in the blockchain itself. Without time the questions of security or immutability wouldn't exist at all as there would be no possibility to create anything of value in the first place. If we look into Bitcoin's white paper,[22] we find the entry shown in Figure 1-7 in the first page.

---

[21]https://grisha.org/blog/2018/01/23/explaining-proof-of-work/
[22]https://bitcoin.org/bitcoin.pdf

third party. Transactions that are computationally impractical to reverse would protect sellers from fraud, and routine escrow mechanisms could easily be implemented to protect buyers. In this paper, we propose a solution to the double-spending problem using a peer-to-peer distributed timestamp server to generate computational proof of the chronological order of transactions. The system is secure as long as honest nodes collectively control more CPU power than any cooperating group of attacker nodes.

Figure 1-7. *Bitcoin white paper mentioning the timestamp server*

The solution to the double-spend problem we already talked about is a *timestamp server* that generates proofs, which are *ordered chronologically*. To get anything of value in Bitcoin demands preventing double spends without exception.

And to double spend something implies the ability of going back in time and executing the same action again, or even multiple times, because without a notion of time, one could "replay" the same action over and over again. To prevent such actions, Bitcoin implements its own timestamp server solution, the blockchain. And because the blockchain defines and controls its own notion of time, there is no way for anyone to take control of it, that is, to redefine timestamps or even make some of them disappear. The time, as defined by the Bitcoin protocol, is *locked* within the blockchain, as it's become an integral part of it. If we look into an early version[23] of Satoshi's Bitcoin source code as shown in Figure 1-8, we can find this comment:

```
1599
1600        // put the main timechain first
1601        vector<CBlockIndex*>& vNext = mapNext[pindex];
1602        for (int i = 0; i < vNext.size(); i++)
1603        {
1604            if (vNext[i]->pnext)
1605            {
1606                swap(vNext[0], vNext[i]);
1607                break;
1608            }
1609        }
```

Figure 1-8. *Snippet from main.cpp from the original Bitcoin Client source code*

---

[23]https://sourceforge.net/p/bitcoin/code/HEAD/tree/branches/ multiplatform/main.cpp

It isn't needed to understand the whole C++ source code, just the line following the highlighted one. We see a *vector or blocks*, which is a term borrowed from mathematics, that means an array of blocks. Instinctively, we'd understand such an array as something *physical*, like a real chain of tangible blocks, put one after another. But, if we instead substitute physical space with time, we recognize the real meaning of the word "timechain" mentioned in the highlighted comment. These blocks aren't ordered *in space* but *in time*. Instead of counting blocks like *block at position 1, block at position 2, block at position 3,* etc. we could say *tick 1, tick 2, tick 3,* etc. And to make those blocks become an orderly line of ticks, we wire them together by using their individual hashes as integral parts of all block headers.

As the blockchain is a clock that's producing ticks, which exist independently from each other, we need hash values to put them in order. Therefore, each block-tick will at some point in time become the input value for the hashing function that will include its result into the header of the next block-tick. A blockchain contains time particles, which can be used to estimate if and when an event did happen. A transaction between two parties, for example, becomes an event that can be positioned in an *orderly line of ticks.* This constitutes the expected *order of things* so that we know, for example, how many bitcoins one has, when someone did spend them, when someone received them, and so on. The Bitcoin white paper itself actually never uses the term blockchain, which also gives us a hint that the correct emphasis should be put on time and not on space or blocks.

The blockchain, being a clock, allows participating nodes to work on creation and validation of blocks without ever communicating with each other, except when a solution has been found. Every node can work for itself, as long as it wants, without ever informing others what it is doing right now. The only thing they need to have in common is the same notion of time, because *each time* a node finds a solution by using the SHA-256 function, it will communicate it throughout the network, and every other node will then validate it by using its own copy of the blockchain (timechain) to reach a decentralized decision, the *Emergent Consensus.*

A possible solution offered by a mining node must be validated by other nodes which (hopefully) use the same blockchain as the one that just sent the candidate block. Therefore, it's in the interest of every node that it works on the same blockchain or, in this case, that it knows what time is.

The validation of solutions is basically a procedure that decides if a block should become the next tick. The time periods between blocks, which are on average 10 minutes as seen from our time perspective, are not known in Bitcoin. There is no time between two blocks that's visible in Bitcoin's network. It's not possible to ask the network what happened between two blocks. The only moment something could happen is when a block got included in the blockchain. There are no "gaps" in Bitcoin.

The question that now arises is, how do the participating nodes actually coordinate without communicating? If every node works for itself, the question of coordination becomes extremely critical. Without some kind of coordination, mining nodes could never be sure that their blocks have indeed been accepted by other nodes, and no single node could ever be sure that it has really validated every block from the correct chain.

The solution for this paradox lies in certain properties of the SHA-256 function.[24] The SHA-256 function is *memoryless*[25] and *progress-free*. These two terms come from statistics and mathematics (Probability). A function is memoryless, when future results are independent from past results. For example, when we're throwing a six-sided dice multiple times, the probability of getting a 6 is still 1/6, no matter how often we've tried it before. The statistical probability remains the same. The same applies for SHA-256 as generated results have no influence over future results. No matter how long a miner has been mining so far, any other miner has the same chance of getting the correct solution. It plays no role if a miner joined the network right now or has been mining for years. The only way to increase the *probability of*

---

[24]https://movable-type.co.uk/scripts/sha256.html
[25]https://en.wikipedia.org/wiki/Memorylessness

finding the Nonce is the hash rate miner provides. The higher it gets, the higher the probability of finding the Nonce will become.

Another aspect of the SHA-256 function is the fact that its *input set*, which means all numerical values one could feed into it, is known in advance. It's an integer value in range between 0 and 2^{256}. Although extremely large,[26] in fact larger than the number of atoms in the known universe, we can still say that every participating node would be able to find out whether a hash value is valid. And if the input set is known and there are no *collisions*, then the output set is known as well.

Every node that participates in Bitcoin's network already has the same set of possible values at its disposal and could anytime check, if a value produced by using a Nonce is indeed below a given target. This in turn also means that every node will only be able to find a value within this set, regardless which of the possible input values it took. This seemingly paradoxical property is what makes finding of hash values so hard and at the same time so easy to prove. Every node knows that a solution is guaranteed to be within the possible set of values of SHA-256, but because of its *memorylessness*, there is no shortcut to find it. This in turn makes it *progress-free*, because no matter how often a node has tried in the past to find a solution, each new step has the same chance as any other. A node could never increase its probability of finding solutions based on how long it has been working so far. A node that just joined the network has the same chance, because they all work within the same *numerical space* that's not giving them any shortcuts.

The problem is not if there is a solution or not but how to find it as quickly as possible. And the only known "optimal" way to find a solution with SHA-256 is by trying every possible Nonce, one by one, also called the Brute-Force method. This of course is anything but performant, and that's what makes Bitcoin's Proof-of-Work so expensive. And it also allows to

---

[26]https://learncryptography.com/cryptanalysis/why-is-2-256-secure

have an indefinite number of working nodes without demanding any kind of communication or coordination between them.

No matter where they are in space, the difficulty remains the same for every node. The only task they should do in public is sending the solution, if they want it. Even if we would be operating a "private mining node" that, for whatever reason, never publishes its Nonces, the aforementioned memorylessness of SHA-256 would keep the finding of future values still progress-free. Therefore, every node that joins the network, no matter for how long, affects the process of finding the valid solution for the current target. And as every node knows exactly what the current difficulty is, the range of possible solutions within the SHA-256 result space is the same for each of them. The difficulty is what drives this clock, as it keeps the velocity of solution finding at a constant rate, for every node, regardless of past results. Each time a node finds a Nonce and thus creates a new block, the blockchain knows that it happened *exactly at this point in time*. The only additional step needed is wiring up those blocks together by using their headers as input values for the hashing function. Bitcoin's blockchain gives us the exact time, which we then use to create an orderly line of back-linked blocks.

Summary

In this chapter we have learned the theoretical fundaments of Bitcoin. Having many faces, Bitcoin is fascinating but also too complex to understand at once. Its usage as money is the most prominent but also the only aspect that doesn't expect any deeper knowledge to start with, at least on a very basic level. From our daily experience with different monetary systems, we instinctively understand what the purpose of Bitcoin as money should be. However, being a truly digital cash, without touching the non-digital world, Bitcoin is hard to understand as technology, that has profound influence on our perception of it but also what money could be or, maybe even, *should be*. Being scarce, censorship-resistant, borderless, premissionless, open source, and trustless, this new kind of money is lots of things at once. So, what makes it "tick"?

This is where we introduce additional concepts like *Decentralized Network, Proof-of-Work,* and *Time*. Bitcoin's Network is based on a decentralized, replicated, append-only database, which we call the blockchain. To prevent replication of data, the so-called double spends, which by the very nature of the digital domain is actually impossible, we wire blocks together and implement the Proof-of-Work functionality to make later changes extremely costly. We also take care of ordering the events that happen in the network by making the blockchain work like a giant, decentralized clock, where every block represents a single "tick". To achieve this, we give Bitcoin its own notion of time that makes it independent from external factors, because Bitcoin knows no authorities or trusted intermediaries. And by using the special properties of SHA-256 hashing function, we take care of providing a global, space- and time-independent, decentralized environment for every participating node.

CHAPTER 2

Bitcoin Technology

In this chapter we will learn the basics of blockchain, addresses, transactions, and Bitcoin's embedded scripting language. We will generate addresses, create transactions, and send them through the network to explore the inner workings of Bitcoin's scripting engine.

Blockchain

Bitcoin's blockchain is an append-only database containing an ordered, back-linked list of blocks that's being replicated over tens of thousands of nodes, which continuously validate new blocks and update their copies according to the current consensus. Very often we can read descriptions of blockchains as decentralized and distributed databases, which I consider only partially correct. Although their decentralized nature is obvious due to the fact that every node maintains its own copy and only accepts those blocks which obey the Consensus Rules embedded in Bitcoin's code, the second part of the definition isn't quite correct. Bitcoin's blockchain isn't distributed but *replicated*, because every node must do the same work by executing the same Consensus Rules, before a block gets accepted as valid.

If the blockchain was distributed, the participating nodes wouldn't do the whole work, but only a part of it, because execution of Consensus Rules would be *distributed over many nodes* thus lowering the pressure on individual nodes. This, however, would be contrary to Bitcoin's design, where every node must execute every task individually in order to make

© Harris Brakmić 2019
H. Brakmić, *Bitcoin and Lightning Network on Raspberry Pi*,
https://doi.org/10.1007/978-1-4842-5522-3_2

changes in the blockchain exceptionally expensive. When every node has to do the same work and validate every transaction, then any attempt to manipulate those entries would become exceptionally expensive for any attacker, because one would have to cheat all of the nodes at the same time. Therefore, we should speak of blockchains as decentralized and replicated structures. The blockchain structure comprises of blocks that carry transactions which in most cases describe transfers of funds between two parties, but there also can be more complex variants with more than two participants as we will see in later chapters. As every block is linked to its predecessor, we call this structure *back-linked* (Figure 2-1).

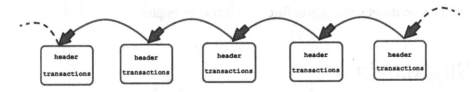

Figure 2-1. *Blockchain structure*

The link between two blocks is the hash value of the header of the preceeding block as we saw it in the previous chapter. Besides the header, every block also contains a list of transactions which carry information about the ownership of coins. A transaction typically assigns funds from one party to another. The technology behind Bitcoin's blockchain implementation is based on Google's LevelDB,[1] which is a very fast on-disk key-value store. Although the word "blockchain" associates with a structure containing *chained elements,* a better description of it would be a *stack*, with elements put on top of each other. In Figure 2-2 we see a stack of blocks, each back-linked to its predecessor.

---

[1]https://en.wikipedia.org/wiki/LevelDB

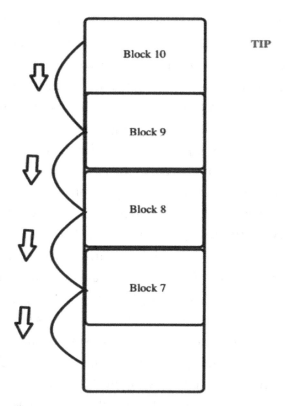

Figure 2-2. *A back-linked stack of blocks*

The topmost block is also called a "tip". Later, when we start learning how to use Bitcoin's RPC API,[2] we will execute commands that give us detailed information about a blockchain's state. Another term often used is "parent block" which means the predecessor of a block. As every block contains a hash as its identifier and links back to its predecessor, this block is then being called "parent" block.

---

[2]RPC stands for *Remote Procedure Call*. API stands for *Application Programming Interface*.

In the previous chapter, we have seen that all blocks in Bitcoin's blockchain ultimately go back to the very first block, the Genesis Block. Every block only has a single parent, but there could exist more than one "child block" that is not yet a *confirmed* member of the blockchain. Each time a new candidate block arrives in the network, there is also a mining entity behind it that wants to win the racing game. Getting blocks included in the chain is the only way to get rewards. And sometimes it comes to situations where multiple miners have created competing blocks which are valid according to Consensus Rules, but because they're representing different possible states of the future blockchain, nodes validating them will have to decide which of them will ultimately become the next "tip".

In such a situation, nodes would temporarily accept every valid block by creating several variants of the blockchain as shown in Figure 2-3. And as miners would continue their racing game by producing more blocks, the ultimate decision will be done later after new blocks have arrived. Those blocks would then extend one of the possible variants of the chain. And because a block can only have one parent, validating nodes would automatically select the variant whose upmost block is the parent of the newly arrived block. In the end, the longest chain variant would win, because it stands for the most work being done. Other variants of the blockchain, also called "forks", will get discarded.

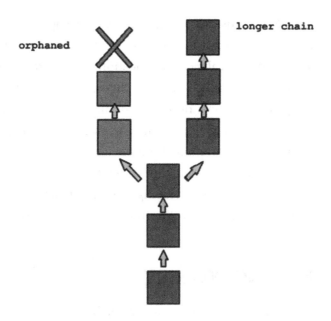

Figure 2-3. *A temporary fork with an orphaned and a winning chain*

These operations are nothing exceptional as the design of Bitcoin allows for this flexibility under the assumption that the majority of mining nodes is honest and not willingly manipulating the chain. But as we have already seen in the previous chapter, the competition in Bitcoin and its aligned system of rewards and punishments is keeping all of its participants acting honestly, because any other behavior would ultimately lead to severe monetary losses. This behavior is also a practical example on how the Emergent Consensus happens in the blockchain. By allowing several forks to exist, the Bitcoin protocol leaves enough room for nodes to find a solution which would be very hard to achieve if there was some hard-coded rule that would ultimately decide on what kind of block "deserves" to become the tip of a valid chain.

Moreover, such a rule would ultimately lead to a dangerous partition of the network, which would render Bitcoin unusable as currency, because several variants of "Bitcoin" could exist at the same time. To prevent this the Emergent Consensus exists, which allows participating nodes to resolve any "disputes" automatically. As Bitcoin nodes can join and leave the network anytime, there is always the question: *What is the current state of the chain?* As we will see on the following pages, a node must first take care of discovering[3] as many peer nodes as possible and also informing them about its own existence, before it can start processing any blocks. Also, it must get enough information about the current state of the chain, for example, about the current height and which services other nodes support. A decentralized network is forcing every node to find its own way "out of the dark", before it can start validating blocks and transactions.

Peer-to-Peer Networking

As no Bitcoin node can function without sharing blockchain information, the question is, how does it find others in the first place? The answer lies in the peer-to-peer, or P2P, network that nodes use to discover each other and exchange data. By default, every node carries a few hard-coded IP addresses and DNS entries that help it kick off the initial discovery procedure. Those nodes, also called *seed-nodes*, contain information about further nodes, which our node can then use to create a more detailed topology of the network. Being decentralized, Bitcoin's network has a *flat structure* without any servers so that every node must find its neighbors on its own, by trying to connect with other IP addresses.

---

[3]https://en.bitcoin.it/wiki/Satoshi_Client_Node_Discovery

A completely new node would use the eight hard-coded seed-nodes[4] to send them certain information about itself by using the *version*-message[5] that contains these entries:

- The protocol version it's following, like *70002*

- The services it supports, like *NODE_NETWORK* or *NODE_SEGWIT*

- The current time

- The IP address of the node it contacted

- Its own IP address

- A string describing the local client version, like */Satoshi:0.18.0/*

- Current blockchain tip[6]

The contacted node would then analyze this message and send *back* an acknowledgement message called *verack*.[7] After the node has contacted some of the hard-coded seed-nodes, it'd then receive a list of IP addresses of other validating nodes, which it can then use to expand its network topology. The seed-nodes are basically special DNS servers[8] that mimic the

---

[4]https://github.com/bitcoin/bitcoin/blob/0.18/src/chainparams.cpp#L123
[5]https://en.bitcoin.it/wiki/Protocol_documentation#version
[6]When a node starts for the very first time, it only has knowledge about the Genesis Block that's included in the Bitcoin source code.
[7]https://en.bitcoin.it/wiki/Protocol_documentation#verack
[8]https://github.com/sipa/bitcoin-seeder

DNS protocol by answering queries on port 53, the default DNS port. Each time a node sends a query on port 53, they send a list of IP addresses back. However, merely querying for IP addresses isn't enough as every node also tries to make other nodes aware of its existence. Therefore, a node would also send *addr*-messages[9] to its peers, which then would forward it to their own peers, thus expanding the reach of the new node. Also, a node can query other nodes by sending *getaddr*-messages to receive its peers' address lists. The strategy of this protocol is clear: to automatically discover, expand, and update the knowledge about the network.

One can also manually define or even disable DNS and peer discovery. To disable DNS completely, the Bitcoin client or daemon can be started with the flag *dnsseed=0*. To add further nodes, one can add their IP addresses and ports in *bitcoin.conf*, the configuration file of the Bitcoin client and daemon, with the entry *addnode*.[10] If peers are using the default TCP port 8333, then only the IP address is needed. If only a single seed-node is needed, the flag *seednode* can be used to define the DNS node to be contacted at the next client or daemon start.

To query information about connected peers, the command *getpeerinfo* can be used. Its output delivers a list of known peers and their client information. The contents returned look like this:

```
{
  "id": 0,
  "addr": "167.71.192.31:8333",
  "addrlocal": "35.200.105.117:59664",
  "addrbind": "192.168.0.87:59664",
  "services": "000000000000040d",
```

---

[9]https://en.bitcoin.it/wiki/Protocol_documentation#addr
[10]https://bitcoin.org/en/developer-reference#addnode

```
"relaytxes": true,
"lastsend": 1567747871,
"lastrecv": 1567747886,
"bytessent": 1574683,
"bytesrecv": 1831044,
"conntime": 1567533523,
"timeoffset": 0,
"pingtime": 0.187978,
"minping": 0.170567,
"version": 70015,
"subver": "/Satoshi:0.18.0/"
}
```

After a node has discovered multiple peers, it will start exchanging its data with them. In case of a completely new node, all it will have to offer is the embedded Genesis Block that starts at chain height 0. It will send a *getblocks* message as shown in Figure 2-4, which contains its highest known block hash. Its peers will find the hash in their own copies of the blockchain and respond with an *inv* message (inventory) containing the first 500 hashes of blocks that came after the last known block of the new node. The queried node then takes the hash provided and tries to find its position in its own copy. If it was able to locate it, it would then generate a list of 500 block hashes that are descendants of the hash from querying node.

The reason why peers answer with only 500 hashes is to prevent overwhelming the asking node. The asking node will then use those 500 hashes to send further *getblocks* messages to other nodes, which then in turn will send another 500 hashes that are located on higher positions in the chain.

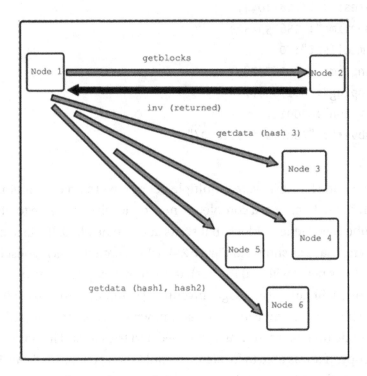

Figure 2-4. *Finding other nodes*

This way a node can easily send many queries that can be combined into an ordered line of blocks. To get full block data, a node would have to send a message called *getdata* that contains the hash of the block whose data should be returned.

The whole procedure of querying and updating peers might seem too complex, but one must not forget that in decentralized networks, every participant can go offline anytime without warning. Therefore, nodes are continuously updating and validating their connections to ensure that they always have the most reliable channels, because only those can ensure access to most recent blockchain data. The quest for peer nodes has always been a vital part of Bitcoin's network, and in the past, it has even used the IRC chat protocol for such tasks. The modern variants of Bitcoin Core client no longer use IRC, but the old source code is still available as an interesting artifact from Bitcoin's past.[11]

Node Types

Another important aspect in Bitcoin's P2P network is the specialization of nodes. Although the protocol itself doesn't distinguish between various types of nodes, there are configuration options available to maintain and operate nodes with different specializations. We have already mentioned the term *Full Node,*[12] without having properly defined it. A Full Node is any node that maintains its own wallet, has a full blockchain copy, and validates transactions without relying on any external service or node. Throughout this book we will be building Full Nodes and later also Lightning Nodes that are based on them.

But these aren't the only available types of Bitcoin nodes. There are also SPV nodes (*simplified payment verification*) that maintain a lighter version of the full blockchain, which needs much less disk space, and are therefore dependent on other nodes with full blockchain copies. One of the use-cases for such nodes are various mobile wallet applications. As the full blockchain copy consumes more than 250GB, we couldn't run such a node on a mobile device. But as we will see later, a mobile node

---

[11]https://github.com/bitcoin/bitcoin/blob/847593228de8634bf6ef5933a474
  c7e63be59146/src/irc.cpp
[12]https://bitcoin.org/en/full-node

only needs to download the headers of blocks which are always 80 bytes long. Currently, the space needed to save all those headers would be less than 50MB, which is not a problem for any modern smartphone. This is possible because blocks are chained together via their block headers so that the second half of each block, the transactions, can be discarded. Only when a mobile node needs information about a certain transaction it would have to issue a request against a Full Node that has the complete information saved in the blockchain. This configuration of course raises another question that has to do with the integrity of information being processed by mobile wallets. As mobile nodes would from time to time need external nodes to process their transactions, one could never achieve the same level of security and independence as possible with Full Nodes. This is a known trade-off that can be mitigated by using own Full Nodes as the only "trusted nodes" to communicate with. Many good mobile wallets offer an option to configure one or more Full Nodes as sources of transaction information.

Another important functionality we already talked about is routing, which is part of every functioning node. And of course, the mining functionality itself is available in every Bitcoin Core client, but only a subset of running nodes in the network are actually using it. Those functionalities can be combined as not every node has to have all of them activated. On the following pages, we will explore different node types and how they are being used.

For example, a mining node that's participating in a mining pool doesn't have to maintain its own blockchain copy and can off-load this responsibility to the pool itself. All it needs to know is the current difficulty and the transactions waiting in the memory pool (Figure 2-5).

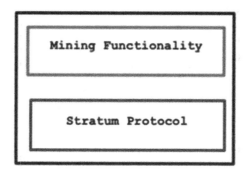

Figure 2-5. *Mining node structure*

Additionally, it uses a protocol for communication with the pool server. Very often this protocol is *Stratum,*[13] but in the future, there will be other mining protocols available, for example, *BetterHash,*[14] that's currently in development.

It is also possible to run a mining node without joining a pool through a technique called *solo mining,* where a node contains a full blockchain copy and takes care of the current difficulty and block generation by itself as shown in Figure 2-6. It doesn't need to join a mining pool as all the information it needs for successful mining is already located inside of it.

---

[13]https://en.bitcoin.it/wiki/Stratum_mining_protocol

[14]https://github.com/TheBlueMatt/bips/blob/betterhash/bip-XXXX. mediawiki

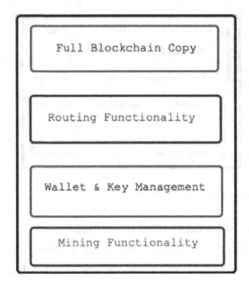

Figure 2-6. *A solo-mining node*

Another example is a mobile application shown in Figure 2-7, where users are only interested in maintaining their wallets and keys. There is no need for them to keep the whole blockchain copy that's currently over 200GB in size.

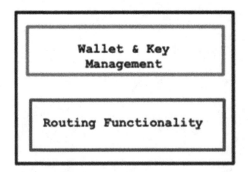

Figure 2-7. *A mobile node*

Mining pool operators too run specific nodes that maintain connections between the original Bitcoin protocol and mining nodes that utilize Stratum or other mining protocols to participate in mining operations. Although this part of the network doesn't belong to the decentralized Bitcoin network, it's still a vital part of the overall ecosystem, as it helps maintaining the communication paths between nodes that create blocks and all others that validate them. However, when it comes to block propagation, this combined or extended Bitcoin network isn't fast enough so that miners utilize yet another network called *Fast Internet Bitcoin Relay Network or FIBRE*[15], which helps minimizing latencies in communication between miners. As we already know, the faster miners propagate new blocks, the higher the chance that they'll get selected as the next chain tip. The Full Nodes we will be building are shown in Figure 2-8. They will contain their own blockchain copy, manage their own wallets, and have routing activated but won't participate in mining operations.

---

[15]http://www.bitcoinfibre.org/

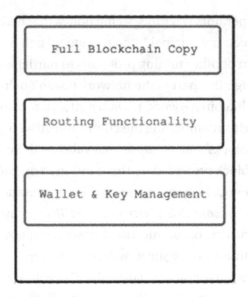

Figure 2-8. *A Full Node*

There is also another type of Full Node which uses a *pruned* blockchain copy to save disk space. Such nodes have the same security level as nodes with full copies but don't keep the whole transaction history locally. Their blockchain copy is of smaller size as they don't keep previous transactions after they have been validated.

Signatures

To control ownership in Bitcoin, we need certain technologies from the field of cryptography, which is a branch of mathematics. Usually, when we say cryptography, we think about writing secret, encrypted texts or development of algorithms, that are very hard to break. But in Bitcoin we aren't that much interested in encrypting information as everything that's written in its blockchain will remain public forever, because it must be accessible for validation of transactions and blocks. What we want instead from cryptography are other, maybe lesser-known tools like *digital signatures* and *keys*.

Bitcoin is not only about technology but also about *ownership*. Before we can spend any bitcoin, we must have provided a proof that we own it. Before someone can send us any "coin", he or she must have included certain information that points at us as future owners. The question of ownership and its transfer is essential to Bitcoin, and this is why it relies on proven cryptographical technologies, which have been available for decades. In fact, Bitcoin rests on several foundations that predate the World Wide Web, and even the DNS protocol.

One of those foundations is the *Public Key Cryptography*,[16] that was invented in the 1970s. With PKC we can generate *key-pairs* that comprise of two keys, one *private* and the other *public*. The private key we always keep to ourselves and never disclose it, while the public key can be used for communication with other parties. The mathematics[17] behind this technique is quite complex and could easily fill several books so that we will only concentrate on its utilization. Both of the keys we can keep in our wallets, which are very often built into the software we're using.

For example, the standard *Bitcoin Core Wallet*, which we'll compile from scratch, is one such software. However, there are other types of wallets like Hardware Wallets, which are small devices that behave like air-gapped computers[18] and never let the private key escape the security chip. Most often we'll be keeping both types of keys in our wallets, but we could also keep private keys only, as the public ones can be easily generated based on private keys. This is due to the nature of PKC, which allows to generate an almost infinite number of public keys based on a single private key, but not vice versa. Therefore, one of the most important features of

---

[16]https://en.wikipedia.org/wiki/Public-key_cryptography
[17]https://en.wikipedia.org/wiki/Elliptic_curve
[18]https://en.wikipedia.org/wiki/Air_gap_%28networking%29

PKC is the fact that it is very easy to go from private key to public key, but practically impossible to find out a private key based on the information provided by a public key. However, although very important, this is not everything we need in Bitcoin. As already mentioned, we aren't interested in creating secret messages but instead in securing ownership of funds written in the blockchain. For this we need an additional feature from PKC, the *digital signatures*.

A digital signature is a number generated by a hash function that's being used in Bitcoin to prove the ownership of funds. If I want to spend bitcoin, I must create a transaction which shows that I am indeed the owner of this bitcoin, because otherwise Bitcoin's scripting engine would refuse to process my transaction. Therefore, I'd use my private key as input data for a *hash function* that will generate a corresponding digital signature, which then can be later checked for validity by using my public key. With hash function we mean functions that can take any kind of input data, whatever their lengths, and return a digest value of a fixed length. No matter how long our inputs are, the returned "fingerprints" will always be of the same length but each time different. And even if we would change only a single element of input data, the generated fingerprint would change drastically. Hash functions are often being used to check the integrity of documents and to ensure that original data hasn't been changed.

Another interesting property of PKC is its asymmetry: one can check a digital signature *created by a private key* by using a *public key* that's related to this private key. The key we use to create signatures isn't the key for checking its validity. One can easily check the results of certain operations (output), but it's practically impossible to calculate back to original (input) values. It is easy to check a digital signature for its validity, which is the output value of an operation done with a private key, but it's impossible to calculate the private key itself based on a signature alone. This directly gives the answer to the question on how one could ever be able to secure funds on a public blockchain. As participants never reveal their private keys and only let others check their ownership claims via public keys and signatures, there is no way for any party to steal funds from any other.

Addresses

One example of a digital signature used in Bitcoin is addresses. Most often addresses are based on hashed values of a public key. However, this is not always the case as addresses can be generated by using various inputs as we will see later. In its infancy, the Bitcoin protocol used raw public keys as addresses without hashing them in any way. Early Bitcoin Wallets could even send funds to IP addresses. This functionality was later removed as it was prone to *man-in-the-middle* attacks.[19] Over time, more complex and also more powerful address types arrived on stage.

To generate an address based on a public key, we'd have to complete a task comprising of several steps that always begins with two hashing functions: SHA256 and RIPEMD160. Written as pseudo-source code, it'd look like this:

```
MyHashValue = RIPEMD160(SHA256(Public Key))
```

We take one of our public keys and let SHA256 generate a hash based on it. Then we use this hash as input value for RIPEMD160 function, which then returns another hash value. Basically, a hash of a hash. However, this is not the final hash value we'll be using as our address, because in the next step, we'd have to encode it in Base58[20] format, which is a subset of the more widely known Base64 format. Base58 prohibits the usage of certain ambiguous characters (0, O, l, and 1) to improve readability. In most

---

[19]https://en.bitcoin.it/wiki/IP_transaction
[20]https://en.wikipedia.org/wiki/Base58

cases the Bitcoin addresses are being generated by using the *Base58Check* format that not only generates the final output but also checks for potential errors. Therefore, the addresses generated by it always contain four additional bytes at the end that represent the checksum of the address, which are being used for validation.

And because we have different types of data in Bitcoin, we will also need to prefix our data with a single byte that represents its version. In our case this would be a zero, because we are creating a Bitcoin address. The checksum that we generate is based on the hashed value and this version byte. To get the checksum, we use double-SHA256 function from which we then take 4 bytes and append to the hash value of our public key we generated at the beginning.

This part comprises of two steps:

- Get Checksum from VersionByte+Data.

- Get Base58Check format from VersionByte+Data+Checksum.

Written in pseudo-code:

```
Checksum = SHA256(SHA256(VersionByte + MyHashValue))
```

```
Address = Base58Check(VersionByte+HashValue+4ChecksumBytes)
```

The final result is a string of alphanumeric characters that begins with a 1 like this:

```
1Q1K26998Y5S7MfV8YwH8R1NfGo4jf73VR
```

This complex procedure can be graphically represented as in Figure 2-9.

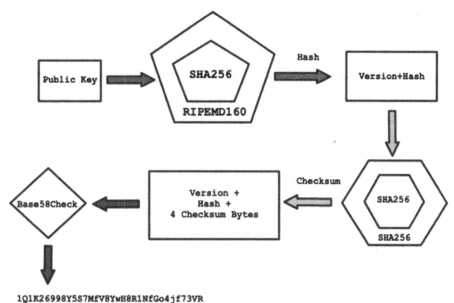

Figure 2-9. *Generating a Bitcoin address*

Here are a few examples of valid Bitcoin address-type variants with their prefixes in bold:

P2PKH: Pay-to-Public-Key-Hash[21]:

1LwQE6PHYyPDVbwmUvttH88hWiAPC74tcp

P2SH: Pay-to-Script-Hash or SegWit[22]:

32LnEubWP9T9FDWJbEk3DzfycH7DnZA7Dx

Bech32 (P2WPKH or P2WSH):

bc1qlm2lv7nw9tede4gwlgq8vhdp0aqu88gphyh4jm

---

[21]https://www.bitaddress.org
[22]https://segwitaddress.org/

The first example represents the oldest address type that directly maps to a public key. This is the address we just generated with our pseudo-code. The other two address types are based on hashes generated from scripts that we will meet in later chapters. A script in Bitcoin means an operation that will be executed during a transaction and whose returned value will decide if this transaction will be accepted or not. The scripts could contain any condition or logic that return Boolean values (true/false). Later, we will learn how to write scripts, but for now we should keep in mind that P2SH and Bech32 addresses can represent more complex structures than mere public keys. Instead of having a hash of a public key, we now have a hash of a whole script, which is an advantage as hashes are of constant length no matter how long the input value was.

These address formats can be used freely and without any constraints. One can send funds from and to other address types without any problems. The reason Bitcoin has different address types is because of historical and technical reasons. For example, P2SH-type addresses aren't based on public keys but instead on hashes of scripts, which must be executed by their respective receivers to receive funds.

To test all those key types, one can use web sites like `https://bitaddress.org`. However, if you are going to generate addresses for private use, you must not generate them in an online browser as there is always a security risk that someone could eavesdrop your communication and steal your private keys. Better download the page and go offline when creating new key pairs. Another way to create them is by using the command `getnewaddress`[23] in the Console Window of the Bitcoin Core client or via the command line tool `bitcoin-cli`. You can also set the type and alias of the address to be generated when executing this command.

To generate a legacy address with `bitcoin-cli,` we type

```
bitcoin-cli getnewaddress "my_first_btc_address" legacy
```

---

[23]`https://bitcoincore.org/en/doc/0.18.0/rpc/wallet/getnewaddress/`

The result will be an address with prefix 1, like this one:

```
1NgaCnCfCaVRZULduiVn2AZAy9zsAd342V
```

The string "my_first_btc_address" is the label for the address. To generate a P2SH-SegWit address a different flag is needed:

```
bitcoin-cli getnewaddress "my_p2sh_address" p2sh-segwit
```

The resulting address would begin with 3, like this one:

```
3JERmTm3qsqDRVpomiEvgj6YRVFV4Ua49s
```

To generate a Bech32-type address, one would use the flag *bech32*. Every public key is a result of a special mathematical operation called the *elliptic curve multiplication*,[24] where the corresponding private key is being used to calculate a public key. To find out the private key of an address, we use the command *dumpprivkey*

```
dumpprivkey 3JERmTm3qsqDRVpomiEvgj6YRVFV4Ua49s
```

The result would be the private key prefixed with K or L:

```
KxRWVQ2nLLoptGHKCK14Jok91RQs6WMkmJNkoa2kjXR4x2WuRPF3
```

If your wallet is encrypted, you will have to unlock it first with command *walletpassphrase*, before you can use *dumpprivkey* and similar operations, which are able to change the contents of a wallet. Of course, such commands should never be used in public or on machines, which are not properly secured, as knowledge of private keys ultimately means ownership of funds associated with them. *Not your keys, not your coins*, is a well-known saying in Bitcoin circles. Another useful command for handling addresses in *dumpwallet*, which is used to export all keys to a

---

[24]https://en.bitcoin.it/wiki/Secp256k1

human-readable local file. The opposite command, for importing such files, is *importwallet*.

The public and private keys being used in Bitcoin can be represented by using different formats. The software itself relies on raw bytes, and most of the time, we won't have to deal with those 256-bit numbers. Instead, we will be using WIF (wallet import format) keys, which combine public key hashes, version prefixes, and checksums.

There are also *testnet*[25] and *regtest*[26] address types, as we will see later, which are being used for testing purposes. In Table 2-1 is shown a list of address types, their Base58 prefixes, and hexadecimal counterparts.

Table 2-1. *List of available address types in Bitcoin*

Type	Hexa	Base58	Example
P2PKH	0x00	1	1JM25UwUUkGuKxzjjWzHGH8a556GTakJFW
P2SH	0x05	3	3GJAAhX7fnR4TDFoLR1gYMroA1ZRVF6Mzg
Private key compressed (WIF)	0c80	K or L	KyiAsiqteZL7yg5qzuPN5HvWHZrE5MbA Utr44YfmE3KpKVcWNhqu
Private key uncompressed (WIF)	0c80	5	5JhEdxAiep1fATDEa6TiTf3wFDc2Q6ri fhMjv2AcY6j3JqdGnMX

---

[25]testnet is a globally available Bitcoin network, that's being used in Bitcoin development.

[26]A regtest (regression testing) is a Bitcoin network, that's run locally for development purposes.

Transactions

Without transactions there would be no Bitcoin. Everything revolves around transactions as only through them the ownership and transfer of funds are made possible. All other parts of the Bitcoin ecosystem are involved in securing, propagating, and processing transactions. Bitcoin transactions are both network signals and blockchain entries, which deal with transfer of funds between parties. Although easily accessible via various blockchain explorers, transactions we see there have little in common with real transactions as they appear in network messages or get written in the blockchain.

Transaction View information about a bitcoin transaction

d6c92078059fcea673ac07246552c976be6cee5d37990486100dfdde220a2134

1K87TMWzsQLzdZb4kUmKAcrCWnQqdVW5QJ	➡	1K87TMWzsQLzdZb4kUmKAcrCWnQqdVW5QJ	11.94413003 BTC
		33eTvUJYuaMLqVh2ejG83UAcYeAgCwgNWW	0.59808344 BTC
			12.54221347 BTC

Summary		Inputs and Outputs	
Size	223 (bytes)	Total Input	12.54321347 BTC
Weight	892	Total Output	12.54221347 BTC
Received Time	2018-11-14 02:34:14	Fees	0.001 BTC
Included In Blocks	**550000** (2018-11-14 02:35:41 + 1 minutes)	Fee per byte	448.43 sat/B
		Fee per weight unit	112.108 sat/WU
Confirmations	34159	Estimated BTC Transacted	0.59808344 BTC
Visualize	**View Tree Chart**	Scripts -	**Show scripts & coinbase**

Figure 2-10. *A transaction shown on blockchain.info web explorer*[27]

---

[27]https://www.blockchain.com/btc/tx/d6c92078059fcea673ac07246552c976be 6cee5d37990486100dfdde220a2134

We will now try to "translate" the data shown in Figure 2-10 into entries as defined by the Bitcoin protocol. Here we see an address on the left that's transferring around 12.54BTC to two addresses. We also see some data under the two target addresses, which describes inputs, outputs, and fees. This is quite a lot of information at once, so let's dissect this transaction by using the commands available via the Bitcoin Client or Bitcoin CLI. In general, all options available via the graphical client are also available via the command line interface (CLI), and very often it's recommended to use the CLI, as this tool can be used to create more complex shell scripts and doesn't require a GUI system. To list the raw data that constitutes the above transaction, we use the command `getrawtransaction`. Afterwards, we use `decoderawtransaction` to turn this long hexadecimal string into a human-readable JSON[28] object, which contains following values ordered as key-value pairs. Each pair has a name (key) and a value assigned to it. This is the JSON object referencing the transaction:

```
{
    "txid": "d6c92078059fcea673ac07246552c976be6cee5d37990486100
    dfdde220a2134",
    "hash": "d6c92078059fcea673ac07246552c976be6cee5d37990486100d
    fdde220a2134",
    "version": 2,
    "size": 223,
    "vsize": 223,
    "weight": 892,
    "locktime": 0,
    "vin": [
```

---

[28]JSON stands for JavaScript Object Notation. More information about it on
  https://json.org

```
{
   "txid": "e5244f26b62119a2bc45e6c7c8975243662e487f7e9369a9
   dcc4fafa0f8190c4",
   "vout": 0,
   "scriptSig": {
      "asm": "3044022051acb984fe96ebc690ac7987c4531875bb39466
      bb557b33ecc952d514842407c02202d691613c6974f53381d938b83
      b883a795e81e40ef07d8917eb9ce115bcc0c0d[ALL] 03ebbc9c063
      50d95f1a50273b3bbb46f51827168afea87b8240bc0c2adc520202e",
      "hex": "473044022051acb984fe96ebc690ac7987c4531875bb3946
      6bb557b33ecc952d514842407c02202d691613c6974f53381d938b
      83b883a795e81e40ef07d8917eb9ce115bcc0c0d012103ebbc9c063
      50d95f1a50273b3bbb46f51827168afea87b8240bc0c2adc520202e"
   },
   "sequence": 4294967295
   }
],
"vout": [
   {
      "value": 11.94413003,
      "n": 0,
      "scriptPubKey": {
         "asm": "OP_DUP OP_HASH160 c6ca904d6c12bd983b983ae21b76
         99dde96a3a5f OP_EQUALVERIFY OP_CHECKSIG",
         "hex": "76a914c6ca904d6c12bd983b983ae21b7699dde96a3a5f88ac",
         "reqSigs": 1,
         "type": "pubkeyhash",
         "addresses": [
            "1K87TMWzsQLzdZb4kUmKAcrCWnQqdVW5QJ"
         ]
      }
   },
```

```
{
    "value": 0.59808344,
    "n": 1,
    "scriptPubKey": {
        "asm": "OP_HASH160 1574b4d35af35f2b7ec7cbe96c9f85adc91a
        0521 OP_EQUAL",
        "hex": "a9141574b4d35af35f2b7ec7cbe96c9f85adc91a052187",
        "reqSigs": 1,
        "type": "scripthash",
        "addresses": [
            "33eTvUJYuaMLqVh2ejG83UAcYeAgCwgNWW"
        ]
    }
  }
 ]
}
```

There's plenty of information as we see, but where does the transfer
of funds happen? We see some addresses, but there is no direct way of
recognizing who gets what. To answer this question, one has to describe
how Bitcoin transactions actually work. As we already know, there are
no "accounts" in Bitcoin, that participants could use for spending or
receiving funds. Being decentralized, Bitcoin offers no option to set up
any kind of registration authority for its users. And because there are no
"user accounts", the first problem we approach is: *How can we safely send
funds from one party to another, if there are no "parties" at all?* One part
of the answer lies in the asymmetric cryptography and digital signatures,
which take care of assigning funds to their owners and prohibiting access

to anyone, who's not able to provide a valid proof of ownership. As we have seen already, digital signatures are related to private keys but can't be used to calculate them. Only owners of private keys are able to access funds assigned to their corresponding signatures. Another important fact is the way Bitcoin protocol sees those funds. Everything that's not been spent is part of the global UTXO set (*unspent transaction output*). In fact, there are no "coins" in Bitcoin. They only exist as a user-friendly concept that's constructed by applications which implement the Bitcoin protocol. The rest of the answer we will discover shortly.

All the network sees is a set of unspent outputs from every owner, regardless when the last transaction happened. Just like with "coins", Bitcoin knows nothing about addresses, as they're mere user-friendly concepts and not directly visible in the blockchain. There is no way for anyone to go from one address to another or track any inputs or outputs. The only structure Bitcoin sees are small programs that get executed by its internal scripting engine. Bitcoin's functionality relies on an embedded programming language that never got a proper name so that we call it "Script". Later we will learn a bit more about it, but for now, we should keep in mind that all Bitcoin does is execute small scripts (programs), which ultimately decide about ownership of funds.

When we want to spend our coins, we have to give exact information which of the parts of the available UTXOs belong to us, that is, we have to provide a valid *proof of ownership* to the network so we can access those funds. Spoken more abstractly, we could say that creating transactions in Bitcoin is actually *changing the state of the UTXO set*. There is actually no option to move any coins in Bitcoin, because there are not only no coins available, but also because there isn't anything that could be moved at all. The only option we have, and this is the essence of every transaction, is to change the ownership information regarding some part of the UTXO set. What moves in Bitcoin is the ownership objects and not the objects themselves.

In many ways, it would be better to use the *land metaphor* to describe ownership in Bitcoin than metallic coins. Just like a person can own a piece of land and hand it over to someone else, without ever being able to move it, the same happens with bitcoins, which one "sends" to someone else. In most cases, the balance is being calculated by the software used to access Bitcoin's network. The sum of all unspent outputs is presented as a certain number of bitcoins, which is just a more convenient way to present the current UTXO state to the user.

And just like any other currency, bitcoins too can be divided into smaller parts. The division can go down to eight decimal positions. The smallest unit is called Satoshi, named after Bitcoin's pseudonymous creator. But one should keep in mind that bitcoins never move inside the blockchain. Moreover, the transactions keep a record of the current state of the global UTXO set. And some of those pieces of UTXO belong to us, because we can provide valid proofs of ownership by using our private keys and digital signatures as shown in Figure 2-11.

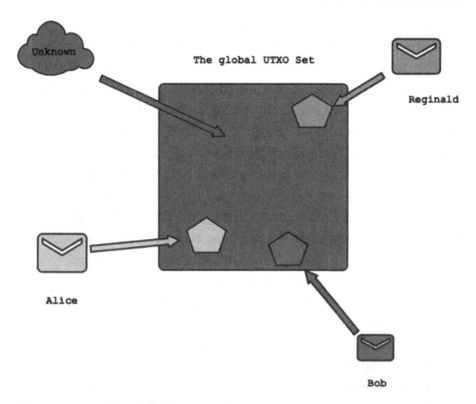

Figure 2-11. *The global UTXO set*

Another important rule regarding UTXOs is that they can only be consumed once and as a whole. There is no way to split up an UTXO before including it in a transaction. This of course raises the question of what should be done when an UTXO contains a value that's higher than the one we would like to spend. If I own two bitcoins, which come from some previous transaction, but want to spend only one in a future transaction, what would happen to my other bitcoin? The rule in Bitcoin protocol states that any bitcoins left automatically get included in transaction fees paid to the miner of the respective block. But we of course wouldn't want to lose our remaining bitcoins.

If we look at the JSON object shown before, we notice the **vin** entry. This is the *input transaction*, that consumes all UTXOs, which we will be using to create a new *output transaction*. Before we can create any outputs, we have to consume some inputs. This is the source of our funds, that we will assign later, in the **vout**-section of the JSON object. There, we see two entries, each with a different **value** and **addresses**. This is the place where the previous input funds get sent to new addresses. In most cases, one of the entries will be a so-called *change address*[29] that's sending the difference back to the creator of transaction. Usually, the software we use would automatically generates such an address. This is the place where we take care of getting back all the bitcoins that we don't want to send (or let miners take them from us). By following this strategy, the Bitcoin protocol elegantly avoids any kind of accounting logic, because everything that deals with the ownership of funds can be maintained by using transactions alone.

However, there are no rules without exceptions, and in this case the exception is a special transaction we already named in the previous chapter: coinbase.[30] This transaction has no input UTXO as we would maybe expect. Instead, its role is to bring new bitcoins into existence and also collect all the fees for transactions included in the block. Both new bitcoins and fees constitute the reward for the miner who created the block. In fact, the input transaction of this special transaction is called coinbase.[31] Here is an example from block 1000 that was generated in 2009.

```
"vin": [
  {
    "coinbase": "04ffff001d02fd04",
    "sequence": 4294967295
  }
],
```

---

[29]https://en.bitcoin.it/wiki/Change
[30]https://bitcoin.org/en/blockchain-guide#transaction-data
[31]https://bitcoin.org/en/glossary/coinbase

```
"vout": [
  {
    "value": 50.00000000,
    "n": 0,
    "scriptPubKey": {
      "asm": "04f5eeb2b10c944c6b9fbcfff94c35bdeecd93df97788
      2babc7f3a2cf7f5c81d3b09a68db7f0e04f21de5d4230e75e6
      dbe7ad16eefe0d4325a62067dc6f369446a OP_CHECKSIG",
      "hex": "4104f5eeb2b10c944c6b9fbcfff94c35bdeecd93df977
      882babc7f3a2cf7f5c81d3b09a68db7f0e04f21de5d4230e75e6db
      e7ad16eefe0d4325a62067dc6f369446aac",
      "reqSigs": 1,
      "type": "pubkey",
      "addresses": [
        "1BW18n7MfpU35q4MTBSk8pse3XzQF8XvzT"
      ]
```

The first entry in its "vin" is *coinbase,* and its "vout"
comprises of a single entry that spends 50BTC, which was the
initial *block reward* before the first halving in 2012, to address
1BW18n7MfpU35q4MTBSk8pse3XzQF8XvzT. Also, we see that the given type
of address is *pubkey.* As mentioned before, the initial protocol version only
used public keys without hashing them. Nowadays, the usage of raw public
keys as addresses is discouraged, and only hashes of public keys (P2PKH)
or pay-to-script-hash (P2SH) should be used. Another important piece
of data is the number associated with *reqSigs* key. This value indicates
the number of required signatures that is needed to unlock the funds.
In both of the JSON objects presented, there was only a single signature
needed, but Bitcoin also supports so-called *multisig*[32] transactions, that is,

---

[32]https://bitcoin.org/en/glossary/multisig

transactions where multiple signatories (each with own private key) create signatures that get included in a particular transaction.

To later access those funds, a certain *minimal* number of parties is needed to prove their ownership of funds by providing signatures, which correspond to previously given public keys. There are various options to create such multi-signature transactions, for example, 2-of-3, 2-of-2, etc. Each combination means that at least a certain number of signatures must be given, before funds can be spent. So, 2-of-3 means that if there were three signatories who locked the funds, later at least two of them must give their consent to spend the funds. Such combinations are very useful when executing contracts created in the real world, outside of blockchain, where parties could get prevented from or deliberately refuse to participate in the unlocking procedure. Also, multi-sig transactions could be used to enhance the security of funds, as one could keep several keys on different machines, or hardware wallets. In case of theft, funds would still be safe, as the attacker would need access to multiple keys, which is less likely to succeed. We will later talk about them and their importance in the Lightning Network in more detail. For now, we will only think about two participants in a transaction: a sender and a recipient.

To complete the analysis of a Bitcoin transaction, we have to understand how bitcoins get spent in the first place. As there is no way to spend anything in Bitcoin without having received it via some *input* transaction, we will now check the parts that make an output transaction possible. This may at first sound illogical; when we say that to be able to send bitcoins out of our wallet, we need an input transaction first, but don't forget that Bitcoin protocol knows no accounts. Therefore, the only way to move anything in Bitcoin is to change the state of the global UTXO set. What makes an output transaction applicable is the existence of a previous input transaction that we use to prove our ownership of bitcoins.

If we look more closely at the example transaction shown previously, we recognize that we don't have a complete knowledge about bitcoins that came in. All we see is a transaction ID (**txid**) and another **vout** key, similar to those we saw in our own output transactions. And there is a large chunk of data under **scriptSig** that contains unreadable hexadecimal strings.

```
"vin": [
    {
        "txid": "e5244f26b62119a2bc45e6c7c8975243662e487f7e9369a9
        dcc4fafa0f8190c4",
        "vout": 0,
        "scriptSig": {
          "asm": "3044022051acb984fe96ebc690ac7987c4531875bb3946
          6bb557b33ecc952d514842407c02202d691613c6974f53381d938b8
          3b883a795e81e40ef07d8917eb9ce115bcc0c0d[ALL] 03ebbc9c06
          350d95f1a50273b3bbb46f51827168afea87b8240bc0c2adc520202e",
          "hex": "473044022051acb984fe96ebc690ac7987c4531875bb394
          66bb557b33ecc952d514842407c02202d691613c6974f53381d938
          b83b883a795e81e40ef07d8917eb9ce115bcc0c0d012103ebbc9c06
          350d95f1a50273b3bbb46f51827168afea87b8240bc0c2adc520202e"
        },
        "sequence": 4294967295
    }
],
```

The solution to this puzzle lies in the way how Bitcoin network and its nodes operate. Each time a node wants to send bitcoins, it will collect the inputs from UTXOs it controls by using its own private keys. Those inputs are coming from other output transactions of course, and by going back in time, we would basically reach the very first transaction in the Genesis Block. Everything in Bitcoin can be traced back, because everything is part of the global UTXO set. The bitcoins never change; only the state of the global UTXO set does. In our preceding case, we want to use "some bitcoins" from the transaction with id:

e5244f26b62119a2bc45e6c7c8975243662e487f7e9369a9dcc4fafa0f8190c4

But as this transaction could have many outputs, we must point at the one where our "input bitcoins" come from. For this we are using the **vout** key and the number 0, which means the *first entry* from the list of outputs coming from this transaction. Here we declare a previous output to become our own input. But as we know, we can't simply point at things in Bitcoin and reclaim ownership. We have to provide a valid proof of claimed ownership. To successfully complete this task, we must also include another piece of code, the *unlocking script*, that will be executed by Bitcoin's scripting engine. The result of this execution must be the Boolean value of TRUE.

If we retrieve and decode this transaction with getrawtransaction and decoderawtransaction commands, we'll find the UTXO containing 12.54BTC together with the *locking script* at the entry **scriptPubKey**.

```
"vout": [
       {
           "value": 12.54321347,
           "n": 0,
           "scriptPubKey": {
               "asm": "OP_DUP OP_HASH160
               c6ca904d6c12bd983b983ae21b7699dde96a3a5f
               OP_EQUALVERIFY OP_CHECKSIG",
               "hex": "76a914c6ca904d6c12bd983b983ae21b7699d
               de96a3a5f88ac",
               "reqSigs": 1,
               "type": "pubkeyhash",
               "addresses": [
```

```
                    "1K87TMWzsQLzdZb4kUmKAcrCWnQqdVW5QJ"
            ]
        }
    }
],
```

These "input" bitcoins have been used to generate the next transaction from the example at the beginning. But they could only have been used after the puzzle given by scriptPubKey has been solved. What we see in scriptPubKey is one-half of the complete script that has to be executed by Bitcoin's scripting engine. The script itself contains a few keywords (*OP_DUP*, *OP_HASH160*, *OP_EQUALVERIFY*) and a hexadecimal value, which will be discussed later. For now, it is sufficient to know that this half of the script demands that anyone who claims to be the owner of these bitcoins must provide the rest of the script so that it can be executed successfully. What's missing right now is the other half: *a signature and a corresponding public key*. This data will be included when the UTXO of this transaction should become input of another transaction, that is, when someone wants to spend those funds. The value in scriptSig from the referencing transaction we discussed previously is the *unlocking logic* we need to spend the funds. The moment these two halves get combined and executed is when the scripting engine checks a transaction for validity. It is also important to know that there is no state during executing of scripts. We say that Bitcoin Script environment is *stateless*, as there are no preconditions for any script to be executed. The Engine takes the two scripts and checks if it can produce a TRUE by executing them one after another. There is nothing else that could ever influence this execution. Either a script contains everything that's needed and it succeeds or it fails.

In the early versions of Bitcoin, both of the scripts were executed together. This was later changed due to security reasons, because it was possible for an attacker to spend funds without being the actual owner. Nowadays, the scripting engine executes scriptSig first, and if there are no errors, it executes `scriptPubKey` as well. If it succeeds at the end, the new transaction will be allowed to spend the referenced `input` bitcoins. This new transaction will later be included in one of the upcoming blocks. But if the attempted transaction fails, it will get discarded and can't make it into a block. This is how Bitcoin ensures that only those who possess private keys can access the corresponding funds. However, unlocking scripts don't have to be signatures and public keys only, but in most cases the unlocking script will contain such data.

In our preceding example, the owner was able to provide valid unlocking logic, and therefore the transaction that wanted to spend 12.54BTC made it into the block. Every input transaction references some output transaction, because for bitcoins to be spent, they must have come from some other transaction. The only exception to this rule is the very first transaction in the Genesis Block, where it didn't have a preceding transaction, because there was no block before Genesis Block itself. This is also the reason why the initial transaction can never be spent, because there is no valid unlocking script for it. The irony is that the very first 50 bitcoins are locked forever. According to some calculations, four million bitcoins have been lost due to various reasons.[33]

Bitcoin Script

Everything that touches the blockchain is a script.[34] From a purely technological perspective, we could say that Bitcoin is a giant script execution engine, because every time we send or receive funds, we do create transactions that carry little scripts of different complexities with them. In most of the cases our scripts transfer ownerships from one address to another. And the language used to execute them started its

---

[33]https://fortune.com/2017/11/25/lost-bitcoins/
[34]https://en.bitcoin.it/wiki/Script

existence as an embedded part of Bitcoin's source code. However, unlike most other programming languages, this one never was designed upfront, with a properly described grammar and syntax. It didn't even have a name, which is the reason why it's still simply being called "Script". Its semantics and structure resemble an obscure language designed in the 1970s, called Forth.[35] Unlike most of the modern programming languages, it uses the *stack* as its machine abstraction. This means that it pushes and pops certain data and operators to and from the stack during execution. To describe its algorithms, it uses the *Reverse Polish Notation.*[36]

For example, to write and execute the addition operation in a language similar to Script, you wouldn't use the familiar 2 + 3 but instead 2 3 +. This notation might look pretty unusual, but as Script uses the stack as its machine abstraction, the Polish Reverse Notation is a perfect match. Let's imagine a stack structure inside our machine's memory that we fill with the preceding data as shown in Figure 2-12. According to our new notation, we'll first have to push the two numbers into the stack. The next step will be to read the operator +.

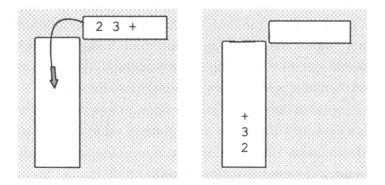

Figure 2-12. *Pushing the elements into the stack*

---

[35]https://en.wikipedia.org/wiki/Forth_(programming_language)
[36]https://en.wikipedia.org/wiki/Reverse_Polish_notation

Now the question is, when is the operation executed? The answer is simple: as soon as our hypothetical scripting engine reads the sign **+,** the two operands will be popped from the stack and used in the addition operation. Subsequently, the result would be pushed back into the stack as shown in Figure 2-13.

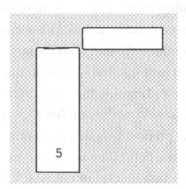

Figure 2-13. *Result got pushed back into the stack*

This is how stack machines work. In Bitcoin's script there is an operator, or Op-Code, named **OP_ADD, that's being used** instead of the + sign. In general, one can push as many data into the stack as the stack memory allows, but as soon as an operator is being read, the stack machine would execute it by taking as many operands as the operator expects and then later pushing back any results into the stack.

When it comes to Bitcoin's scripting engine, as long as the last value returned is a Boolean TRUE or any other nonzero value, the execution is considered successful. The last value remaining in the stack must be of that type to mark the respective transaction as valid.

Of course, if we provide scripts with missing operands or wrong operators, we'd get an error. There's also a memory limit regarding script sizes, so the flexibility of putting as many data as one wants is only in theory. To prevent spam and other attacks, Bitcoin's scripting engine imposes several constraints. As every participating node must validate each script, the possibility of running "bloated" scripts would open an attack surface for DDoS-ing[37] the whole network.

Let's now try to follow the execution of the locking script from scriptPubKey in the JSON-formatted transaction structure we used previously. The operators are prefixed with OP_, while the only operand is the hexadecimal value in the middle of the script.

OP_DUP OP_HASH160 c6ca904d6c12bd983b983ae21b7699dde96a3a5f
OP_EQUALVERIFY OP_CHECKSIG

We see two operators: OP_**DUP** and OP_**HASH160** (we will from now on write operators without the **OP_** prefix). Then we see a hexadecimal value, probably a hash. At the end of the string, we see two more operators **EQUALVERIFY** and **CHECKSIG**. In total, we have four operators but only one operand. This script doesn't look like it could be executed successfully. Indeed, this script could never succeed, because it is designed to remain incomplete as long as there is no valid unlocking script, which we have to take from scriptSig in the input transaction that spends those 12.54 bitcoins. As we already talked about UTXOs, to be able to spend them, one must provide a valid unlocking script. In most cases the unlocking script contains a signature and a public key of the spender, but there are also other ways to define them. We will for now stick with this option as it represents the majority of unlocking scripts. The content under the key hex in vin of the spending scriptSig look like this:

473044022051acb984fe96ebc690ac7987c4531875bb39466bb557b33ecc95
2d514842407c02202d691613c6974f53381d938b83b883a795e81e40ef07d
8917eb9ce115bcc0c0d012103ebbc9c06350d95f1a50273b3bbb46f518271
68afea87b8240bc0c2adc520202e

---

[37]https://en.wikipedia.org/wiki/Denial-of-service_attack

This is the serialized content of spender's digital signature and public key. The term *serialization* means that the binary representation of data in memory gets converted into its physical form, for example, as an entry in a text file. The opposite of it, *deserialization*, is the process of reconstructing data in memory based on some physical representation.

The reason we use signatures and public keys here is to express a *commitment* to a certain transaction. We are referencing a previous transaction, whose data we want to use as inputs for our spending, or *output* transaction. Our transaction therefore is the message we're sending to the network. And to prove that we are indeed allowed to spend claimed bitcoins, which are the *inputs* referenced by our transaction, we provide our signature and public key. In the next step, every validating node would receive our message and validate it. By utilizing the properties of the asymmetric cryptography, every node will then execute the combined locking and unlocking scripts to check for validity of our claim of ownership. This is how a complete script and operation on it would look like. The parts in bold are from our `scriptSig`.

[Sig] [PK] OP_DUP OP_HASH160 [PKHash] OP_EQUALVERIFY OP_CHECKSIG

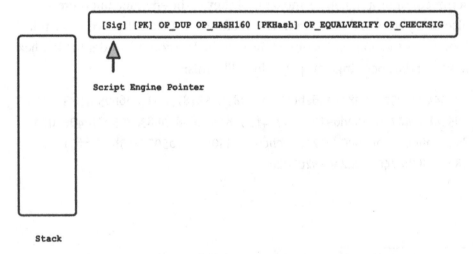

Figure 2-14. Script content before execution

In Figure 2-14 we see that Bitcoin Script has prepended the signature and public key to the locking script taken from `scriptPubKey`. We now have the complete script that can be executed. The execution is done by reading data and commands from left to right. In the preceding figure, we see the script execution pointing at the first entry and moving further to the right. By default, the scripting engine pushes data into the stack until it reads an Op-Code. The Op-Codes don't get pushed into the stack but executed as they aren't data but code with certain logic embedded. Often, an Op-Code requires a certain number of elements to be popped from the stack and returns a value to be pushed back into the stack.

However, a command can never take an element from the stack that's below the topmost element. The only way to pop the elements is one by one, beginning with the topmost element. In our case the engine pushes two elements, one after another, onto the stack: a signature and a public key. Then, after the stack pointer has read DUP, it would execute its logic, in this case it's *duplication of elements*, by popping the first element, the public key, and then pushing back two public key elements into the stack, one after another of course. The pointer now moves further to the right and reads another command (Figure 2-15).

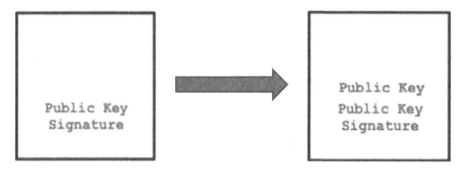

Figure 2-15. *Execute DUP*

The command we execute next is HASH160 as shown in Figure 2-16. This command pops one element, the Public Key, and returns its hash.

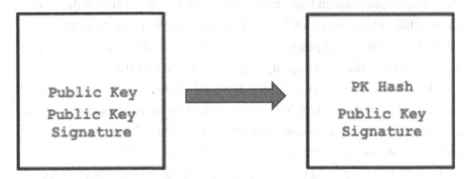

Figure 2-16. *Hashing the Public Key*

We then push the Hash value from the script into the stack (Figure 2-17).

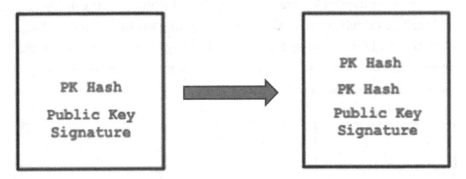

Figure 2-17. *Pushing the hash value from script into the stack*

The next command shown in Figure 2-18 is EQUALVERIFY that checks for equality between two hashes and therefore will pop two topmost values to complete its operation. The goal of this operation is to check if the expected public key hash from the *locking script* equals to the hash of the provided public key from the unlocking script. If the result is not TRUE, the script execution would fail immediately. Otherwise, it would continue reading the next data or Op-Code. Unlike previous operations,

EQUALVERIFY[38] returns nothing. There exists a related operation called EQUAL which would return TRUE, but in our case we need no return value but instead a continuation of script execution that is given by using EQUALVERIFY.

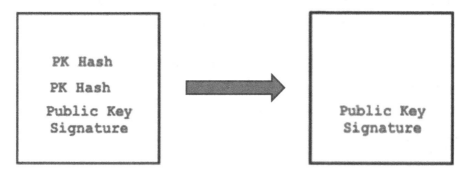

Figure 2-18. *Checking for hash equality*

Our last step is shown in Figure 2-19. Here we have to check if the given signature corresponds to the public key. If successful, the **CHECKSIG** operation would push a TRUE into the stack, which would signal the Script Engine to accept the transaction and allow the UTXO in question to be spent.

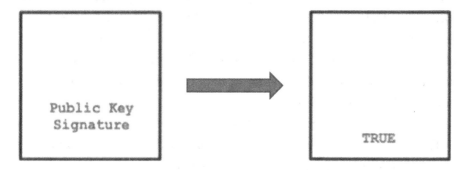

Figure 2-19. *Checking if signature corresponds with Public Key*

---

[38]Internally, EQUALVERIFY executes another Op-Code, VERIFY, that returns a Boolean value. Every Op-Code with suffix "VERIFY" does this.

Although Script offers a wide range of Op-Codes and even branching in form of special **IF-ELSE** constructs, it is still not a *Turing complete*[39] programming language. This means that Script has no loop constructs like most other languages do (*for-each, while-do, loop-until,* and similar semantics). This design choice was deliberate to prevent code execution that could exhaust node's resources. Imagine a script with a never-ending for-each loop. This would be disastrous as nodes could never complete their validations tasks, which would ultimately lead to a halt of the blockchain.

Wallets

The term wallet in Bitcoin is both a misnomer and something that means very different things. For example, the standard Bitcoin Core application is called a wallet. Additionally, the structure that is managing keys inside the application is called wallet too. And then there are hardware wallets, small devices for keeping private keys in a secure way. But irrespective of its particular usage, the term wallet still remains misleading as it suggests that it's containing bitcoins, which is impossible as those never leave the chain. More precisely, bitcoins don't exist at all as Bitcoin protocol only deals with UTXOs, the unspent transaction outputs. The visual representation in form of bitcoin balances is done in the application stack that is located above the raw Bitcoin protocol environment. Therefore, it'd be much better to call all those different "wallets" *keychains*, because that's what they really do: *keeping and managing key pairs.*

There exist two variants of wallets, *nondeterministic* and *deterministic.* The nondeterministic wallets are available since the very first version of

---

[39]https://en.wikipedia.org/wiki/Turing_completeness

Bitcoin Core software and basically mean that each key pair is created separately from any other key pair. Such wallets are basically sets of randomly generated key pairs. This of course makes them pretty hard to manage and restore, as we would have to keep track of every key pair and also make sure of not using an address twice, which is always a bad practice as it reveals too much information about our transactions and funds. In general, the usage of nondeterministic wallets is strongly discouraged.

The deterministic wallets,[40] also called **HD**[41] (hierarchical deterministic) **wallets**, are wallets, whose private keys are derived by using a one-way function that consumes a special input data called "seed". The seed is technically a randomly generated number that later gets combined with additional data like index number and "chain codes" to generate private keys. The advantage of deterministic wallets is that one only needs seed data to restore a complete wallet, regardless how many private keys have been generated already. Unlike nondeterministic wallets, the private and public keys in deterministic wallets are derived one from another. Therefore, to recreate such a wallet, only the initial seed is needed. The rest would follow automatically.

It is also possible to reuse the seed between different software and hardware tools as long as they support the same regeneration schema. Currently, there exist two variants of deterministic wallets, Type-1 and Type-2. Type-1 wallets use their seeds to create private keys, which in turn can be used to produce further private keys, and so on. Basically, they create a linear structure with the seed at the top as shown in Figure 2-20. The technique behind this key generation lies in the application of the

---

[40]More about the history and development of deterministic wallets: https://thebookofbitcoin.github.io/html/storage/deterministic_wallets.html
[41]https://github.com/bitcoin/bips/blob/master/bip-0032.mediawiki

random number. We start with the seed that produces the first private key; the second private key then will be generated by using a random number that's related to seed's random number. The second private key will then be based on random data from the previous key and so on. This way we only have to keep the seed as all other random numbers will be directly or indirectly based on it anyway.

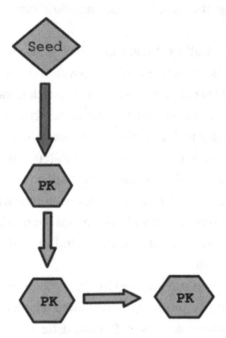

Figure 2-20. *Type-1 deterministic wallet*

Although sufficient for private use, such wallets have a significant weak point: it is not possible to create public keys without having access to corresponding private keys. This of course makes them unusable for use-cases where keys are exposed to untrusted public, for example, merchant applications. Imagine a web-facing shop application that offers a *Pay-with-Bitcoin* option. To generate a public key for each new invoice, this web server would have to have access to seed and private keys simultaneously, which would make it an ideal target for attacks. In such cases we need an option to generate public keys without having access to any private key.

To overcome this problem, a new variant of nondeterministic wallets, Type-2, was created. Such wallets are able not only to generate keys based on a single seed but can create whole sequences of child-keys, which in turn can have their own child-keys and so on. Also, Type-2 wallets can generate public keys without having access to private keys, which solves the abovementioned problem as we see in Figure 2-21.

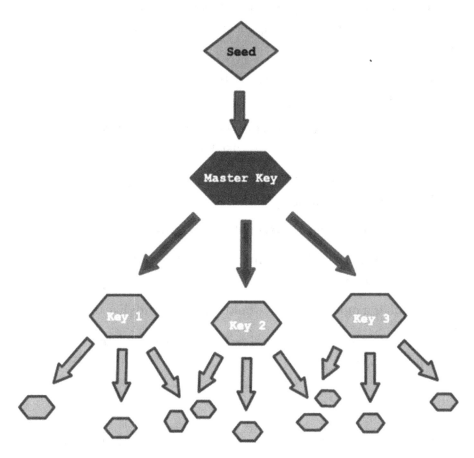

Figure 2-21. *Type-2 deterministic wallet*

With Type-2 wallets we can create different *branches* that could, for example, represent divisions within a company. Each division could have its own "root" private key that would not disclose any of its siblings, thus making it impossible to guess other keys and their structures. Also, a branch could be solely based on a public key alone like in the web-facing merchant application mentioned previously.

The most important part of HD wallets is of course the seed which can be expressed by using *mnemonics* that are words used from a vocabulary of 2048 words, which are based on one of the supported human languages. The BIP[42] that defines it is BIP39.[43] The HD wallet is defined in BIP32. The creation of a seed is done by application of several mathematical functions:

- Generate a random sequence between 128 and 256 bits.

- Calculate a checksum of the above sequence by taking the first 4 bytes from its SHA256 hash.

- Expand the sequence by adding the checksum (it now becomes 132 bits long).

- Split the sequence into equal 11-bit chunks.

- Map those chunks to words from a 2048-word vocabulary.

The result is a mnemonic that would contains words like these:

strategy hunt session whale galaxy vocal skull better evoke tool inhale hybrid

---

[42]BIP stands for Bitcoin Improvement Proposal, a standard way of introducing improvements in the Bitcoin protocol.

[43]https://github.com/bitcoin/bips/blob/master/bip-0039.mediawiki

The corresponding *root private key* would look like this:

xprv9s21ZrQH143K2doWLwAwAvkbicMRWfL7tZrtfSVUqNu8n56q9iKUH8
G7zChrm1maSVVBt44DyktN6GXEag8L2sY6ee8FofNRGdZwEfikPSM

As we see, this private key looks quite differently from those we saw before. It is longer and it has a different prefix, **xprv**. This is because after we have created the mnemonic sequence, additional steps need to be taken to produce the actual seed number. The human-readable mnemonic is only meant for us to be kept in a safe environment. The next steps are what create the actual numeric seed value.

- Apply the *PBKDF2* [44]algorithm by giving it the mnemonic and a "salt" value as inputs. Optionally, the *salt* can be expanded by entering a passphrase that adds additional randomness to the procedure. If no passphrase was entered, the value of salt would only contain the string value "mnemonic".

- *PBKDF2* algorithm would then stretch the original mnemonic by applying 2048 rounds of hashing with *HMAC-SHA512* algorithm. The resulting value would be 512-bit long. This is the *actual seed.*

This seed is then used to create the master private (**xprv**) and public (**xpub**) keys as shown in Figure 2-22.

---

[44]https://en.wikipedia.org/wiki/PBKDF2

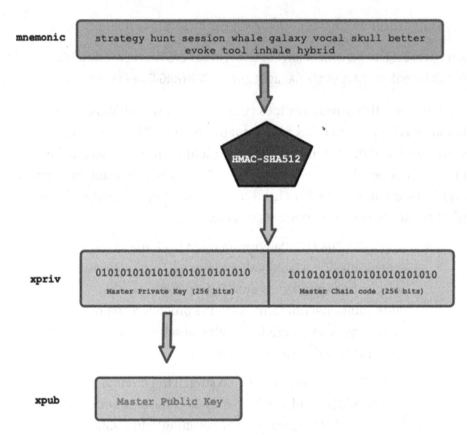

Figure 2-22. Generating master private and public keys

These keys can later be used to create "normal" private and public keys. The seed also contains the chain code (the right 256 bits of the 512-bit seed), which is used to create different key chains within the tree structure. This way we can split up the wallet into several divisions, each with its own master private key and child-keys.

The optional passphrase should not be understood as "password" but moreover as a way of creating different wallets based on the same word mnemonic. This strategy can be applied to create different "wallet variants" that could serve different purposes. In extreme cases, for example, extortions, a person could "give away" the seed without giving the accompanying passphrase. The wallet based on seed alone would, for example, contain only a small amount of funds. The "correct" wallet, the one with larger amounts, could only be recreated with the passphrase. The passphrase is actually a pointer to a variant of a wallet, as there can be many of them based on the same seed but with different passphrases.

To experiment with the technology behind HD wallets a web site located at `https://iancoleman.io/bip39/` is recommended. The various options offered there allow for testing of different scenarios. It is also possible to run this page locally, without a network connection, which should always be done when creating wallets for real-world usage.

Summary

In this chapter we have learned how Bitcoin works and what its most important parts are. We have looked into the Blockchain, the peer-to-peer network, with its various node types and the Bitcoin's scripting engine. We have learned to understand scripts and have written and executed one that's sending funds from one address to another. We have learned that Bitcoin only sees transactions and that everything else revolves around this concept. Without transactions Bitcoin wouldn't be possible. Although Bitcoin knows nothing about "coins", we have learned that various applications can help us abstract away many complexities from the underlying architecture. However, we have also learned that Bitcoin maintains a specific structure called the UTXO set, which transitions from one state to another each time a new block gets created. To send funds in Bitcoin actually means to change the UTXO set, which is the number of unspent transaction outputs. Ultimately, we have learned that the ecosystem around Bitcoin offers different options on how to keep our private keys safe, from old wallet types that carry around bunches of keys to highly sophisticated industry standards like HD wallets, which help us create and maintain separate key chains. We have delved into the technology behind HD wallet creation and followed the various steps toward a complete HD wallet based on a single seed mnemonic that can be safely stored outside any software application or device.

CHAPTER 3

Environment Setup

In this chapter we will get more practical and prepare our Raspberry Pi hardware, Bitcoin's source code, and the C++ compiler toolchain. Our first goal will be to install and configure Raspberry's operating system, which is a variant of Linux. Afterward, we will setup the environment for both the Bitcoin daemon and the GUI wallet application.

Hardware

In most cases a standard Raspberry Pi of type Zero W, Pi3, or Pi4 with a cheap 64GB SD card would be sufficient for all the tasks done in the testnet or regtest, the two Bitcoin networks designed for development and testing. For real-world usage in the mainnet of Bitcoin, a much larger SD card, or SSD, is needed. As the mainnet blockchain is currently over 240GB in size, either a 400GB SD card or 512GB SSD is needed. However, SSDs are strongly recommended as SD cards have a much shorter lifetime than SSDs, especially when used in scenarios with frequent read/write operations as it's the case with Bitcoin. In Table 3-1 you can find the list of needed hardware for a successful operation of Full Nodes.

© Harris Brakmić 2019
H. Brakmić, *Bitcoin and Lightning Network on Raspberry Pi*,
https://doi.org/10.1007/978-1-4842-5522-3_3

Table 3-1. *Hardware Requirements*

Hardware	Zero W	Pi3	Pi4
SSD	512GB	512GB	512GB
SD card	400GB U3	400GB U3	400GB U3
HDMI	Micro-HDMI-adapter	HDMI-port available	Micro-HDMI-adapter
CPU Cooling	passive	passive	passive
Keyboard	Wireless with USB-receiver	Wireless with USB-receiver	Wireless with USB-receiver
Power Supply	Standard cable or Power Bank	Standard cable	Standard cable

All of our practical examples can be applied on Pi 3, Pi 4, and Zero W without any additional modifications. Due to its operating system-agnostic nature, Bitcoin's source code can be compiled and run on various devices and needs only a few sets of packages like C++ compiler, optional graphic libraries from Qt Framework, and a portable database library BerkeleyDB. In the upcoming chapters, we will learn to install and compile them in a step-by-step fashion. In Figures 3-1, 3-2, and 3-3, different variants of Raspberry hardware are shown. As the processing power and available RAM between them differ greatly, not all scenarios should be tried on any hardware. For example, the smaller Zero W device is not to be used in GUI-based environments as it simply lacks enough RAM capacity for setting up the whole Bitcoin environment. It's not impossible to run a GUI with Zero W, but the overall speed of its GUI environment is simply not comparable with other Raspberry variants. When Zero W is used, it is much better to compile everything via SSH without ever activating its GUI. However, console-based environments require a certain amount of experience with the Linux system so that inexperienced users should maybe better use the bigger Raspberry variants.

Figure 3-1. *Raspberry Pi3*

Figure 3-2. *Raspberry Pi4*

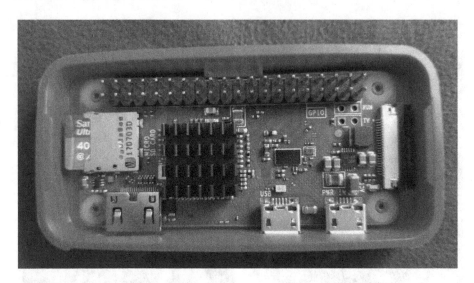

Figure 3-3. *Raspberry Pi Zero W*

For "mobile scenarios" with Raspberry Pi Zero W, there is an option to run it without direct power supply by using a power bank. Such a configuration is shown in Figure 3-4.

Figure 3-4. *Raspberry Pi Zero W with a power bank*

It is possible to run the OS and Bitcoin on a single micro SDXC card. As those cards are getting cheaper, the operating system as well as Bitcoin software could be run together on a relatively inexpensive 400GB micro SDXC card. At least for now, because Bitcoin's blockchain is continuously getting bigger and currently demands more than 200GB. But if one is running a pruned[1] Full Node, which are nodes that discard already validated transaction data, then a variant with a micro SDXC card might be a good alternative. Of course, in such cases one doesn't need a large SDXC card as the pruned data can be less than 1GB in size. We will explore this option, but in general it's advisable to use an external SSD hard drive when using Bitcoin for managing funds. A micro SDXC card simply can never be as robust as an SSD. We will also need an HDMI cable to connect with our monitor and an external keyboard. For setups involving Pi Zero and Pi 4, one would need a micro HDMI-to-HDMI adapter. Although the initial setup will be done by using a directly connected monitor and keyboard, it's not required for future tasks as we will later activate SSH and VNC servers for remote access. It is also strongly recommended to use passive heat sinks as shown in Figure 3-5.

---

[1]https://bitcoin.org/en/release/v0.11.0#block-file-pruning

Figure 3-5. *Passive heat sinks applied on Raspberry Pi 3*

In general, after being installed and synchronized with its network, Bitcoin nodes can be safely left alone without further investing much time into configuration and maintenance. The conservative nature of the Bitcoin project and strict avoidance of introducing incompatible changes in the Consensus Protocol, the so-called *hard forks*,[2] delivers a high degree of compatibility and stability, which saves much time on the administration side. Instead of keeping up with the latest updates, owners of Bitcoin Full Nodes can concentrate on the actual application of Bitcoin technology. For example, by running applications that utilize the Lightning Network, which we will meet in later chapters, when we introduce the so-called 2nd-layer payment solutions.

---

[2]https://bitcoin.org/en/glossary/hard-fork

Linux Installation

Our future Full Nodes will run the standard Raspberry Pi OS Raspbian that can be installed by using the NOOBS package available on their home page[3] (Figure 3-6).

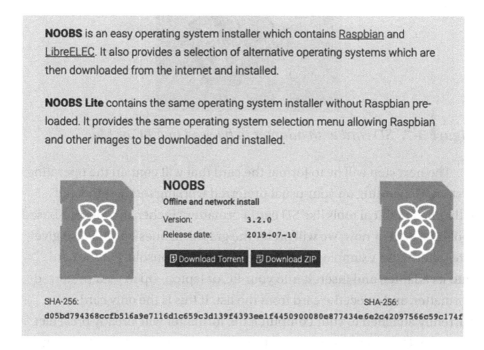

NOOBS is an easy operating system installer which contains Raspbian and LibreELEC. It also provides a selection of alternative operating systems which are then downloaded from the internet and installed.

NOOBS Lite contains the same operating system installer without Raspbian pre-loaded. It provides the same operating system selection menu allowing Raspbian and other images to be downloaded and installed.

NOOBS

Offline and network install

Version: 3.2.0
Release date: 2019-07-10

⬇ Download Torrent   ⬇ Download ZIP

SHA-256:   SHA-256:
d05bd794368ccfb516a9e7116d1c659c3d139f4393ee1f4450900080e877434e6e2c42097566c59c174f

Figure 3-6. *The official Raspbian image download page*

Download the ZIP file of the *"offline and network install"* variant by either using direct download or with a Torrent client. Then unzip the file with an unpacker of your choice. You will get a new directory named *NOOBS_v3_2_0* that contains the installation data, which we will later copy to the SDXC card. However, we will only transfer *the contents of this*

---

[3]https://www.raspberrypi.org/downloads/noobs/

directory and not the directory itself. Very often, beginners make a mistake by directly copying the directory, which leads to a non-bootable card.

Figure 3-7. *SD card with adapter to be used in a PC or Mac*

The next step will be to format the card that will contain the operating system. Depending on your usual preferred working setup, this could either be graphical tools like SD card Formatter,[4] Etcher,[5] or console-based tools like *dd*. For now, we will prefer the graphical ones but will also give later alternative examples that can be run on the console. Put the card into its adapter, and insert it into your PC or laptop. Open your preferred Formatter, and select the card from the list. If this is the only card currently attached to your computer, the formatter will already preselect it for you. However, double check the selection to prevent accidental data loss. A typical format window is being shown in Figure 3-8.

---

[4]https://www.sdcard.org/downloads/formatter/index.html
[5]www.balena.io/etcher/

Figure 3-8. *SD card Formatter*

Click the *Format* button, and confirm operation in the window that will pop up as shown in Figure 3-9.

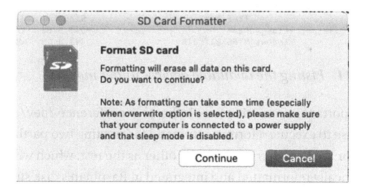

Figure 3-9. *Formatting confirmation window*

The formatting operation will take a few moments to complete. If everything was completed successfully, you'll be presented a confirmation window like in Figure 3-10.

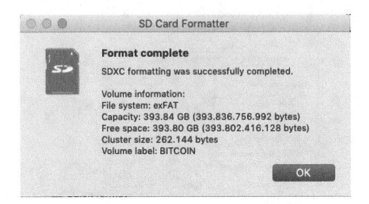

Figure 3-10. *Format completed*

An alternative way to format card in the console could, for example, be the diskutil tool that's available on macOS.

First, I check the availability of my card by using diskutil list. The resulting list in Figure 3-11 shows all available drives, and one of them, usually at the end of the list, will be your SD card.

```
/dev/disk3 (internal, physical):
   #:                       TYPE NAME                  SIZE       IDENTIFIER
   0:      FDisk_partition_scheme                     *393.9 GB   disk3
   1:              Windows_NTFS BITCOIN                393.8 GB   disk3s1
```

Figure 3-11. *Listing the available devices under macOS*

The important information here is the device reference /dev/disk3 that I will use to execute a format command for creating two partitions on it, one for the Raspberry OS and the other as the rest, which will then be automatically reformatted and integrated in Raspbian's disk structure during the installation.

diskutil partitionDisk **disk3** 2 MBR MS-DOS **BITCOIN** 10G\ ExFAT **remaining** R

This command creates two partitions on *disk3*. The first one is a MSDOS-formatted 10GB partition named BITCOIN, and the rest comprises of all the unused disk space left behind those 10GB. It is named *remaining* and the letter R means "rest of the available space".

Your machine would then show you two new disks. In the last step before installation, we select all available files from the NOOBS_v3_2_0 directory and copy them to our BITCOIN partition or any other partition name you chose.

name	ext	size	modified	kind
Macintosh HD › Users › brakmic › Downloads › NOOBS_v3_2_0				
..		DIR	20.07.19, 10:50	folder
defaults		DIR	10.06.19, 13:18	folder
os		DIR	10.07.19, 17:03	folder
overlays		DIR	10.06.19, 11:50	folder
bcm2708-rpi-b-plus	dtb	23 KB	10.06.19, 13:18	
bcm2708-rpi-b	dtb	23 KB	10.06.19, 13:18	
bcm2708-rpi-cm	dtb	23 KB	10.06.19, 13:18	
bcm2708-rpi-zero-w	dtb	24 KB	10.06.19, 13:18	
bcm2708-rpi-zero	dtb	23 KB	10.06.19, 13:18	
bcm2709-rpi-2-b	dtb	25 KB	10.06.19, 13:18	
bcm2710-rpi-3-b-plus	dtb	26 KB	10.06.19, 13:18	
bcm2710-rpi-3-b	dtb	26 KB	10.06.19, 13:18	
bcm2710-rpi-cm3	dtb	25 KB	10.06.19, 13:18	
bcm2711-rpi-4-b	dtb	39 KB	10.06.19, 13:18	
bootcode	bin	52 KB	10.06.19, 13:18	Mac...chive
BUILD-DATA		303 by...	10.06.19, 13:18	data
INSTRUCTIONS-README	txt	2 KB	10.06.19, 13:18	text
recover4	elf	761 KB	10.06.19, 13:18	
RECOVERY_FILES_DO_NOT_EDIT		0 bytes	10.06.19, 13:18	data
recovery	c...	121 byt...	10.06.19, 13:18	
recovery	elf	684 KB	10.06.19, 13:18	
recovery	img	3 MB	10.06.19, 13:18	Clas...mage
recovery	rfs	28,6 MB	10.06.19, 13:18	
recovery7	img	3,2 MB	10.06.19, 13:18	Clas...mage
recovery7l	img	3,4 MB	10.06.19, 13:18	Clas...mage
riscos-boot	bin	10 KB	10.06.19, 13:18	Mac...chive

Figure 3-12. *Copying Raspbian contents to SD card with a file manager*

An alternative way to create bootable SD cards is by using Etcher, a formatting tool that is capable of writing the downloaded Raspbian image without expecting the user to unpack it first. One only needs to select the package, and the rest will be done by Etcher itself (Figure 3-13).

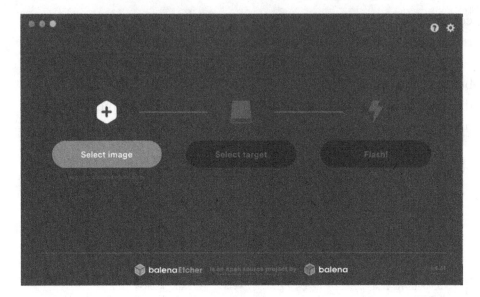

Figure 3-13. *Etcher automatically unpacks and writes images to disks*

We will now put the card into the slot on the Raspberry and connect the needed cables.

Figure 3-14. *Inserting the SD card into Raspberry*

Depending on your preferences, you might be using a different keyboard variant, monitor type, and network. Here, I am using a wireless keyboard with an adapter, a LAN cable, and an HDMI adapter for my monitor (Figures 3-15 and 3-16).

Figure 3-15. *Keyboard adapter*

Figure 3-16. *Micro-HDMI-adapter*

After we have activated our device, it will welcome us with a screen where we can select packages, set up a WLAN connection, and also edit configuration files. In our case, all we need is a standard Raspbian installation (Figure 3-17).

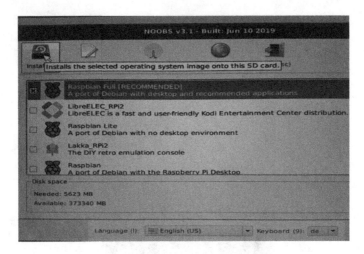

Figure 3-17.   *Package selection*

To start the installation, click the button *Install*. The warning window should be closed with "**Yes**"(Figure 3-18).

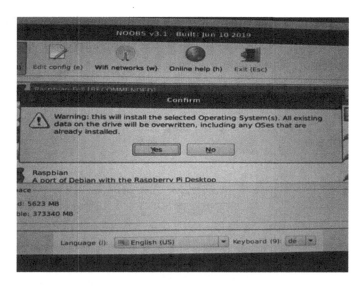

Figure 3-18. *Starting the installation of Raspbian*

The installation will now start, and for the time being, you will see this screen (Figure 3-19) with progress updates shown at the bottom.

Figure 3-19. *Installation progress*

If there were no errors, the final result will be a small message box informing you about the successful operating system installation. Click the button *OK* to restart your Raspberry device.

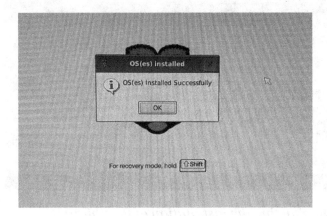

Figure 3-20. *Message showing that the installation has completed successfully*

Linux Configuration

After we have installed our system, a few configuration settings will have to change to activate the VNC server, the SSH server, and also the settings regarding the language and keyboard we use (Figure 3-21).

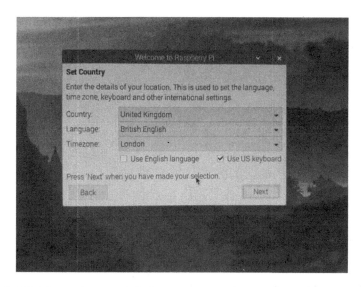

Figure 3-21. *Language and time zone settings*

After we have set up our language and keyboard, we'll have to set a
password for the default user pi (Figure 3-22).

Figure 3-22. *Password settings*

Throughout this book we'll be using the default user pi, but you can anytime create another one. This can be done with the command adduser on the console.

```
pi@raspberrypi:~ $ sudo adduser bitcoiner
Adding user `bitcoiner' ...
Adding new group `bitcoiner' (1002) ...
Adding new user `bitcoiner' (1002) with group `bitcoiner' ...
The home directory `/home/bitcoiner' already exists.  Not copying from `/etc/skel'.
New password:
Retype new password:
passwd: password updated successfully
Changing the user information for bitcoiner
Enter the new value, or press ENTER for the default
        Full Name []: Bitcoin Maximalist
        Room Number []: 2140
        Work Phone []: 20090103
        Home Phone []: 0001
        Other []:
Is the information correct? [Y/n]
```

Figure 3-23. *Executing adduser command to create a new Raspbian user*

Depending on your monitor type and resolution, you might want to activate the *black-border*-setting (Figure 3-24).

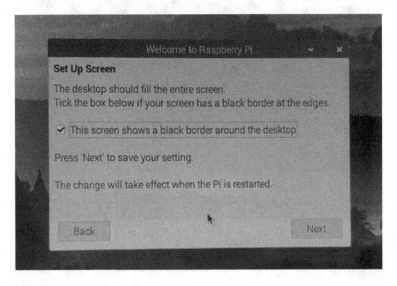

Figure 3-24. *Black-border setting*

If you prefer to use WLAN, you can open a connection in the following screen (Figure 3-25).

Figure 3-25. *WLAN settings*

The configuration wizard will also ask us to check for OS updates, which is always a good idea. A working Internet connection is required (Figure 3-26).

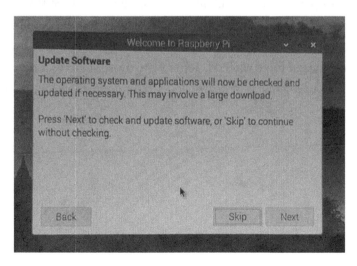

Figure 3-26. *Software update*

Depending on your connection speed and the number of updates, it could take some time until the update process has completed. Just let the Raspbian install all the packages without interfering with the system. After the update has completed, your Raspberry will be ready for a reboot. Click the button *OK* to restart the device (Figure 3-27).

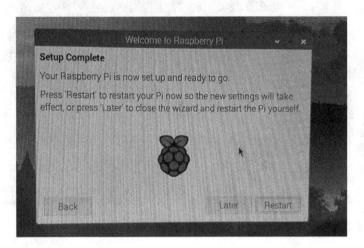

Figure 3-27. *Setup complete*

Our first step after reboot will be to configure VNC and SSH servers for remote access. If you only prefer to use GUI tools for remote configuration, then ignore the SSH settings and vice versa. Throughout the book we'll be using console-based tools via SSH. To activate those services, open the main menu and select *Preferences* ➤ *Raspberry Pi Configuration* (Figure 3-28).

Figure 3-28. *Configuring Raspberry Pi device*

In the configuration window, open the tab *Interfaces,* and enable SSH and VNC (Figure 3-29).

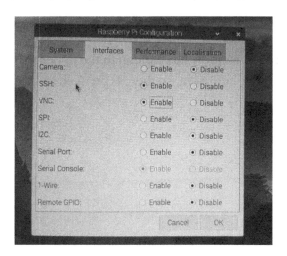

Figure 3-29. *Activating additional interfaces*

After clicking the OK button, you'll get a warning about a mandatory restart. Accept it and reboot your device (Figure 3-30).

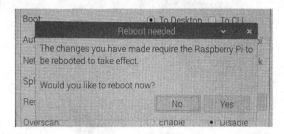

Figure 3-30. *Rebooting after system change*

After restart the taskbar will show a new icon signaling the existence of a VNC server. Click it to open the configuration window (Figure 3-31).

Figure 3-31. *VNC service is active*

The configuration window has a menu in the upper right corner, but the default settings are sufficient, so there is no need to change anything (Figure 3-32).

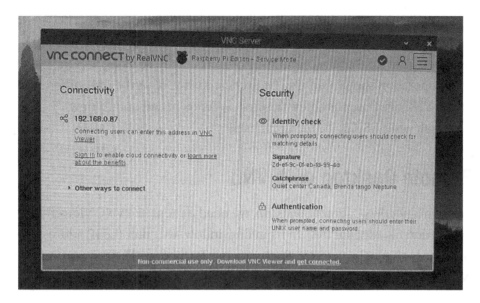

Figure 3-32. *VNC server settings*

All we need to know for now is the IP address that is shown in the *Connectivity* area of the VNC window. Next, we will check the SSH server. For this we open a console in another device, like a laptop or PC, and enter the below SSH command. The IP address given in the example should of course be replaced with your device's IP address.

```
ssh pi@192.168.0.87
```

To issue this command under Windows, we'll need a Unix-like environment like Cygwin[6] or Windows Subsystem for Linux.[7]

If we are trying to connect with SSH server for the first time, our machine might not know the remote server and will send a warning regarding its public keys. The error message would contain a message like this:

```
The authenticity of host '192.168.0.87' can't be established.
```

---

[6]www.cygwin.com/

[7]https://docs.microsoft.com/en-us/windows/wsl/install-win10

In our case, we should ignore the warning and accept the keys by typing *yes* in the console. We now have opened an SSH connection to our Raspberry device. For the rest of the book, we'll only be using SSH, but every operation shown can also be executed via VNC as the only difference is that VNC client opens a new desktop, where we then open a new terminal, while SSH is the terminal itself.

Remote Desktop with VNC

To open a new VNC remote desktop, we need a client like VNC Viewer[8] that can be downloaded for free. In its main window, we enter the IP address previously shown by the VNC Server on our Raspberry. The connection Name can be anything (Figure 3-33).

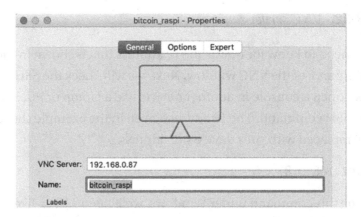

Figure 3-33. *VNC connection setup*

The default settings in the area below should be left unchanged (Figure 3-34).

---

[8]https://www.realvnc.com/en/connect/download/viewer/

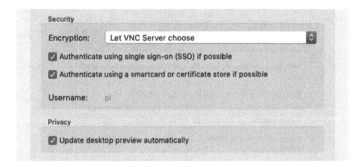

Figure 3-34. *VNC's default settings*

To set the default VNC user, we switch to *Expert* tab and enter pi under the option UserName (Figure 3-35).

Figure 3-35. *VNC username*

Now we can open a connection which will immediately show a warning window, because the VNC server isn't known to our client. We should click on *Continue* to open the connection (Figure 3-36).

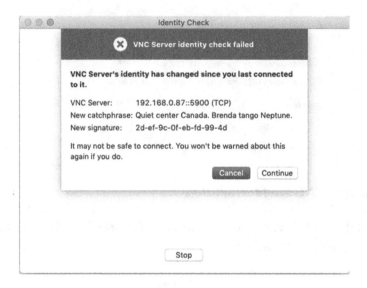

Figure 3-36. *VNC warning regarding an unknown server*

Ultimately, we'll be presented the desktop window, which we can use to remotely manage our device (Figure 3-37).

Figure 3-37. *Default Raspbian desktop*

Updating Raspbian

Although we have updated our packages during OS installation, it is always a good practice to check for new packages every now and then. This is done with the *apt* package management tool that's included by default. This tool is based on Debian's original *apt* tool and is available for many different Debian-based distributions. Our OS, Raspbian (**Rasp**berry De**bian**), is such a distribution. To check for any changes of installed packages, a single command is needed:

```
sudo apt update
```

As this tool needs special permissions to manipulate the state of the OS, we must execute it together with the sudo command that elevates user permissions. Usually, one would first have been granted such elevation rights, but as the user pi is by default given such rights, we don't have to do anything. To apply new updates retrieved via update, a second command is needed:

```
sudo apt upgrade
```

You will get a list of applicable updates that you should confirm with ENTER.

Getting Bitcoin Sources with Git

Bitcoin's source code is located at GitHub, a very popular software development collaboration platform (Figure 3-38).

Figure 3-38. *Bitcoin project's GitHub page*

To use GitHub's service, one needs the source code management tool called *git*. As this package is already available on your Raspbian, there is no need to install anything. All you need to get Bitcoin's source code is a single command typed in the console. If you have never used git before, a simple "git tutorial" search will provide you many competent resources.[9]

```
git clone https://github.com/bitcoin/bitcoin.git
```

The git tool will now connect the repository and ask for the latest changes from the master branch. As Bitcoin is a complex project with hundreds of developers, they don't work on the same branch all the time but rather implement their code changes in separate branches. In general, one should use the latest stable branch which at this point is *0.18.0*. After the preceding command has completed, we will get a new directory called bitcoin.

---

[9]http://rogerdudler.github.io/git-guide/

114

We enter it with cd bitcoin and check for available branches with git branch --all. We'll get a list of currently available remote repositories.

```
master
remotes/origin/0.14
remotes/origin/0.15
remotes/origin/0.16
remotes/origin/0.17
remotes/origin/0.18
remotes/origin/HEAD -> origin/master
remotes/origin/master
```

As we see we're by default on the master branch, which is the default development branch with the latest code changes. This of course means that the latest and not completely tested code is available for our local compilation. However, we don't want to run a potentially unstable Bitcoin variant, and therefore we switch to the current stable branch with git checkout 0.18. The returned result would be

```
Switched to branch '0.18'
Your branch is behind 'origin/0.18' by 4 commits, and can be
fast-forwarded.
  (use "git pull" to update your local branch)
```

A branch in git means a separate variant of the source code that contains new implementations, bug fixes, and other changes. A branch other than master represents a version of the source code that could later become part of the final version. Often, only parts of branches get included or merged into the master branch. It is advisable to check for code changes and especially bug fixes. This can be done easily with the command git log that lists changes and their metadata like comments.

To include latest changes from a git repository, one needs to execute the git pull command. If there were any changes, the git tool would download the changes and merge it with our local source code copy.

Setting Up the Build Environment

First, we will install build and configuration packages with

```
sudo apt-get install build-essential libtool\
autotools-dev automake pkg-config bsdmainutils python3
```

As most of them are already installed by default, the whole procedure will run more like an update process, if there are any updates available. The next step is the installation of Boost,[10] libevent, and SSL libraries which Bitcoin needs to operate.

```
sudo apt-get install libssl-dev libevent-dev\
libboost-system-dev libboost-filesystem-dev\
libboost-chrono-dev libboost-test-dev libboost-thread-dev
```

You will now be asked if you want to install the new boost libraries. Accept with ENTER.

After a few moments, the operation will complete. We will also install two additional packages: *ZMQ*[11] and *libupnpc*.

```
sudo apt-get install libminiupnpc-dev
sudo apt-get install libzmq3-dev
```

Depending on your preferences, you might avoid the installation of automatic port mapping feature (*upnpc*) and messaging service (*ZMQ*). As these libraries aren't vital for Bitcoin Client's operation, you can safely

---

[10]www.boost.org/

[11]http://zeromq.org/

ignore them. However, some future setups might demand *ZMQ* and *upnp* and is therefore recommended to install them.

Another optional package is the collection of libraries that constitute the Qt framework, which is the default GUI framework of Bitcoin's reference client. If you plan to run Bitcoin's *daemon* only, then you won't need to install them. In some scenarios, like Zero W, it is strongly recommended to run Bitcoin without the GUI, and thus no Qt packages are required. But as we are using Pi 3 as our reference hardware, the installation of Qt's libraries is acceptable.

```
sudo apt-get install libqt5gui5 libqt5core5a libqt5dbus5\
qttools5-dev qttools5-dev-tools libprotobuf-dev\
protobuf-compiler
```

Additionally, we will also install the library for QR code generation which is required for scenarios where we use QR codes instead of typing raw addresses, for example, when scanning addresses with mobile apps.

```
sudo apt-get install libqrencode-dev
```

The final step is the installation of the Berkeley DB 4.8, which is mandatory for all scenarios that must have access to wallets. If you are planning to run a node that doesn't need any wallet operations, then you can ignore this step and later use the flag `--disable-wallet` when executing the `configure` script. However, most of the scenarios in this book will need a wallet. As there are no precompiled versions of BDB4.8 for Raspbian, we will have to compile those libraries by hand. Luckily, there is a script available that executes the whole configuration and compilation procedure for us. From within the bitcoin directory type this command in your console.

```
./contrib/install_db4.sh `pwd`
```

A lengthy installation procedure will start that will download BDB's source code, configure it, and ultimately compile the binaries. Be patient, and don't use your device for anything else to avoid slowing down the procedure. Ultimately, the installation script will finish with this message.

```
db4 build complete.
```

```
When compiling bitcoind, run `./configure` in the following way:
```

```
Export BDB_PREFIX= '/home/pi/bitcoin/db4 '
./configure BDB_LIBS= " -L${BDB_PREFIX}/lib -ldb_cxx-4.8" BDB_
CFLAGS= " -I${BDB_PREFIX}/include" ...
```

It is very important to use the preceding paths when executing the configure script later. Without them the Bitcoin compilation procedure would fail by producing weird errors. The first of the two should be included in your user's .bashrc script to make it available by default each time you open a new shell. However, instead of using the recommended shell variable named BDB_LIBS and BDB_CFLAGS, you should use LDFLAGS and CPPFLAGS, which we will see later when we start compiling Bitcoin software.

For this open your profile script with

```
nano ~/.bashrc
```

and add this line at its end:

```
export BDB_PREFIX= ' /home/pi/bitcoin/db4'
```

Save changes with *CTRL+O* and ENTER, then close **nano** editor with *CTRL+X*.

The next step we have to make is executing the autogen.sh script inside the bitcoin directory. You will get a console output like this:

```
glibtoolize: putting auxiliary files in AC_CONFIG_AUX_DIR,
'build-aux'.
glibtoolize: copying file 'build-aux/ltmain.sh'
glibtoolize: putting macros in AC_CONFIG_MACRO_DIRS, 'build-
aux/m4'.
```

```
glibtoolize: copying file 'build-aux/m4/libtool.m4'
glibtoolize: copying file 'build-aux/m4/ltoptions.m4'
glibtoolize: copying file 'build-aux/m4/ltsugar.m4'
glibtoolize: copying file 'build-aux/m4/ltversion.m4'
glibtoolize: copying file 'build-aux/m4/lt~obsolete.m4'
```

After a few moments, the autogen-script will complete by leaving the console open.

Now we can execute the configuration script which will generate all the Makefiles we need to build a working Bitcoin Client. Depending on flags we use, the outcome might differ greatly. configure is a powerful script that offers many flags, which we can list with ./configure --help.

```
`configure' configures Bitcoin Core 0.18.0 to adapt to many
kinds of systems.

Usage: ./configure [OPTION]... [VAR=VALUE]...
```

In our case we want to configure a standard Bitcoin Core wallet with GUI, QR code support, UPnP, and messaging services. Additionally, we will disable compilation of test and benchmarking binaries, because we don't participate in Bitcoin's development. Usually, one should always test software being used in production, but in this case, we rely on test results generated by the Bitcoin Core team itself. This strategy simply saves some of compilation time on our small Raspberry devices. We also decide to build a binary that doesn't rely on dynamically linked libraries but instead integrates all of them into a single file.

```
./configure LDFLAGS="-L${BDB_PREFIX}/lib\
-ldb_cxx-4.8" CPPFLAGS="-I${BDB_PREFIX}/include"\
--with-gui=qt --disable-tests --disable-bench\
--disable-shared
```

The preceding command will kick off a lengthy procedure. You will see many configuration tests, checks, and results which in the end will produce a working build environment that can be used many times and as long as no vital changes are required. If everything went as expected, the final result will contain information about our future binaries. We're now ready to compile Bitcoin's binaries.

Compiling Bitcoin

However, before we type in make and wonder why the compilation freezes or even throws weird compiler errors around, we should first provide enough swap space for our Raspbian system. Any Linux system needs some kind of swap space, and their sizes might differ greatly. In our case, the swap space is essential as the compilation procedure will activate many processes which will be continuously reading and writing temporary data. By default, Raspbian configures a very small swap space defined in /etc/dphys-swapfile. We open this file with

```
sudo nano /etc/dphys-swapfile
```

The variable CONF_SWAPSIZE is by default set to 100MB which is not enough. Therefore, we increase its value to 2048 and save the file. In scenarios where the OS and application run both on a single card, the above change is sufficient. If you are using an external hard drive, which is recommended, you should add another line that would move the swap file to your hard drive. By default, the swap file is located in /var, which is less performant. Here is an example of a hard drive mounted on one of the USB ports.

Figure 3-39. *Raspberry with an external hard drive*

To check for external disks, you can use the mount command or the file commander GUI, if your Raspberry is running with desktop activated. In the example from the preceding picture, the disk got automatically mounted at /mnt/sda2 so that the entry for the alternative swap file path would be like this:

```
CONF_SWAPSIZE=2048
CONF_SWAPFILE=/mnt/sda2/swap.file
```

In any case, the new settings must be activated by executing this script.

```
sudo /etc/init.d/dphys-swapfile restart
```

Now it's time to kick off the compilation. For this, we use the make script, which we can tweak a bit by using the -j flag that allows us to define the number of CPU cores to be used during compilation. As Raspberry Pi 3 and 4 have Quad-core CPU's, it is advisable to run make with -j4 flag. This way make will always try to compile four different source files at the same time, which makes the overall compilation procedure much faster.

121

As the compilation time greatly differs depending on the scenario, there is no correct estimation available. During compilation the console will be filled with numerous C++ compiler warnings, which you can safely ignore. However, the final output will always look the same.

```
make[1]: Nothing to be done for 'all-am'
make[1]: Leaving directory '/home/pi/bitcoin'
```

Ultiamtely, we'll get five binaries (or four in non-GUI setups): `bitcoind`, `bitcoin-cli`, `bitcoin-tx`, `bitcoin-wallet,` and `bitcoin-qt`. To make them available system-wide, we type `sudo make install` as our final command.

Summary

In this chapter we have learned about the hardware needed to run Bitcoin Full Nodes. We have learned how to install and configure the Raspbian OS, which is the standard Linux variant for Raspberry computers. We have configured the C++ build environment for our future compilation tasks. We have learned how to use standard Linux tools for package management and installations. We also have learned how to use `git`, the decentralized source code management tool. We cloned the current Bitcoin source code and used configuration scripts to set up certain functionalities in our Bitcoin installation. And to make our daily tasks with Raspberry devices easier, we learned how to set up and run VNC and SSH servers.

CHAPTER 4

Running Bitcoin

In this chapter we will learn how to configure Bitcoin's reference client, also called Bitcoin Core. We will explore some of its many configuration options and learn how to synchronize with its decentralized network. We will also try out the console-based tools and the GUI wallet software. For testing and development, we will learn how to use Bitcoin's *regtest* and *testnet* networks.

Configuration

After having compiled and installed the binaries in the previous chapter, we will now take care of providing proper settings to our Bitcoin daemon and GUI application. In general, most of the settings provided in Bitcoin's default config file `bitcoin.conf` apply both to the daemon, a noninteractive process that runs in the background, as well as the Qt-based GUI application called "Bitcoin Core Wallet", which is recommended to less tech-savvy users. The usage of the GUI interface depends on the Raspberry variant. For P3 and P4 users there is enough memory available so that the graphical interface could be left running all the time, while Zero W users should prefer the Bitcoin's daemon only. In later chapters we will also talk about daemon configuration scripts that will take care of proper starts and shutdowns to avoid user interactions.

© Harris Brakmić 2019
H. Brakmić, *Bitcoin and Lightning Network on Raspberry Pi*,
https://doi.org/10.1007/978-1-4842-5522-3_4

To create a proper configuration file for Bitcoin, we will first create a new, hidden directory in our home path with mkdir .bitcoin. By default, our home path is /home/pi. If you are using a different username, please adapt the command accordingly.

Inside this new directory, we open a new file called bitcoin.conf[1]. Bitcoin's configuration file comprises of key-value pairs. The lines preceded by a hashmark are considered comments and are being ignored by Bitcoin's software. Since v0.17 of Bitcoin, a valid configuration must separate non-mainnet settings by indicating designated areas with [test] and [regtest] as their respective headers. This also helps keeping equally named settings separated from each other and only in use when running on the respective network. In older versions of Bitcoin, one had to comment out such settings. When we run on *testnet,* our bitcoin.conf would have these settings activated. The same settings can also be used for *mainnet.*

```
testnet=1
[test]
listen=1
server=1
daemon=1
rpcuser=raspiuser
rpcpassword=mypassword
rpcallowip=127.0.0.1
rpcbind=127.0.0.1
rest=1
deprecatedrpc=generate
txindex=1
```

---

[1]https://github.com/bitcoin/bitcoin/blob/master/share/examples/
 bitcoin.conf

```
zmqpubrawblock=tcp://127.0.0.1:28332
zmqpubrawtx=tcp://127.0.0.1:28333
zmqpubhashtx=tcp://127.0.0.1:28334
zmqpubhashblock=tcp://127.0.0.1:28335
```

The first entry *testnet*[2] indicates that we want to run on testnet. However, there is another network available for testing, called *regtest*.[3] Unlike testnet, it can only be run locally and is mostly useful for debugging and local tests. To get a more "realistic" environment for testing without having to risk real bitcoins, the *testnet* is a much better alternative. Throughout this book we will be using both *regtest* and *testnet*.

The entry listen activates the listening mode, which means that our node will be allowed to answer requests from other nodes, for example, for sending blocks and transactions. The next entry, server, activates the local RPC (remote procedure call) server, which we can use to query the state of our node. The setting daemon=1 is only useful for bitcoind, the daemon process, which means that after having started it from the console, the binary will continue running in the background and unblock the console. Without this setting, bitcoind would keep the console blocked and using it as output for its log entries. Using the daemon binary on the console is discouraged as it offers no meaningful interfaces. Instead, run the daemon as background process, and control it via the bitcoin-cli tool that uses the account data from bitcoin.conf and communicates with bitcoind over RPC. More precisely, it uses the TCP port 8332 that is the default port for Bitcoin's RPC server. To stop the daemon, one only needs to issue a stop command via console like this:

```
bitcoin-cli stop
```

---

[2]https://en.bitcoin.it/wiki/Testnet
[3]https://bitcoin.org/en/glossary/regression-test-mode

The next two entries in `bitcoin.conf`, `rpcuser` and `rpcpassword`, define the RPC user and password to prevent unauthorized access to our RPC server. The next two entries, `rpcallowip` and `rpcbind`, bind the RPC server to our local IP address and only allow local RPC queries from the same address. In general, when `rpcallowip` is being used `rpcbind` should be used as well. Failure to do so would provoke a warning in the log entries.

```
WARNING: option -rpcallowip was specified without
-rpcbind; this doesn't usually make sense
```

The next entry, `rest`, activates the HTTP-based API which can be used as alternative to the older RPC-API. Many Bitcoin web explorers use this API to query data, because it delivers them in JSON-format that can be directly consumed by web-based clients. The entry `deprecatedrpc` can be used to activate deprecated APIs, that is, APIs which will be removed in future but are still available for compatibility reasons. In our case, we want to use the `generate` functionality, which is very useful in *regtest*. This command would not make much sense in *testnet*, because a Raspberry Pi could never compete with *testnet*-mining devices. Here it serves as a mere example and will be used in *regtest* scenarios only. The next entry, `txindex`, instructs the Bitcoin node to create its own index of transactions which is very useful for searching transaction data. The last four entries prefixed with `zmq` have all to do with Bitcoin's messaging interface that we will learn to use in later chapters.

First Run—Console

Over the next couple of pages, we will keep the configuration file focused on *mainnet,* and will now start the daemon simply by typing `bitcoind` on the console. As we have activated the setting `daemon=1,` we will see no data coming out in the console and thus should open Bitcoin's log file

./bitcoin/debug.log by using one of the available tools for continuous file reading. One such versatile tool is *multitail* that can be easily installed with

```
sudo apt install multitail
```

To start reading the log file we call it with:

```
multitail -f ./bitcoin/debug.log
```

I assume that we are currently in our home directory, so I don't use the $HOME prefix for paths. Otherwise, just type

```
multitail -f $HOME/.bitcoin/debug.log
```

The log file will always begin with the header indicating Bitcoin's software version, its paths, and access settings. It also displays data about its internal data structures and sizes (Figure 4-1).

```
2019-07-24T10:53:01Z Bitcoin Core version v0.18.1rc1 (release build)
2019-07-24T10:53:01Z Assuming ancestors of block 0000000000000000000f1c54590ee18d15ec70e68c8cd4cfb
2019-07-24T10:53:01Z Setting nMinimumChainWork=0000000000000000000000000000000000000000051dc8b82f4
2019-07-24T10:53:01Z Using the 'standard' SHA256 implementation
2019-07-24T10:53:01Z Default data directory /home/pi/.bitcoin
2019-07-24T10:53:01Z Using data directory /home/pi/.bitcoin
2019-07-24T10:53:01Z Config file: /home/pi/.bitcoin/bitcoin.conf (not found, skipping)
2019-07-24T10:53:01Z Using at most 125 automatic connections (1024 file descriptors available)
2019-07-24T10:53:01Z Using 16 MiB out of 32/2 requested for signature cache, able to store 524288
2019-07-24T10:53:01Z Using 16 MiB out of 32/2 requested for script execution cache, able to store
2019-07-24T10:53:01Z Using 4 threads for script verification
2019-07-24T10:53:01Z HTTP: creating work queue of depth 16
2019-07-24T10:53:01Z No rpcpassword set - using random cookie authentication.
2019-07-24T10:53:01Z scheduler thread start
2019-07-24T10:53:01Z Generated RPC authentication cookie /home/pi/.bitcoin/.cookie
2019-07-24T10:53:01Z HTTP: starting 4 worker threads
2019-07-24T10:53:01Z Using wallet directory /home/pi/.bitcoin
2019-07-24T10:53:01Z init message: Verifying wallet(s)...
2019-07-24T10:53:01Z Using BerkeleyDB version Berkeley DB 4.8.30: (April  9, 2010)
2019-07-24T10:53:01Z Using wallet /home/pi/.bitcoin
2019-07-24T10:53:01Z BerkeleyEnvironment::Open: LogDir=/home/pi/.bitcoin/database ErrorFile=/home/
2019-07-24T10:53:01Z init message: Loading banlist...
2019-07-24T10:53:01Z Cache configuration:
2019-07-24T10:53:01Z * Using 2.0 MiB for block index database
2019-07-24T10:53:01Z * Using 8.0 MiB for chain state database
2019-07-24T10:53:01Z * Using 440.0 MiB for in-memory UTXO set (plus up to 286.1 MiB of unused memp
2019-07-24T10:53:01Z init message: Loading block index...
2019-07-24T10:53:01Z Opening LevelDB in /home/pi/.bitcoin/blocks/index
2019-07-24T10:53:01Z Opened LevelDB successfully
2019-07-24T10:53:01Z Using obfuscation key for /home/pi/.bitcoin/blocks/index: 0000000000000000
2019-07-24T10:53:01Z LoadBlockIndexDB: last block file = 0
```

Figure 4-1. *Bitcoin log entries*

Of course, Bitcoin's *mainnet*-blockchain is a giant structure comprising of more than 240 gigabytes of data so that the initial download and synchronization could take many days and maybe even weeks.

Another important aspect is the usage of fast hard drives like SSDs. Although it's possible to run the whole system on a single drive, like SD cards, which I prefer for local tests, the usage of such hardware configurations in production is discouraged for several reasons. First, the speed of a separate SSD that's only working on the blockchain and not being used for any other operations is unmatched. Second, by having separated the operating system from the actual data, one also takes care of avoiding single points of failure in case something goes wrong with the system or Bitcoin software.

The hardest part in creating an initial Bitcoin configuration on small devices like Raspberry Pi's is setting up the blockchain data and synchronizing it properly. Therefore, it is recommended to keep configuration and compilation of Bitcoin software separated from Bitcoin's payload data, that is, its blockchain data. This can be done easily by starting `bitcoind` with an argument indicating an alternative path for its data directory. The same could be achieved by putting the flag `datadir` in `bitcoin.conf` as well.

```
bitcoind -datadir=/mnt/media/bitcoin
```

Now the daemon would automatically search for configuration data in the given directory. If you have entered the above setting in the default configuration in `.bitcoin/bitcoin.conf,` then the daemon would read all other settings first, apply them, and then start downloading blockchain data in the given location. In this case one should first move an existing `wallet.dat` file, that contains public and private keys, from default data directory to the alternative one. `bitcoind` and `bitcoin-qt`, the GUI application, by default always create a new `wallet.dat` when the data directory has none.

In cases when a complete copy of blockchain data isn't needed, there is an option to run a node as a so-called *pruned node*. These nodes have the same security level as ordinary full nodes, with the difference that old transaction data gets discarded after having been validated. A pruned node always checks blocks and transactions, but it doesn't keep the whole index of all past transactions as full nodes do. Therefore, they need a much less disk space. However, a pruned node can't be switched back to a full node without re-downloading the whole blockchain again.

Also, the indexing of transactions with pruned nodes isn't possible so that certain settings won't be available, for example, txindex=1 can't be used in the configuration files. By default, a node only builds an index of transactions for the current user, that is, the local *wallet data* being used by a node. But, if you want to have a full index of all transactions, you will need to create an index, by using the aforementioned setting. However, this is only possible if you have data about all transactions since 2009, which is not given when you're running a pruned node. The same applies to rescanning the chain, rescan=1, as there is simply no full chain data available to be scanned.

Therefore, one should carefully compare the pros and cons before activating the pruned mode. For example, by setting prune=550, one would activate pruning mode that would delete any old blocks to stay under the specified size of 500MB. This of course could be either set as configuration option or used as one of the flags when starting bitcoind or bitcoin-qt. In general, most of the options used in Bitcoin's configuration file can also be used as arguments in the console.

However, pruned nodes offer the same level of security as full nodes as they are still validating all incoming data without relying on any external factors or authorities. The only real difference is that full nodes also offer support for the overall Bitcoin network by providing synchronization to services to other nodes. Just like our node started by only knowing the Genesis Block and asking for all other blocks from external nodes, the same way would new nodes ask our node to provide them information to update their blockchain copies. To operate a full node not only means to be an independent validator but also to provide services for other participants in this decentralized network. Therefore, putting aside the questions regarding disk space, electricity costs, and invested time, to run a full node also means to make Bitcoin's network stronger, more decentralized, and more independent. Every single node, even a small one like our Raspberry Pi, has an impact in Bitcoin's network. The more nodes we run, the more resilient our network becomes against attacks and manipulations.

First Run—GUI

To run Bitcoin Wallet GUI, we'll have to open a VNC connection first. Of course, you can do the same directly via plugged-in keyboard and mouse. The easiest way to run *Bitcoin Core wallet*, as the software is being called, is just by typing bitcoin-qt in the console. However, this is not exactly the most elegant way to open a GUI application, and therefore we will create a proper menu entry. For this we open with nano a new configuration file:

```
sudo nano /usr/share/applications/bitcoin.desktop
```

The following data we enter there will instruct the desktop environment to create a new menu entry. The icon-path should contain a properly sized bitcoin image that can be found easily via image search on the net.

```
[Desktop Entry]
Type=Application
Exec=/usr/local/bin/bitcoin-qt --datadir=/mnt/data
Icon=/home/pi/Pictures/bitcoin-logo.png
Name=Bitcoin Core v1.8.1
GenericName=Bitcoin Core Wallet
Categories=Internet
```

The path pointing at `bitcoin-qt` application is critical. Make sure you have installed the binaries with `make install` after the compilation. The flag `datadir` should point at the directory, where your blockchain data is located. After we have saved the file, we execute the following command to update our desktop environment.

```
sudo update-desktop-database
```

Now we can open our desktop's main menu and go to the "Other"menu-group (Figure 4-2).

Figure 4-2. *Bitcoin Core Wallet menu entry*

From now on, we can comfortably start our Bitcoin Core client with a mouse click. The first window we will see is a noninteractive splash screen that will remain visible until Bitcoin has completed internal tasks (Figure 4-3).

Figure 4-3. *Bitcoin client splash screen*

Afterward, you'll be presented the GUI indicating the download process, which can take a long time. Therefore, it's strongly recommended to use fast SSD drives and cable-based Internet connection to speed up this process.

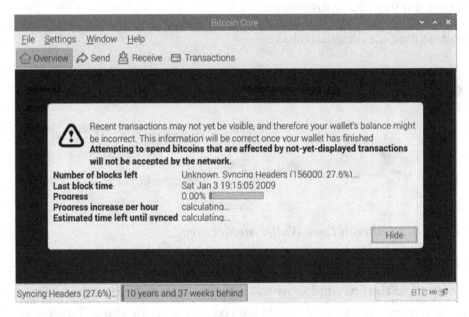

Figure 4-4. *Initial blockchain download*

By clicking the button Hide, we switch to the actual GUI of the client (Figure 4-5).

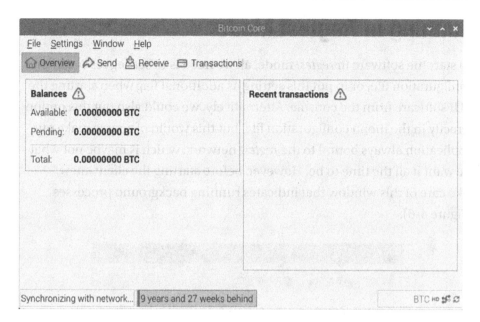

Figure 4-5. *Bitcoin Core Wallet main window*

As long as the client is downloading data, all operations regarding sending and receiving bitcoins aren't considered valid until the chain has been completely synchronized. However, we can still explore the wallet and its many functions, but a much better way to do so is by running the client in `testnet` or `regtest` mode. To experiment with the available tools and commands, one doesn't need to use the *mainnet* blockchain. Most of the functionality offered in the "real" Bitcoin network can be reproduced in a local `regtest` mode, for example. This is also the preferred when developing Bitcoin-based software as we will see in later chapters, when we will be using *JavaScript* and *Python* to call various functionalities and APIs.

Running in Regtest Mode

To start the software in *regtest* mode, all we need is to set `regtest=1` in the configuration file, or to put this setting as additional flag when starting the GUI software from the console. Alternatively, we could also put this option directly in the menu configuration file, but this would of course make our application always bound to the *regtest* network, which is maybe not what we want it all the time to be. However, before starting the client anew, take care of this window that indicates running background processes (Figure 4-6).

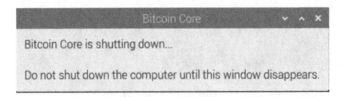

Figure 4-6. *Shutdown window*

This window will remain visible as long as there are unfinished Bitcoin processes. You should not shut down the device or try to start a new Bitcoin Core instance.

After having started the GUI with this setting, the splash screen would look a bit differently than the one from *mainnet*, indicating a different blockchain environment (Figure 4-7).

Figure 4-7. *Regtest splash screen*

We see in the tile of the splash screen the *regtest* indicator. Also, the color of the Bitcoin logo is no longer orange but turquoise. The main GUI will look the same, and even the blockchain download window will be shown. However, as *regtest* is a *local-only* chain, there is no way to synchronize it with any external node. There are simply no external nodes at all. How can we use *regtest* for anything if there are no blocks? The answer is simple: we will create new ones by ourselves. We first click the *Hide* button to close the download indicator and then select the menu *Window* ➤ *Console* (Figure 4-8).

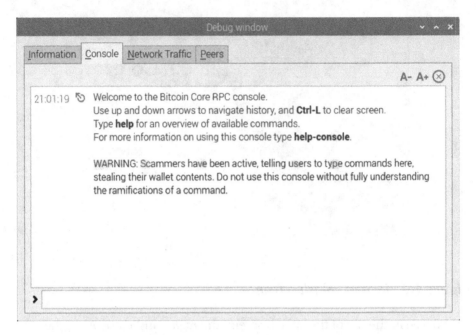

Figure 4-8. *Debug window with console*

This window offers the same functionality we can find in the console by using `bitcoin-cli`. As we are now in GUI mode, it is more user-friendly to execute such commands via Debug window, but there is also nothing that would prevent a user from sending same commands via `bitcoin-cli`. In our case, we will need an address first, because for *regtest*-blocks to be generated, we have to provide a "miner's address" by typing the command `getnewaddess` and confirming it with ENTER.

An address with 2 as prefix will be returned, for example:

`2NBP3w5m425n12RePYQoJfsznTXnJr4yGiY`

Figure 4-9 shows how the execution of this command looks like in the GUI.

```
21:09:16  ↻  getnewaddress
21:09:16  ↻  2NBP3w5m425n12RePYQoJfsznTXnJr4yGiY
```

Figure 4-9. *Executing a command in Bitcoin's console window*

Our next step will be to generate a few blocks, which we instantiate with the command generatetoaddress.

generatetoaddress 5 2NBP3w5m425n12RePYQoJfsznTXnJr4yGiY

The number 5 indicates the number of blocks we want to be generated. The address is the recipient of the block rewards that come with each block. We also get a tool tip informing us about the incoming transactions (Figure 4-10).

Figure 4-10. *Tooltip informing about incoming transactions*

Now our client's main window doesn't show the download indicator anymore (Figure 4-11).

Figure 4-11. *Bitcoin Core Wallet showing transaction entries*

Summary

In this chapter we have learned how to configure and run `bitcoind`, the Bitcoin daemon. We have also learned how to use the GUI interface of Bitcoin, the Bitcoin Core Wallet. We have seen a few important options for setting up Bitcoin's configuration file, `bitcoin.conf`. We have learned about available Bitcoin networks, because not only the "real" network, `mainnet`, exists, but also `testnet` and `regtest`, which are recommended for learning about Bitcoin or developing software based on it. We have also learned about the command line-based management tool called `bitcoin-cli` that can be used to issue commands against Bitcoin Daemon's RPC API. To make using Bitcoin Core Wallet more user-friendly, we have created a menu entry for our desktop environment. Ultimately, we have learned how to run the GUI in `regtest` mode and how to mine `regtest` bitcoins via Debug console.

PART II

Using Bitcoin

CHAPTER 5

Bitcoin Core Wallet

In this chapter we will learn how to configure and control our Wallet
GUI. We will also learn how to prepare and execute transactions as well
as message signing and verification. Bitcoin Core Wallet is a powerful tool
that can do much more than executing monetary transactions. Properly
used, it can function as a bank on your desk, or in your pocket.

Wallet Encryption

As we have already learned, the Bitcoin Core Wallet is directly accessing
our *wallet.dat*, which means that this application has a raw access to our
most important data: private keys. Therefore, it is strongly recommended
to encrypt wallet data to prevent unauthorized movement of funds. In case
your device becomes compromised, an attacker would only need to create
new transaction and move all your funds to another address.

There is no recovery possible. To prevent such situations, go to menu
Settings / Encrypt Wallet (Figure 5-1).

Figure 5-1. *Encryption menu entry*

© Harris Brakmić 2019
H. Brakmić, *Bitcoin and Lightning Network on Raspberry Pi,*
https://doi.org/10.1007/978-1-4842-5522-3_5

Then type in twice your new password in this window (Figure 5-2).

Figure 5-2. *Entering the new password for the wallet*

After you have confirmed it with OK, you'll get a warning window informing you about the importance of your new password (Figure 5-3).

Figure 5-3. *Warning message about wallet password*

If you ever lose your password, you'll also lose access to your funds. After having clicked the button *Yes*, the encryption will start. This process will need a few moments to complete. Let the application finish the work without doing anything else with it. Ultimately, you'll get a confirmation window (Figure 5-4) informing you that your wallet is now fully encrypted. This means that whenever in the future you try to execute a "sensitive" operation, you'll have to enter this password. Sensitive operations are, for example, new transactions, dumping of private keys, or manipulation of any data located in *wallet.dat*.

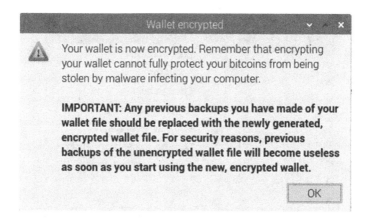

Figure 5-4. *Wallet encryption completed successfully*

We can now test this security measure by trying to export or "dump" the private key of one of our addresses. For this we switch to Transactions Tab (Figure 5-5) in our main window and copy the address we used previously as target for our mining rewards.

File Settings Window Help		

⌂ Overview ⮡ Send 🖳 Receive ▤ Transactions		

| All ▾ | All ▾ | Enter address, transaction id, or label to search |

Date ▲	Type	Label
✅ 9/20/19 21:13	Mined	↗ (2NBP3w5m425n12RePYQoJfsznTXnJr4yGiY)
✅ 9/20/19 21:13	Mined	↗ (2NBP3w5m425n12RePYQoJfsznTXnJr4yGiY)
✅ 9/20/19 21:13	Mined	↗ (2NBP3w5m425n12RePYQoJfsznTXnJr4yGiY)
✅ 9/20/19 21:13	Mined	↗ (2NBP3w5m425n12RePYQoJfsznTXnJr4yGiY)

Figure 5-5. *Transactions Tab*

To copy an address, we open the context menu with a right click on one of the available entries and select the option "Copy address" (Figure 5-6).

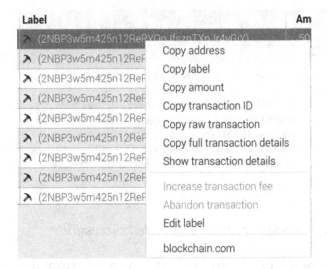

Figure 5-6. Copying an address from Transactions Tab

In the next step, we open the Debug Console Window by selecting the menu Window ➤ Console (Figure 5-7).

Figure 5-7. Window menu in Bitcoin Core Wallet

In the newly opened Console window, we enter the below command. You will of course be using a different address.

```
dumpprivkey 2NBP3w5m425n12RePYQoJfsznTXnJr4yGiY
```

However, the Bitcoin Core Wallet is not following our orders as the *wallet.dat* is now encrypted (Figure 5-8).

```
dumpprivkey 2NBP3w5m425n12RePYQoJfsznTXnJr4yGiY
Error: Please enter the wallet passphrase with walletpassphrase first. (code -13)
```

Figure 5-8. *Error message in Console window*

To be able to execute such operations, we have to unlock our wallet first. For this we use the command `walletpassphrase` that accepts two parameters: our password and a timeout for keeping the passphrase in memory. The timeout we set is a numerical value indicating the number of seconds. After we have typed in our password and timeout data, the application will return nothing, and the wallet will be unlocked.

```
walletpassphrase YOUR_PASSWORD TIMEOUT
```

The result would be just a simple entry "null" stating that there were no errors, and our wallet is now available for more sensitive operations (Figure 5-9).

```
walletpassphrase(...)
null
```

Figure 5-9. *A successful walletpassphrase command execution*

Now we can try again to dump the private key of our "mining" address (Figure 5-10).

dumpprivkey 2NBP3w5m425n12RePYQoJfsznTXnJr4yGiY

cTHvUeQjXxAEJmiZSHMK7ra9WcX7hhrUGChrbqnpnpZ9avKty7E8

Figure 5-10. *Getting the private key*

This time we were successful and could get the private key. This example of course should also serve as a clear warning that an attacker doesn't need to have full access to a device to steal funds. All that is needed is a temporary access to an unencrypted wallet. A simple check of the transaction list is sufficient to find out which of the addresses have the most funds. Therefore, wallet encryption **should always** be activated. Also, funds that are not moving very often should better be moved to addresses controlled by hardware wallets. A running Bitcoin Full Node is basically a "hot wallet", because of its constant connection with the Internet.

Having a great freedom with software that mimics a small bank should never be treated as a product that only needs to be plugged in somewhere. Quite contrary, it's a *continuous process* that needs great care and a healthy dose of "paranoia". Not encrypting your wallets and leaving unneeded funds in Internet-connected nodes is a recipe for disaster, which in most cases could have been easily avoided by following a few simple rules.

Sending and Receiving Funds

Our Wallet GUI makes sending and receiving funds much easier than done with console-based tools. However, it is still possible to execute any GUI-based operation via the Debug Console window. In later chapters, when we will be using the console management tool `bitcoin-cli`, we will use such commands as well. But for now, we will stick with the more user-friendly GUI variants. But before we send any funds, we should activate *Coin Control Features* first. For this we select the menu *Settings* ➤ *Options*, and in the *Options* window, we switch to tab *Wallet*, where we activate the checkbox "Enable coin control features" (Figure 5-11).

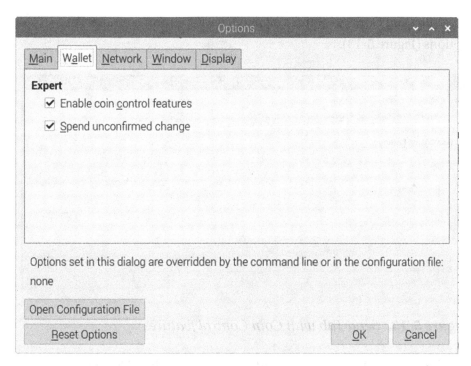

Figure 5-11. *Activating Coin Control features*

Coin Control features allow us to select our spending addresses individually. Also, we get the option to set the change address. Without the coin control features being activated, our *Send* tab would look like this (Figure 5-12).

Figure 5-12. *Send Tab without Coin Control features*

With Coin Control features enabled, we get a more granular set of options (Figure 5-13).

Figure 5-13. *Send Tab with Coin Control features*

By clicking the button *Inputs*, we get a complete list of all matured funds that could be spent. *Mature funds* in Bitcoin means that an UTXO we own got at least 100 confirmations, that is, the number of blocks being mined.

The number of confirmations is shown in the rightmost column (Figure 5-14).

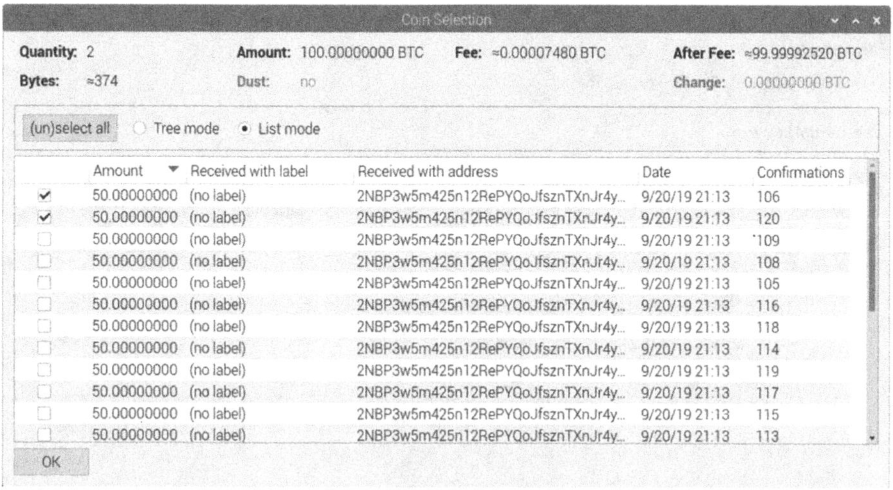

	Amount ▼	Received with label	Received with address	Date	Confirmations
✔	50.00000000	(no label)	2NBP3w5m425n12RePYQoJfsznTXnJr4y...	9/20/19 21:13	106
✔	50.00000000	(no label)	2NBP3w5m425n12RePYQoJfsznTXnJr4y...	9/20/19 21:13	120
☐	50.00000000	(no label)	2NBP3w5m425n12RePYQoJfsznTXnJr4y...	9/20/19 21:13	109
☐	50.00000000	(no label)	2NBP3w5m425n12RePYQoJfsznTXnJr4y...	9/20/19 21:13	108
☐	50.00000000	(no label)	2NBP3w5m425n12RePYQoJfsznTXnJr4y...	9/20/19 21:13	105
☐	50.00000000	(no label)	2NBP3w5m425n12RePYQoJfsznTXnJr4y...	9/20/19 21:13	116
☐	50.00000000	(no label)	2NBP3w5m425n12RePYQoJfsznTXnJr4y...	9/20/19 21:13	118
☐	50.00000000	(no label)	2NBP3w5m425n12RePYQoJfsznTXnJr4y...	9/20/19 21:13	114
☐	50.00000000	(no label)	2NBP3w5m425n12RePYQoJfsznTXnJr4y...	9/20/19 21:13	119
☐	50.00000000	(no label)	2NBP3w5m425n12RePYQoJfsznTXnJr4y...	9/20/19 21:13	117
☐	50.00000000	(no label)	2NBP3w5m425n12RePYQoJfsznTXnJr4y...	9/20/19 21:13	115
☐	50.00000000	(no label)	2NBP3w5m425n12RePYQoJfsznTXnJr4y...	9/20/19 21:13	113

Figure 5-14. *Coin Selection window*

In Figure 5-14 we have selected two spendable inputs. The application automatically subtracts the future mining fee from it, thus leaving us with 99,99992520 bitcoins that the receiving address could get from us. After we have clicked the *OK* button and entered the receiving address, our *Send* tab would now look like in Figure 5-15. Additionally, we have entered the change address, because we are sending 90 bitcoins. This address would then receive the change of about 10 bitcoins. We also decide to subtract the mining fee from the amount we are sending. Therefore, we won't be sending whole 90 bitcoins but a slightly lower sum.

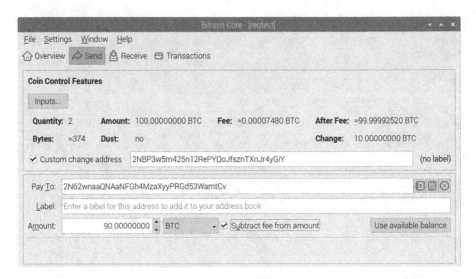

Figure 5-15. *Sending funds to another address*

We don't have to type those addresses as there are more convenient "address book" and "paste from clipboard" options available (Figure 5-16).

Figure 5-16. *Address book selection and clipboard*

For a more complex scenarios, there is also the option available to add several recipients that will be defined separately but in the same window. By clicking the button "Add Recipient", an additional address area will be shown to enter additional recipient's data and the amount of funds to be sent (Figure 5-17).

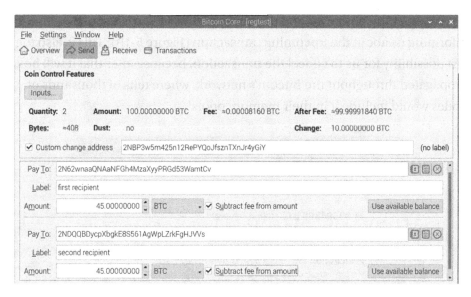

Figure 5-17. *Sending funds to multiple recipients*

This of course is a very convenient way of sending funds to multiple recipients. If we now go back to our initial transaction with one recipient and try to send funds, the first thing we will see is the window asking us for password (Figure 5-18).

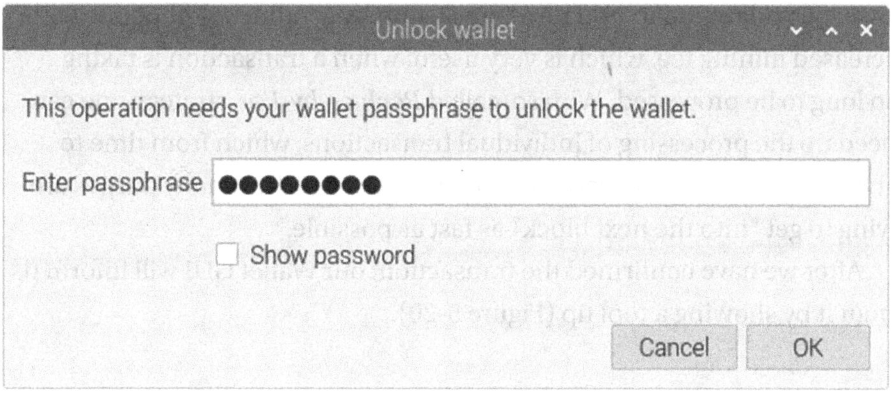

Figure 5-18. *Unlock window*

We enter the password and the next window we see is the one informing us about the upcoming transaction (Figure 5-19). This is also the last possibility for us to cancel the transaction, because after that it will be propagated throughout the Bitcoin's network, where tens of thousands of nodes would include it in their memory pools[1].

Figure 5-19. *Confirmation window*

From this point on, no transaction could be made "undone". There is, however, and option to update a transaction by sending another one with increased mining fee, which is very useful when a transaction is taking too long to be processed. With so-called *Replace-by-Fee*[2] strategy one can speed up the processing of individual transactions, which from time to time becomes a pressing issue in the Bitcoin network as many parties are trying to get "into the next block" as fast as possible.

After we have confirmed the transaction, our Wallet GUI will inform us about it by showing a tool tip (Figure 5-20).

---

[1]As we are dealing with *regtest* here, there won't be any real network propagation
[2]https://en.bitcoin.it/wiki/Replace_by_fee

Figure 5-20. Tooltip transaction confirmation

Also, our main window would automatically switch to the Transactions tab (Figure 5-21).

Date	Type	Label	Amount (BTC)
9/21/19 10:32	Payment to y...	(n/a)	-0.00005120
9/21/19 10:30	Payment to y...	(n/a)	-0.00005120
9/21/19 08:48	Mined	(mpm26BniAWAfiQWuZLsxdrHFijEupa9mwP)	[50.00000000]
9/21/19 08:48	Mined	(mpm26BniAWAfiQWuZLsxdrHFijEupa9mwP)	[50.00000000]
9/21/19 08:48	Mined	(mpm26BniAWAfiQWuZLsxdrHFijEupa9mwP)	[50.00000000]
9/21/19 08:48	Mined	(mpm26BniAWAfiQWuZLsxdrHFijEupa9mwP)	[50.00000000]

Figure 5-21. Transaction tab

If we double click the transaction we just sent, we'll get a window showing its details (Figure 5-22).

Details for 476b2a54908eb18f8...0f1df787c1cd9e9aee017b83697   ⌄ ᴧ ✕

Status: 0/unconfirmed, in memory pool
Date: 9/21/19 10:32
Total debit: -99.99994880 BTC
Total credit: 99.99994880 BTC
Transaction fee: -0.00005120 BTC
Net amount: -0.00005120 BTC
Transaction ID:
476b2a54908eb18f8be3ae08b51be464448cd0f1df787c1cd9e9aee017
b83697
Transaction total size: 418 bytes

Close

Figure 5-22. *Transaction Information window*

This transaction too will now need several confirmations before it
can be accepted as settled. In Bitcoin's network the minimum amount
of confirmations needed before any party should accept a transaction as
finalized is six blocks. After six blocks have passed, we can be pretty sure
that there is no practical way to reverse any transaction as the amount
of energy (and money) needed to manipulate the blockchain wouldn't
be economical in any way. The well-aligned system of incentives and
punishments in Bitcoin is keeping any adversarial parties at bay, while
those who support the network by investing energy and other resources
can reap the benefits in form of *coinbase* transactions, that is, the "block
rewards", and mining fees paid by those who are using the network to send
funds. Just like we did it now.

As we are sending our transactions in *regtest* mode, we will need to
issue another `generate` or `generatetoadress` command in the Debug
console to move the chain for a few blocks (Figure 5-23). As the *regtest*
mode has no high-difficulty requirements regarding block creation, it is no
problem to create even hundreds of blocks at once. In general, the *regtest*
mode should be used to learn basic functions like sending and receiving
funds, creation of signed messages, and working with wallet data like
private key exports and imports.

```
generate 10
```

```
[
  "5908f60cfb1646225fcaa2d7933a8558218afd3bdcd9d26568e1aa0c3e8f2eeb",
  "4e238f100e4b705ac6edd3c771272b3fedc6725e7bb7053f910ddf80fcb7a11b",
  "227cd1e6e789f9c1a8a6434053e328e5127863e64a7c0e8533e07ddba700090f",
  "58c8f3de857a7dcbe4b5ff975389f7c71015cb2cd80419be23e42b475cd5544b",
  "1a61c9a16c128a3733e33960b5b898fe4995aee3f2888c06f4d8c09d74c6a1d8",
  "1d349111d949e99db110153f3140b5bfbfe3b610ed991393534fc2c56952aa0b",
  "7dbdaf01ed94d6be204d640eeccd7c425aaef230522068b4582d7c89721d1cfd",
  "6672692703ab08b444f2df717bc6e812112a21e54d911bdf0e6d68d73334e7a4",
  "4d8576d04a65d6a417a8771e38dee6a3d06a039b23c79e1bd2d52b4dd38d4cab
",
  "02807bf066ffa42697bc753ed57de80117826df0e1e4e590e0cf6f9ddd4acd8d"
]
```

Figure 5-23. *Generating 10 more blocks in regtest mode*

To receive funds, we have an easy-to-use functionality behind the *Receive* tab (Figure 5-24). There we can not only insert our address but also the amount we expect to receive. Additionally, we can create Bech32 addresses that provide several benefits. One of them are the much lower transactions fees. In later chapters, when we will be talking about the Lightning Network, these addresses will become very important to us.

Figure 5-24. *Receive Tab for creating payment requests*

After having clicked the button *Request Payment*, a new window will appear (Figure 5-25).

Figure 5-25. *Request Payment window with QR code*

This window shows a QR code that could be scanned by a mobile app or sent via e-mail for later processing. It also shows an URI that encodes the request, which can be used in web sites, for example. The information about our payment requests gets saved internally and is shown in the list below the request editor (Figure 5-26).

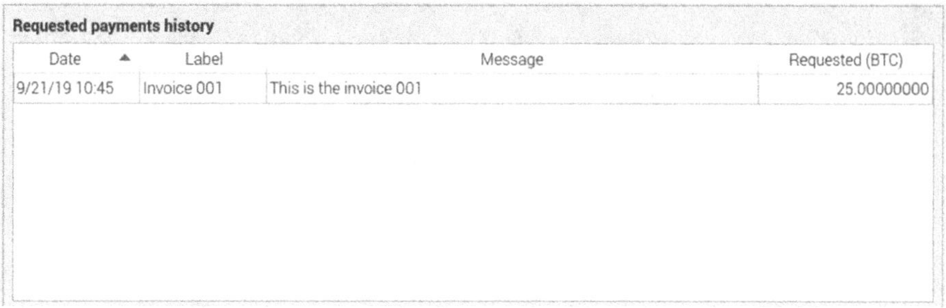

Requested payments history			
Date ▲	Label	Message	Requested (BTC)
9/21/19 10:45	Invoice 001	This is the invoice 001	25.00000000

Figure 5-26. Requested payments history

Clicking twice on the entry opens the window with QR code again. The practice of generating QR codes and encoding expected sums in them is always recommended to prevent transaction errors. Senders only need to scan the payment request without entering any values by hand, and recipients can be sure that the expected amounts will be sent.

Message Signing and Verification

Bitcoin Core Wallet offers message signing and verification functionalities. With them we can prove that we own certain addresses so that senders can be sure that we will receive those funds. As transactions made in the Bitcoin network are irreversible, the message signing procedure can provide additional level of security before sending funds to an address. To sign a message, we select the menu *File ➤ Sign Message*. A window with three fields will be opened (Figure 5-27).

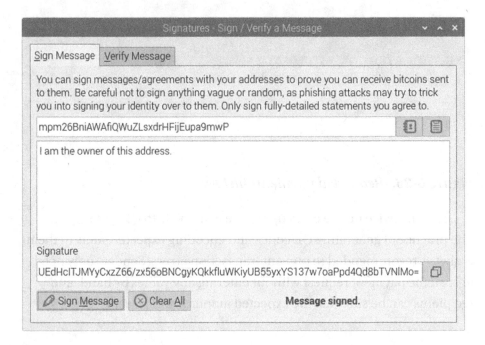

Figure 5-27. *Signing a message with own key*

To successfully sign a message, we need an address, which is shown in the first field in Figure 5-27. In this example, I have selected one address from my *regtest* environment. In the textbox below the address, we enter any message we want. Then we click the button *Sign Message* to generate the message signature that will be shown in the third field. Our message signing procedure is now complete, and we can give the signature to other parties.

However, message signing is not to be confused with encryption. We aren't writing secret messages but creating proofs of ownership of certain addresses. As we own the private key associated with the address we used to sign the message, we are able to prove our ownership of it. Other parties would then be able to use our public key to check if the signature generated indeed fits to a given address. Here, again, we utilize the asymmetric nature of public-key-cryptography to generate proofs and let others check them for validity without ever disclosing our private keys.

To validate our signed message, we use the other tab in the same window (Figure 5-28). There we enter the address, the exact message, and the signature.

Figure 5-28. *Message Verification tab*

However, take into account that message signing and verification can't help you to check if a party has indeed generated a certain transaction. Message signing and verification have nothing to do with the UTXO's (unspent transaction outputs) and transactions related to it. All it can do is to prove that a receiving address belongs to a certain party.

Client Settings

Bitcoin Core Wallet offers many interesting configuration options easily accessible via the *Options* window that can be selected in the *Settings* menu. Over multiple tabs one can change various application behaviors regarding network, disk space consumption, proxies, language, and currency settings (Figure 5-29).

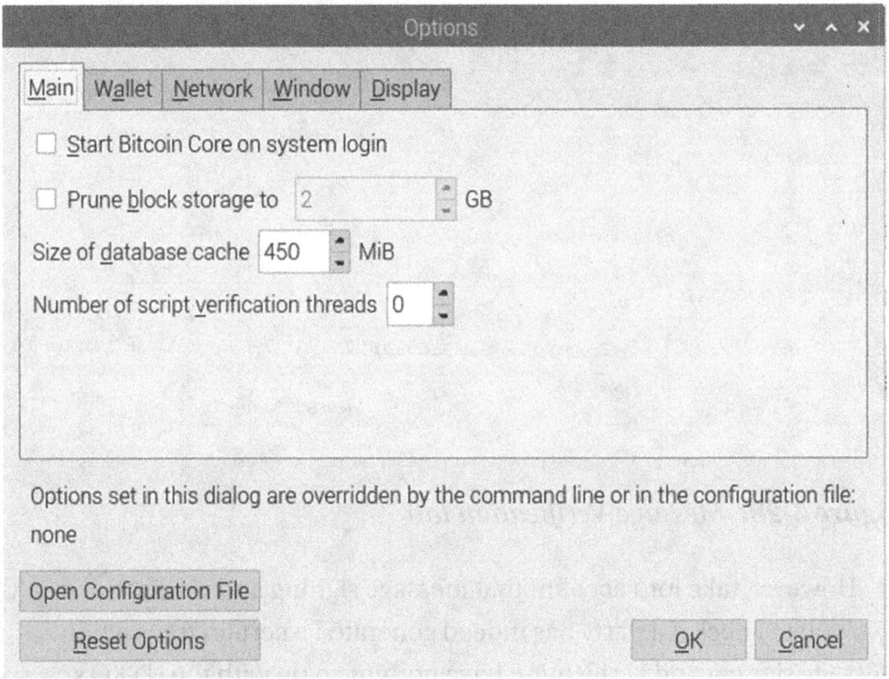

Figure 5-29. Options window

In the first tab (*Main*), we can activate the autostart function for our client as well as the size of pruned storage. As already mentioned in previous chapters, Full Nodes can also be run as pruned nodes, that is, nodes that discard old transactions after they have been validated once. However, take into account that this option can only be selected once and that there is no way to go back to a Full Node with complete blockchain data.

In such case one would have to re-download the whole blockchain again. The other two options deal with data caching and CPU core utilization. By default, the client uses all available cores minus one for checking scripts in Bitcoin transactions. This behavior can be changed if you experience heavy slowdowns of your machine.

The *Wallet* tab offers two options regarding Coin Control features we used previously and spending of unconfirmed change (Figure 5-30).

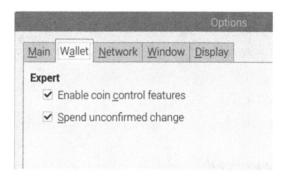

Figure 5-30. *Wallet tab*

The option to send unconfirmed change means that we allow our client to create transactions that could include UTXOs from previous transactions that haven't been confirmed yet. Usually, it takes at least six blocks for a transaction to count as confirmed.

In the *Network* tab, we can modify our node's communication behavior. For example, we can decide if it should accept incoming connections or not. Also, it is possible to configure additional proxies like Tor.[3] If we use UPnP port mapping, we can activate it there as well (Figure 5-31).

---

[3]https://github.com/Actinium-project/Actinium/wiki

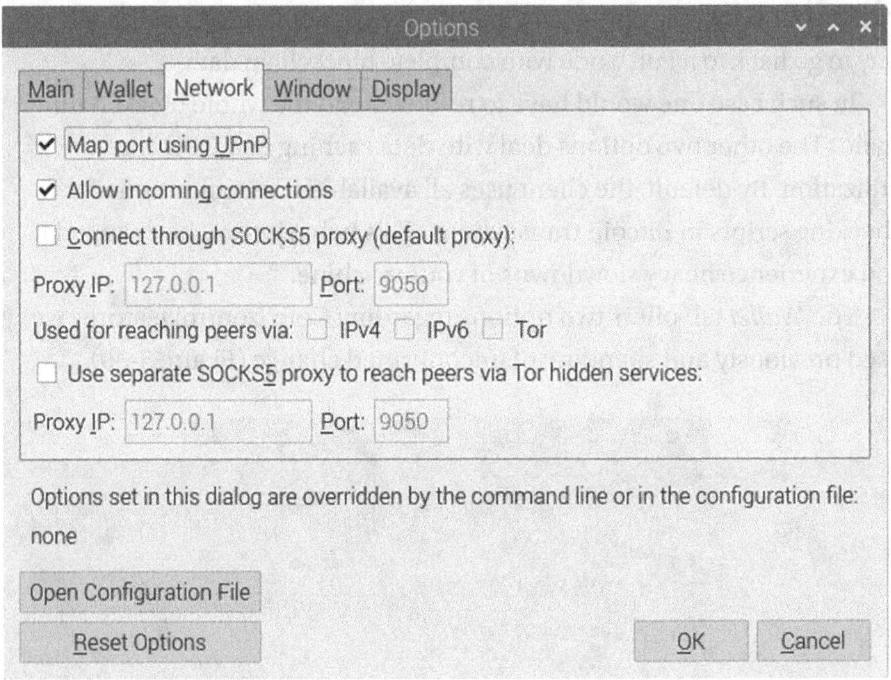

Figure 5-31. *Network tab*

The visual behavior can be changed in the *Window* tab (Figure 5-32).

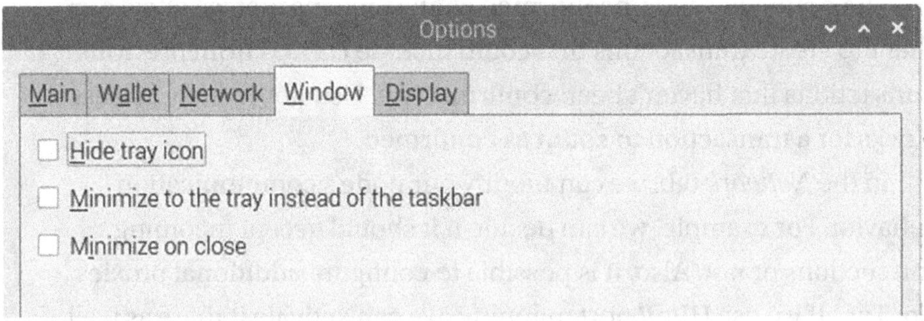

Figure 5-32. *Window tab*

The last tab, *Display*, contains options for setting up the language, the bitcoin units, and the URL for querying transaction data via 3rd-party explorers. In Figure 5-33 I have selected one such explorer. As those addresses belong to external parties, one should take care of properly setting up their template URLs. The placeholder for the transaction ID is %s, while the rest describes the URL to be accessed.

Options				⌄ ^ ✕

Main	Wallet	Network	Window	Display

User Interface language: (default)

Unit to show amounts in: BTC

Third party transaction URLs   https://blockchain.com/btc/tx/%s

Options set in this dialog are overridden by the command line or in the configuration file: none

Figure 5-33. *Display tab*

After having changed the settings and restarted the client, we can now access the URL in the *transaction list* by opening the context menu for a transaction (Figure 5-34).

sl   Edit label

      blockchain.com

Figure 5-34. *Querying transaction data with external explorers*

163

Summary

In this chapter we have learned how to use and configure the Bitcoin Core Wallet application. This application is the standard reference client that dates back to 2009, the year Bitcoin came into existence. This application has seen many changes, but its core functionalities remained the same. We have learned the most important basics: creating addresses, sending funds, encrypting our wallet, and signing and verifying messages. We have also learned about the many options that can be changed in the Options window.

CHAPTER 6

bitcoind

In this chapter we will learn how to control the Bitcoin Daemon, bitcoind,[1] via Bitcoin's command line interface, bitcoin-cli. Every function we explored before in the Bitcoin Core Wallet can be replicated in the console as well. This of course makes Bitcoin easy to integrate with other tools and services. We will also learn to use Bitcoin's API and messaging service.

Configuration

It is not required to run Bitcoin as Core Wallet, because the same functionality can be provided by using its daemon, bitcoind. As the daemon always gets compiled together with other parts of the system, the only difference is that we have to call this binary in the console to start the non-interactive daemon process.

To find out where your bitcoind is located, use this command:

```
which bitcoind
```

Usually, the path returned would be /usr/local/bin/bitcoind that is globally known. To start bitcoind from the console, just type its name and confirm with ENTER.

---

[1]https://en.bitcoin.it/wiki/Bitcoind

© Harris Brakmić 2019
H. Brakmić, *Bitcoin and Lightning Network on Raspberry Pi*,
https://doi.org/10.1007/978-1-4842-5522-3_6

However, to start the daemon with our individually selected configuration settings and directories, we should take care of giving it the correct path of our `datadir`, which is the directory where the configuration file and blockchain data reside. In cases where the `datadir` is located separately from the configuration file, an explicit `datadir` parameter must be given in `bitcoin.conf`. We also add the flag `daemon` to instruct the daemon to release the console. This is not needed if this flag is already active in *bitcoin.conf*. A typical start of `bitcoind` from console would look like this:

```
bitcoind -datadir=/home/pi/.bitcoind -daemon
```

To see what's happening in the background, we can use a tool called *multitail* that can be installed with `apt`, the Raspbian's package manager.

```
sudo apt install multitail
```

All `bitcoind` logfiles will be located in the given `datadir`, but it depends on the chain currently being used which of the logfiles we should be read. If we're using the *testnet,* then the logfile would be located in *.bitcoin/ testnet3/debug.log*. For *regtest* the logfile would be in *.bitcoin/regtest/ debug.log*. The number after the *testnet* name is the version of the *testnet* chain, which implies that there were older variants that later got abandoned.

As `bitcoind` is a non-interactive process, we need another tool that can communicate with it. For this we use `bitcoin-cli`, the command line interface, that communicates via RPC (remote procedure call) with `bitcoind`. To be able to communicate with it, we need a few settings in our bitcoin.conf.

```
server=1
daemon=1
rpcuser=raspiuser
rpcpassword=mypassword
rpcallowip=127.0.0.1
rpcbind=127.0.0.1
rest=1
```

The daemon process can be configured to activate access to its API by using the option server=1 in bitcoin.conf. The daemon also offers the JSON-HTTP[2] API that can be activated by using the option rest=1. The option "rest" stands for REST,[3] which is an architectural software design style that defines a set of constraints for creation of web services.

In short, the flag rest allows bitcoind to operate a web service that's often being used by various web-based tools as their backend service. Without it, most of the services available on the web today wouldn't exist. This also makes it accessible for tools that use the same protocol and transport format, like the popular HTTP client curl.

The settings rpcuser and rpcpassword are needed to activate authentication-based service access. To further lock down the access to our service, we define a set of allowed IP addresses and also *bind* the service to a single IP address. In our case we only need to allow the localhost IP 127.0.0.1, but if there were more addresses that needed access, we would only have to repeat the command multiple times, each with another address.

The list of available API calls comprises of commands ranging from diagnostic data to complex transaction creation commands. Here we will query the current block hash and subsequently get more detailed data on this block.

```
bitcoin-cli getbestblockhash
```

It would return the hash of the highest block:

```
02807bf066ffa42697bc753ed57de80117826df0e1e4e590e0cf6f9ddd4acd8d
```

---

[2]https://en.bitcoin.it/wiki/API_reference_%28JSON-RPC%29
[3]https://en.wikipedia.org/wiki/Representational_state_transfer

This data can then be used to query more detailed information about this block:

```
bitcoin-cli getblock \ 02807bf066ffa42697bc753ed57de80117826df0
e1e4e590e0cf6f9ddd4acd8d
```

The data we get will be in JSON format:

```
{
  "hash": "02807bf066ffa42697bc753ed57de80117826df0e1e4e590e0cf
  6f9ddd4acd8d",
  "confirmations": 1,
  "strippedsize": 228,
  "size": 264,
  "weight": 948,
  "height": 130,
  "version": 536870912,
  "versionHex": "20000000",
  "merkleroot": "0f5f2c23ec74091df5ce7f33d8db73e5183e4e1243daf
  8595762a45221d546c2",
  "tx": [
    "0f5f2c23ec74091df5ce7f33d8db73e5183e4e1243daf8595762a45221
    d546c2"
  ],
  "time": 1569055284,
  "mediantime": 1569055283,
  "nonce": 1,
  "bits": "207fffff",
  "difficulty": 4.656542373906925e-10,
  "chainwork": "0000000000000000000000000000000000000000000000
  00000000000000106",
```

```
    "nTx": 1,
    "previousblockhash": "4d8576d04a65d6a417a8771e38dee6a3d06a039
    b23c79e1bd2d52b4dd38d4cab"
}
```

Accessing bitcoind

By hosting a RESTful web service, `bitcoind` offers an alternative way for querying data. Here I have used `curl` to execute `getnetworkinfo` to query network information. To colorize the returned JSON-text, you can pipe it into **jq**,[4] a tool for formatting JSON data, that can be installed with apt.

```
curl --user raspiuser:mypassword --data-binary \ '{"jsonrpc"
:"1.0","id":"1","method":"getnetworkinfo",\ "params":[]}' -H
'content-type:application/json;' \ http://127.0.0.1:18332 | jq
```

As the access to Bitcoin's web service is protected, we have to pass user data configured in *bitcoin.conf*. The declaration of the command to be executed is done in a separate JSON-structure that must follow certain conventions, like JSON-RPC version, method name, and parameters, if needed. At the end of the command line, we enter the web service URL, which in our case is the local Raspberry Node running on a *testnet* chain. Therefore, its port number is 18332 instead of 8332, which is the standard port number of the *mainnet* chain.

With *curl* we can access all of the available APIs offered by `bitcoind`. However, as we see, the configuration is a bit more complex, because we have to describe our queries in great detail. In cases where we don't need to deal with such details, the usage of `bitcoin-cli` is recommended, as it keeps these complexities away from us. This of course makes `bitcoin-cli` less suitable for developing own solutions like web-based blockchain explorers that rely on REST style and HTTP protocol. But as long as we

---

[4]https://stedolan.github.io/jq/

are using our node only in private, bitcoin-cli will be sufficient enough. Here is how we would query the same data with it.

```
bitcoin-cli getnetworkinfo
```

Transactions with bitcoin-cli

To create a transaction without using the Core Wallet UI, we have several options offered by bitcoin-cli. The easiest one is sending funds to an address. This way we don't touch the raw data needed to create a process transaction but simply concentrate on spending funds. As we are operating in *regtest* network, we append the flag -regtest to every call.

```
bitcoin-cli -regtest sendtoaddress\ 2Mth369tgSr976Hi3WsHHngCp7Q
GmqFGwqa 10
```

In the above example, we have sent 10 bitcoins to a *regtest* address. The success of our transaction is confirmed by returning the transaction ID.

However, before trying to send any funds, you will likely have to unlock your wallet first. An error message will appear:

```
error code: -13
error message:
Error: Please enter the wallet passphrase with walletpassphrase
first.
```

This is done similarly to the example from the previous chapter, only this time on the console by entering this command:

```
bitcoin-cli -regtest walletpassphrase PASSPHRASE TIMEOUT
```

After having unlocked the wallet and sent the transaction, we will now analyze its structure by executing the gettransaction command in the console:

```
{
  "amount": 0.00000000,
  "fee": -0.00003320,
  "confirmations": 0,
  "trusted": true,
  "txid": "2dd96f4af992a9ab22bd8b2a44d63b2230fd020c94ad3d53eadb
  bb110fa21f1e",
  "walletconflicts": [
  ],
  "time": 1569059524,
  "timereceived": 1569059524,
  "bip125-replaceable": "no",
  "details": [
    {
      "address": "2Mth369tgSr976Hi3WsHHngCp7QGmqFGwqa",
      "category": "send",
      "amount": -10.00000000,
      "label": "",
      "vout": 1,
      "fee": -0.00003320,
      "abandoned": false
    },
    {
      "address": "2Mth369tgSr976Hi3WsHHngCp7QGmqFGwqa",
      "category": "receive",
      "amount": 10.00000000,
      "label": "",
      "vout": 1
    }
  ],
```

"hex": "0200000000010102ccd2a4bdd28fb96a952f2d8c81a0a9d935ac2
ad8b59ab554bbf6e558409c8400000000171600144e0dcbd747e2bc0f003b5b
44f0bbdf21a80d4a39fefffffff0208a29dd00000000017a9146d2d9017e0adc
f0f4511cea5b109ce0f2da1f4438700ca9a3b0000000017a9140fd9d7cacd31
409f4cdde68b5439e36e6f1734118702473044022053db9124b89f8feba8ade
b05b35c625b3c96c8e80f96f428202e3f64444d063e02202db976c7d2c2d8a7
e57c7b8b82c6e4faf792cbb38fcef435bbee6a6d5e99d5960121039a45cc55c
2f2fa7d6c3fa66f8c6f5be3d166c61e2d7cd194cb771d89c50c836c82000000"
}

As we can see in the JSON structure, our transaction was successful, but there are no confirmations right now. We have to generate a few more blocks to get our transaction properly confirmed. For this we can use the command generate. Although this command is marked as deprecated and in future generatetoaddress will exist as the only alternative, we will use it now as *generate* doesn't need any address to be given as parameter. To activate the usage of deprecated APIs, we have to add another parameter in our bitcoin.conf:

```
deprecatedrpc=generate
```

After every change in bitcoin.conf, we must restart the daemon. If it's already running, we can stop it with

```
bitcoin-cli -regtest stop
```

If your current daemon is running in another mode, replace the flag -regtest with -testnet or -mainnet. These flags let the daemon know which parts of the configuration file it should use when running. After having updated the configuration file, we start the daemon again:

```
bitcoind -regtest
```

We can now generate three blocks and then check the previous transaction again to see if it got confirmed.

```
bitcoin-cli -regtest generate 3
```

The returned data will contain hashes of generated blocks:

```
[
"725a73922ef8281c694288ddb8d806c67908bfd05bdacadab44667dfcb767
9bd",
"1dfcbb1af7c89f548281344fdddb518a96a07a73fcb18e56c9e9fff7920fa
4cd",
"1a2e27dbe2ba5c0be32b4fcd222bbdc531757c9cf1a03047790053d2d3191
c26"
]
```

When we now query the same transaction again, the returned JSON would show a different confirmations property. However, this isn't the only way to deal with transactions. There is also a command to show raw transaction data:

```
bitcoin-cli -regtest getrawtransaction \ 2dd96f4af992a9ab22bd8
b2a44d63b2230fd020c94ad3d53eadbbb110fa21f1e
```

We will get a long hexadecimal string:

0200000000010102ccd2a4bdd28fb96a952f2d8c81a0a9d935ac2ad8b59ab55
4bbf6e558409c84000000000171600144e0dcbd747e2bc0f003b5b44f0bbdf21
a80d4a39feffffff0208a29dd00000000017a9146d2d9017e0adcf0f4511cea
5b109ce0f2da1f4438700ca9a3b0000000017a9140fd9d7cacd31409f4cdde6
8b5439e36e6f1734118702473044022053db9124b89f8feba8adeb05b35c625
b3c96c8e80f96f428202e3f64444d063e02202db976c7d2c2d8a7e57c7b8b82
c6e4faf792cbb38fcef435bbee6a6d5e99d5960121039a45cc55c2f2fa7d6c3
fa66f8c6f5be3d166c61e2d7cd194cb771d89c50c836c82000000

Although this structure is not human readable, there is a way to create transaction data in the same format and send it directly to the network for further processing. This hexadecimal data structure is also called "serialized data", as it reflects the data structure represented internally in the software.

The individual byte values, which are read as hexadecimal pairs, represent different chunks of data[5] like version numbers, number of inputs and outputs, and other data. On the following pages, we will create such a transaction manually. But first, let's examine the parts that constitute them.

Transaction Structure

Serialized transaction data as shown in the previous example is a structure comprising of these elements:

- **Version** number

- Its **inputs**

- Its **outputs**

- **Witness data** (*SegWit transactions only*)

- **Locktime**

As an example, we will dissect the representation of transaction

e571d40d9b73ad7714e53c07076e0c6e4bc3c8c26400ee83ee320096b2f1 b251

at block height 593895 from Bitcoin's *mainnet*.

---

[5]https://en.bitcoin.it/wiki/Protocol_specification#tx

010000000001011cd9276965223987985c0edbfb0eacad943e6191aeb5
cb15e647d8a66cedc9d61e0100002322002014f37431ff22d0e9f9ee66
8626998309d2bde923b485babeec865e508ad51fd6ffffffff010e9003
000000000017a914d9706a3046f9f6a0173d14c8142acaa3f706473b87
0400483045022100be654032dd5189b9c34bb8560fc0c33d00dcd5472e
79d89775e7da5e90f8199102203bf8f4057c5699b566503bbb3e8f4cac
ee6bacc2a6cce7a6bce2e92ae953db170147304402206f8169e0237b5a
552e805ecb45d3635d1f9279de4a236811b5d01570118274230220597 0
8b4ed39ca4f7ce550cabb8d913b21fbb8f29ea1a94a35ce23cdecddec2
a8016952210312bd32f29bab8fbfdcda964df1da8734318a0e81a995f0
49050fc674271963e7210321d9d7a25a3337ea4b4c34418fbe5d870bf3
a600bd573ca162b2dbab85def6ef21027162c82cd0535b6032622f7b8d
d560671e34220a2e7e0b7fc32956c207b2e61853aee50f0900

Figure 6-1. *Serialized transaction*

The colors in Figure 6-1 represent different elements, while the underlined part 0001 will be discussed later, when we talk about SegWit.

The individual size and serialized length of a transaction depend on several things, like input number, output number, and if it's a SegWit transaction. Non-SegWit transactions carry *witness* data, which are signatures needed for providing proofs of ownership. This of course makes them bigger than their SegWit counterparts.

In the transaction shown in Figure 6-1, the version we're using is 1 which is indicated at the beginning of its serialized structure. Every byte of data is indicated by *two hexadecimal elements*. For example, the version byte containing number 1 is written as 01. As the whole data structure for version number reserves 4 bytes, the available space is not used completely, which leads to several zeroes after the 1. It is also important to know that the serialized data is in *Little-Endian* format, which is the exact opposite to how we write numbers in real life. In Little-Endian the smallest numbers come first.

The second part, the *input*, is where the funds for spending are declared and proofs of ownership given. This means that there we reference previous transactions and provide proofs that we are indeed eligible to spend them. Every input transaction starts with a number indicating how many inputs are available. In this case there was only one input transaction referenced. Also, as this transaction is of type SegWit, the witness data was separated from input transaction itself. Instead of carrying signature data, its `scriptSig` field is empty as the signatures have been moved to a separate field called "witness" that is underlined in the example above. Inside our input data is of course the ID of the previous transaction we're referring to:

1cd9276965223987985c0edbfb0eacad943e6191aeb5cb15e647d8a66cedc9d6

This data is also written in Little-Endian-Format which we must convert to Big-Endian before trying to extract further information from it. This is how the "reversed" transaction ID should look like:

d6c9ed6ca6d847e615cbb5ae91613e94adac0efbdb0e5c98873922656927d91c

The whole input data block from Figure 6-1 comprises of these parts, with a special handling of the 2 bytes at the beginning[6].

<u>0001</u>011cd9276965223987985c0edbfb0eacad943e6191aeb5cb15e647d8a6
6cedc9d61e0100002322002014f37431ff22d0e9f9ee668626998309d2bde9
23b485babeec865e508ad51fd6ffffffff

- SegWit **marker**
- SegWit **flag**
- Number of **inputs**
- Previous **transaction ID**

---

[6]The data inside our serialized transaction comprises of additional elements like lengths and Op-Code numbers, which we're not showing here. Jimmy Song's book *Programming Bitcoin* has a very detailed description of various transaction types

- Previous **Index** that points at the output from this transaction

- **scriptSig**

- **Sequence** (which is mostly unused, unless it's needed for CHECKLOCKTIMEVERIFY as in Lightning Network transactions)

The underlined part is only relevant to nodes that support SegWit. Other nodes would serialize this data differently and would never see those two bytes. To get more information about this particular transaction, we can use one of the available web explorers, for example

https://www.blockchain.com/btc/tx/d6c9ed6ca6d847e615cbb5ae91613
e94adac0efbdb0e5c98873922656927d91c?show_adv=true

Creating Raw Transactions

The first step we take is getting an UTXO that we will use in the upcoming transaction. For this we use the command *listunspent*.

```
bitcoin-cli -regtest listunspent
```

As every node would give a different list of unspent transaction outputs, the transaction we will be using in the following pages should be replaced with those from your wallet.

```
{
    "txid": "fce1294d8b38ea17c1a64e4956d8eff648df839bf3d82f814f8
    0463da28f06f4",
    "vout": 0,
```

```
    "address": "2NBP3w5m425n12RePYQoJfsznTXnJr4yGiY",
    "label": "",
    "redeemScript": "0014d46fdaa84262a27cd923ed1b7b4d873c9769
    6084",
    "scriptPubKey": "a914c6ed32ba1058fb436e5cc594710f30bd22a3
    916987",
    "amount": 50.00000000,
    "confirmations": 126,
    "spendable": true,
    "solvable": true,
    "desc": "sh(wpkh([d697f246/0'/0'/0']029533e360bc3d270c0ace8
    9dd5527190d1d3394a269cae64c89860d20fea701eb))#wj2c7p26",
    "safe": true
  },
```

We have 50 bitcoins in this UTXO with output index, vout, at 0. We will also need to know the transaction ID. As we already know, a transaction can only spend something that comes from another transaction as UTXO. Therefore, we will need this transaction ID to refer to those 50 bitcoins later. As we are working in the bash shell, we create two variables to make this data available for later processing.

```
MY_UTXO_TXID=fce1294d8b38ea17c1a64e4956d8eff648df839bf3d82f814f
80463da28f06f4
MY_UTXO_VOUT=0
```

These two variables are basically pointers which our future transaction will use to reference the correct UTXO. Out next step will be to create a new address that will be the recipient of those funds. As usual, we execute the getnewaddress command and save it in another shell variable, RECIPIENT_ADDRESS. We then create a second address that will serve as our change address and put it in the shell variable CHANGE_ADDRESS.

```
bitcoin-cli -regtest getnewaddress
RECIPIENT_ADDRESS= 2MsjDqTpNzHKF3CC91swUiGQD44fG8SNfF5
CHANGE_ADDRESS= 2NFG69VfkBYLTzbp8xSaWgNt9Y2gSLjywrQ
```

The next step is to create a JSON structure that will represent the transaction and include data we just saved in our shell variables. As direct writing of below structure is rather hard and could lead to various errors, I recommend editing JSON data in a separate editor first and then appending it to the command createrawtransaction shown below.

```
bitcoin-cli -regtest createrawtransaction
'[{
        "txid" : "'$MY_UTXO_TXID'",
        "vout" : '$MY_UTXO_VOUT'
}]'
'{
        "'$RECIPIENT_ADDRESS'": 25,
        "'$CHANGE_ADDRESS'": 24.99
}'
```

In our JSON structure, we have referenced a transaction and defined one recipient and a change address. From the available 50 bitcoins, we will be sending 25 to our recipient and 24.99 back to us, which means that miners would take the remaining 0.01 bitcoins as fees.

If our JSON structure was correct, the executing of the above command would deliver a raw transaction representation in hexadecimal form as shown in Figure 6-2 that is structurally similar to the *mainnet* transaction we referred to in Figure 6-1.

0200000001**f4068fa23d46804f812fd8f39b83df48f6efd856494ea6c1
17ea388b4d29e1fc**0000000000ffffffff0200f90295000000017a914
054b851d49d9c9ffca96ef8d781bbfac5b6ee34a87c0b6f39400000000
17a914f17ca3410e454656105b854fd7827ecd1ecbbedd8700000000

Figure 6-2. *New transaction in serialized format*

The hexadecimal data in bold is our input transaction from which we are getting those 50 bitcoins for spending. This ID of course is in Little-Endian format too.

Our next step is to put this data in another shell variable, MY_RAW_TX.

```
MY_RAW_TX=0200000001f4068fa23d46804f812fd8f39b83df48f6efd85649
4ea6c117ea388b4d29e1fc0000000000ffffffff0200f902950000000017a9
14054b851d49d9c9ffca96ef8d781bbfac5b6ee34a87c0b6f3940000000017
a914f17ca3410e454656105b854fd7827ecd1ecbbedd8700000000
```

As we already know, in Bitcoin we have full responsibility for anything we do. And before we try to change anything or send any data, we must check it for validity first. To check a raw transaction for validity, we have the command decoderawtransaction. If it returns valid JSON data, we can be sure that our transaction will be accepted by the network.

```
bitcoin-cli -regtest decoderawtransaction $MY_RAW_TX
```

The output would be in JSON format as shown in Figure 6-3.

```
pi@raspberrypi:~ $ bitcoin-cli -regtest decoderawtransaction $MY_RAW_TX | jq
{
  "txid": "4fa6c02b2e9df3b0f2de94d7b1e73aa4218d95d82d4aa6fc994b007230b000d5",
  "hash": "4fa6c02b2e9df3b0f2de94d7b1e73aa4218d95d82d4aa6fc994b007230b000d5",
  "version": 2,
  "size": 115,
  "vsize": 115,
  "weight": 460,
  "locktime": 0,
  "vin": [
    {
      "txid": "fce1294d8b38ea17c1a64e4956d8eff648df839bf3d82f814f80463da28f06f4",
      "vout": 0,
      "scriptSig": {
        "asm": "",
        "hex": ""
      },
      "sequence": 4294967295
    }
  ],
  "vout": [
    {
      "value": 25,
      "n": 0,
      "scriptPubKey": {
        "asm": "OP_HASH160 054b851d49d9c9ffca96ef8d781bbfac5b6ee34a OP_EQUAL",
        "hex": "a914054b851d49d9c9ffca96ef8d781bbfac5b6ee34a87",
        "reqSigs": 1,
        "type": "scripthash",
        "addresses": [
          "2MsjDqTpNzHKF3CC91swUiGQD44fG8SNfF5"
        ]
      }
    },
```

Figure 6-3. *A successfully decoded raw transaction*

We see our UTXO and the recipient's address. Our transaction looks good. Now it's time to sign it with our private key. For this we will be using another command called signrawtransactionwithwallet.

```
bitcoin-cli -regtest signrawtransactionwithwallet \
$MY_RAW_TX
```

The data returned would contain the information about the transaction that got signed and if the operation was successful:

```
{
  "hex": "02000000000101f4068fa23d46804f812fd8f39b83df48f6efd85
6494ea6c117ea388b4d29e1fc0000000017160014d46fdaa84262a27cd92
3ed1b7b4d873c97696084ffffffff0200f9029500000000017a914054b851
```

d49d9c9ffca96ef8d781bbfac5b6ee34a87c0b6f3940000000017a914f17
ca3410e454656105b854fd7827ecd1ecbbedd8702473044022045062190bc
ae5940360d16d6f9764226b5cad65fd41153de7ff955a2a6460a5c902200b
3bcd9c83a34635ab46fe2111124d7e991b5e50a20380a21e2911539ae8724
e0121029533e360bc3d270c0ace89dd5527190d1d3394a269cae64c89860d2
0fea701eb00000000",
    "complete": true
}

There also exists an alternative command for signing transactions:
signrawtransactionwithkey

This command can be used when only a certain private key should be
used for signing. In our case we are fine with any of the private keys our
wallet uses.

In older versions of Bitcoin, the command for signing was called
signrawtransaction, which got deprecated in version 0.18.

Our next step is now to save this signed transaction into another shell
variable, MY_SIGNED_RAW_TX. Our signed transaction is located in the
property hex from the previous JSON object.

MY_SIGNED_RAW_TX=02000000000101f4068fa23d46804f812fd8f39b83df48f
6efd856494ea6c117ea388b4d29e1fc0000000017160014d46fdaa84262a27cd
923ed1b7b4d873c97696084ffffffff0200f902950000000017a914054b851d4
9d9c9ffca96ef8d781bbfac5b6ee34a87c0b6f3940000000017a914f17ca3410
e454656105b854fd7827ecd1ecbbedd8702473044022045062190bcae5940360d
16d6f9764226b5cad65fd41153de7ff955a2a6460a5c902200b3bcd9c83a3463
5ab46fe2111124d7e991b5e50a20380a21e2911539ae8724e0121029533e360b
c3d270c0ace89dd5527190d1d3394a269cae64c89860d20fea701eb00000000

Our last step will be to send our transaction by using the command
sendrawtransaction:

```
bitcoin-cli -regtest sendrawtransaction $MY_SIGNED_RAW_TX
```

We will get a transaction ID back:

dda761617c08b443ef652be64485b1741e128fe63b79d689186f0e974ef0b1be

This means that our transaction now got included in the node's memory pool, often abbreviated as *mempool*. And it will probably be included in the one of the upcoming blocks. This of course depends on the fee we are willing to pay and how many older transactions are already waiting for inclusion. As we are working in *regtest* mode, this is not an issue for us, but in *mainnet* it could very quickly become one if we aren't careful enough.

Now we can use *gettransaction* to check data it's referring to:

```
bitcoin-cli -regtest gettransaction \
dda761617c08b443ef652be64485b1741e128fe63b79d689186f0e974ef0b1be
```

Again, a JSON object will be returned (Figure 6-4).

```
pi@raspberrypi:~ $ bitcoin-cli -regtest gettransaction dda761617c08b443ef652be(
{
  "amount": 0,
  "fee": -0.01,
  "confirmations": 0,
  "trusted": true,
  "txid": "dda761617c08b443ef652be64485b1741e128fe63b79d689186f0e974ef0b1be",
  "walletconflicts": [],
  "time": 1569065696,
  "timereceived": 1569065696,
  "bip125-replaceable": "no",
  "details": [
    {
      "address": "2MsjDqTpNzHKF3CC91swUiGQD44fG8SNfF5",
      "category": "send",
      "amount": -25,
      "label": "",
      "vout": 0,
      "fee": -0.01,
      "abandoned": false
    },
    {
      "address": "2NFG69VfkBYLTzbpBxSaWgNt9Y2gSLjywrQ",
      "category": "send",
      "amount": -24.99,
      "label": "",
      "vout": 1,
      "fee": -0.01,
      "abandoned": false
    },
```

Figure 6-4. *Transaction JSON*

Our next step will be to create a few more blocks and to check if one of them has included our transaction. Again, we execute the command generate

```
bitcoin-cli -regtest generate 6
```

We then query our transaction and check if the property blockhash in the returned JSON is visible.

```
bitcoin-cli -regtest gettransaction \
dda761617c08b443ef652be64485b1741e128fe63b79d689186f0e974ef0b1be
```

The result of this call will of course be different; but in any case, you should get a blockhash at the beginning of the JSON object:

```
"blockhash": "3db92d9c1c938f3198e2ba34bf9d95d5c40814fac9404c1d6
96acc7a3a7c16f0"
```

We can now use the command getblock to retrieve block data and search for our transaction within. The result will be a JSON structure that contains two transactions (Figure 6-5). The first one is of course the *coinbase* transaction generated by the miner of this block and contains the rewards and fees collected from transactions included in this block. The second entry in transaction list is our own, which confirms that it got included in this block.

```
{
  "hash": "3db92d9c1c938f3198e2ba34bf9d95d5c40814fac9404c1d696acc7a3a7c16f0",
  "confirmations": 10,
  "strippedsize": 366,
  "size": 511,
  "weight": 1609,
  "height": 137,
  "version": 536870912,
  "versionHex": "20000000",
  "merkleroot": "a5e05277028767b66e8648ab6614a0d7f69fce217271f8422c0691a1f2f78115",
  "tx": [
    "6447f207b01721f5aed87054e01d2ba70f148e4000fca1ffe191a6f87bc1d377",
    "dda761617c08b443ef652be64485b1741e128fe63b79d689186f0e974ef0b1be"
  ],
  "time": 1569066024,
  "mediantime": 1569060592,
  "nonce": 0,
  "bits": "207fffff",
  "difficulty": 4.656542373906925e-10,
  "chainwork": "0000000000000000000000000000000000000000000000000000000000000114",
  "nTx": 2,
  "previousblockhash": "640f6ea400dbda5f7d04b7e05de8fe9abe379056bcbbbe38f8a47a8dc83e283b",
  "nextblockhash": "275586a7f1e04b35ae087fa2834f5f75e48f50dd9d4c869a6f8f4528e77fae27"
}
```

Figure 6-5. *Block data*

Messaging with ZeroMQ

Bitcoin contains a fast, asynchronous messaging library called
ZeroMQ[7] that can be used in scenarios where distributed or concurrent
applications are needed, for example, applications that inform clients
in real time about incoming transactions and blocks. To achieve such
goals, Bitcoin daemon can be configured for broadcasting information
to connected clients. The ZeroMQ library offers various messaging
interfaces that implement different notifiers. The one being used in
Bitcoin is the *publish–subscribe*, a method where a single publisher
defines a socket for sending information via certain predefined topics
that many clients can subscribe to (Figure 6-6).

---

[7]http://zeromq.org/

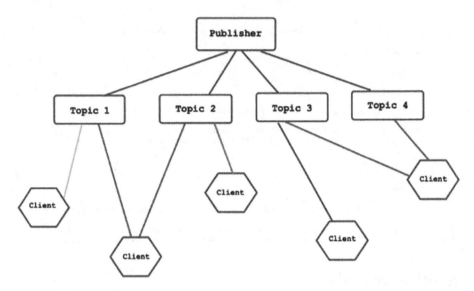

Figure 6-6. *Publish–subscribe with ZeroMQ*

Currently, `bitcoind` offers four topics:

- Block hashes via `zmqpubhashblock`

- Transaction hashes via `zmqpubhashtx`

- Raw blocks via `zmqpubrawblock`

- Raw transactions via `zmqpubrawtx`

These topics can be activated in `bitcon.conf`.

```
zmqpubrawblock=tcp://127.0.0.1:28332
zmqpubrawtx=tcp://127.0.0.1:28333
zmqpubhashtx=tcp://127.0.0.1:28334
zmqpubhashblock=tcp://127.0.0.1:28335
```

The port number can be any free port, and the protocol being used can be other than TCP, but this depends on the operating system being used. In our case it's Linux, and therefore we could also have used IPC for inter-process communication. However, in the following example, we will stick to TCP.

As the information being published is independent from any OS or hardware type, any kind of client could connect to bitcoind as long as it's capable of reading the message format being used by ZeroMQ. Luckily, the ZeroMQ library supports dozens of programming languages and can run on almost every available OS. Due to the nature of ZeroMQ message handling, there is no need to set up any additional logic for message buffering as every single message is self-contained and needs no additional processing.

It's then up to the client to decide what should happen with the data delivered in a message. *bitcoind* does only one task and that is spreading information via topics to its connected clients. There is no direct communication between clients and bitcoind. This of course makes the publish–subscribe pattern ideal for concurrent application setups, where publishers don't have to invest resources for managing clients.

After we have activated ZQM in our bitcoin.conf, we restart the daemon and check if the topics got activated.

```
bitcoin-cli -regtest getzmqnotifications
```

We see the four topics we defined previously (Figure 6-7). Our ZMQ interface is running and waiting for clients. But as we have no client available, this interface remains unused for now. It now depends on our experience in programming networking applications, which solution we'd prefer.

```
[
    {
      "type": "pubhashblock",
      "address": "tcp://127.0.0.1:28335",
      "hwm": 1000
    },
    {
      "type": "pubhashtx",
      "address": "tcp://127.0.0.1:28334",
      "hwm": 1000
    },
    {
      "type": "pubrawblock",
      "address": "tcp://127.0.0.1:28332",
      "hwm": 1000
    },
    {
      "type": "pubrawtx",
      "address": "tcp://127.0.0.1:28333",
      "hwm": 1000
    }
]
```

Figure 6-7. *ZMQ notifications*

One of the easier ways to test ZMQ is by using *JavaScript* programming language in NodeJS[8] environment. NodeJS is an engine that runs JavaScript in the backend, without using any browser. One of the strengths of the NodeJS ecosystem is the availability of hundreds of thousands of packages for every possible use-case. Therefore, instead of writing a complete Bitcoin client, we will install an already existing package that will help us communicate with bitcoind and its ZMQ interface.

For this we have to download the archive file of the Linux (ARM) binary that's compatible with our Raspberry. The location of available downloads is at https://nodejs.org/en/download/, and we should copy the current link first (Figure 6-8).

---

[8]https://nodejs.org

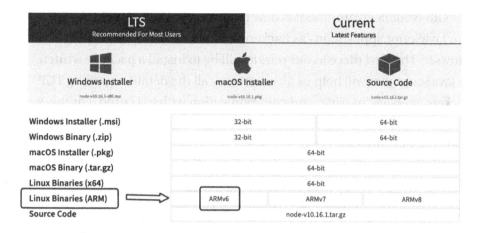

Figure 6-8. *NodeJS download page*

We download this archive with wget to our local system and extract it with tar.

```
wget https://nodejs.org/dist/v10.16.3/node-v10.16.3-linux-
armv6l.tar.xz
tar xf node-v10.16.3-linux-armv6l.tar.xz
```

A new directory with the same name as the package will be created. It contains precompiled binaries and other files which we will copy to our system-wide path *in /usr/local*. This way we will be able to access NodeJS from everywhere. We go into this directory with

```
cd node-v10.16.3-linux-armv6l
```

and copy its contents to */usr/local* with

```
sudo cp -R * /usr/local
```

Ultimately, we test if the node binary is now available in the global path:

```
which node
```

This should return the path to /usr/local/bin/node

Our NodeJS environment is now ready to use. With NodeJS we can run JavaScript applications as backend processes without using any browser. The next piece in our puzzle will be to install a package written in JavaScript that will help us abstract away all the details regarding TCP sockets, message passing, and communication with bitcoind. For this we use a console-based app that comes with the NodeJS environment: the node package manager, npm.

Our first step is to create a new directory for our source code and project settings. We go back to our home directory with cd $HOME directory and create a new directory for for our ZMQ project with

```
mkdir zeromqtest
```

We enter this directory with cd zeromqtest and use npm to set up our initial project structure:

```
npm init
```

The setup process comprises of few questions that could be completed just by pressing ENTER a few times:

```
package name: (zeromqtest)
version: (1.0.0)
description: a zeromq messaging project
entry point: app.js
test command:
git repository:
keywords: bitcoin
author: Harris Brakmic
license: (ISC)
```

At the end of the process, the script will ask you if the information you entered is correct. Confirm with ENTER.

```
About to write to /home/pi/zeromqtest/package.json:
Is this OK? (yes)
```

If we now execute the `ls` command inside this directory, you'll recognize a new file, `package.json`, that contains data we just entered. This file is very important, and every NodeJS project has one. It contains the descriptions of scripts to be used in development, testing, and debugging. It also contains all external packages that we are referencing in our NodeJS project.

There exist several NodeJS libraries for accessing various ZeroMQ functionalities. In our case we will be using the `zeromq` package that we install with:

```
npm install -S zeromq
```

The flag -S is here to instruct NodeJS to save the `zeromq` as library reference in our `package.json`. This way we keep all references persisted in one place and can later reinstall them all by issuing this command in our package's directory.

```
npm install
```

The installation of *zeromq* package will take some time, because it has to compile the ZeroMQ source code itself and reference a bunch of other packages as well. After having installed it, our next step is to write a JavaScript application that will use it to receive ZeroMQ messages via Bitcoin's publish–subscribe interface.

For this we open a new file called `app.js` in directory *zmqtest*.

```
nano app.js
```

It depends on your preference what type of editor you'll be using. The console-based editors like `vim` or `nano` are already included, but one can also use UI-editors like `leafpad` or `geany`, which can be found in the main menu of Raspbian's desktop.

Our application will execute as follows:

- Load the ZeroMQ library.

- Connect with `bitcoind` at its ZeroMQ port.

- Subscribe to a topic we're interested in.

- Define an "event handler", a function for processing ZMQ messages.

```
// load zmq library
let zmq = require('zeromq');
let sock = zmq.socket('sub');

// connect with bitcoind
sock.connect('tcp://127.0.0.1:28335');

// subscribe to topic "hashblock"
sock.subscribe('hashblock');

// write diagnostic mesage to console
console.log('Connected to port 28335');

// setup even handler for processing incoming messages
sock.on('message', function(topic, message) {
  console.log('TOPIC: ', topic, ' - Block Hash:', message);
});
```

Lines 2 and 3 reference the ZeroMQ library and a socket of type SUB. As ZeroMQ supports different kinds of sockets, we have to precisely define which one will be used in our script. Without having properly selected a socket, the whole communication logic would fail.

Line 6 is where we declare the communication channel to our bitcoind instance. This is where we enter the previously defined ZMQ interface from bitcoin.conf.

Line 9 is where we subscribe to the topic "hashblock" that will be sending hashes of newly generated blocks.

Line 15 is where we define an "event handler", that is, a function that will be called each time a new message arrives. This part of the code is where we define the actual logic of our application. Here we can do whatever we want with the data we receive. In our case we declare that on any "message" we receive, our function should write contents of variables topic and message to the console.

After the application has started, the further processing of our script will be halted. Our program will actually "never end" as the method subscribe would open the channel and after that the application will be patiently waiting for new messages to arrive.

All that is left now is to save this code and execute the application by using the *npm* package manager. As we have previously initialized our NodeJS application to use the app.js file as the entry point of our application, there is only a single command needed to execute it:

```
npm start
```

However, if we execute this command right now, NodeJS would complain that there is no script with name "start".

```
missing script: start
```

We have to define it first. This is done by entering a new line in package.json which is located in the same directory where our app.js is. NodeJS environment accepts different scripts which can be individually configured and executed. We can create as many scripts as we want, but there are a few standard ones like start and *test* that can be executed by simply appending their names to npm. Any nonstandard scripts must be executed by using the command run, for example, npm run myscript. To make the execution of app.js available as "start" script, we add a new entry within the "scripts" area in *package.json*.

```
"scripts": {
   "start": "node app.js",
 }
```

One must be very careful when editing JSON files as those don't accept any comments and are unforgiving regarding even the slightest errors, like missing commas or incomplete quotations.

We save the file, and now we can execute our application by using npm start. Our client application has successfully connected to *bitcoind* and subscribed to the topic "hashblock".

```
>zmqtest@1.0.0 start /home/pi/zmqtest
>Node app.js >

Connected to port 28332
```

Now we have to generate some blocks to see if it works.

```
bitcoin-cli -regtest generate 5
```

Indeed, our client received some data, but the output is not human readable.

```
TOPIC:  <Buffer 68 61 73 68 62 6c 6f 63 6b>  - Block Hash:
<Buffer 7b fc f8 95 c8 12 25 43 32 fe 11 0c 86 ad e2 93 43 69
04 12 6e dd 96 5f 03 74 64 17 e9 30 83 f7>
TOPIC:  <Buffer 68 61 73 68 62 6c 6f 63 6b>  - Block Hash:
<Buffer 1d 4c 95 eb c4 d7 9e 30 c5 2a 3a 76 5f 32 d5 56 5d d9
fd cd 10 a5 af d3 09 ec 79 2a ed 6e 51 78>
```

This has to do with the fact that ZMQ only sees raw bytes and doesn't care about any particular encoding or format. We have to be more explicit when dealing with ZMQ messages. Luckily, there are functions available in JavaScript that can convert raw data into more readable formats. We expand our event handler function a bit by calling toString() methods for topic and message. Additionally, bytes coming with message will be shown in hexadecimal format.

```
sock.on('message', function(topic, message) {
  console.log('TOPIC: ', topic.toString(), ' - Block Hash:',
  message.toString('hex'));
});
```

We then start our client and generate a few more blocks with generate command.

Now we will be able to print the topic name as standard string and the block hashes in hexadecimal format .

```
TOPIC:   hashblock   - Block Hash: 50f4e8c44be17f12dc2d82f2df55d
                       2c5a53ff7260371ffebdb228169d83ad18a
TOPIC:   hashblock   - Block Hash: 61b49e88f9479428b43a2b9f8009f
                       5a57caa14643697f9ee8a773014d52b9811
```

Using Bitcoin's ZMQ Interface with C

As ZMQ's primary interface is written in C, we should not end this chapter without having written a similar implementation in this programming language. Just as in JavaScript, we are interested in receiving messages from any of the available ZMQ interfaces our bitcoind process offers. To be able to successfully compile the below source code, we must install the following libraries first:

```
sudo apt install libzmq3-dev libczmq-dev libczmq4
```

We need these packages to reference the correct headers and libraries to be linked with our chainlistener console application. To compile it, we use the default GCC compiler:

```
gcc -o chainlistener chainlistener.c \
-I/usr/local/include -L/usr/local/lib -lzmq -lczmq
```

We reference `include` directories where ZMQ headers reside as well as two libraries to be linked with our program. The first library is ZMQ itself, while the other brings us the ZMQ C-API with several functions we will be using in our demo program.

```c
#include <czmq.h>

int main(int argc, char ** argv) {
  char *zmqserver;
  char *topic;
  if (argc < 3) {
    printf("\nUSAGE:\nchainlistener <tcp://localhost:port>
    <topic>\n\n");
    return 0;
  } else {
    zmqserver = argv[1];
    topic = argv[2];
  }

  zsock_t *socket = zsock_new_sub(zmqserver, topic);
  assert(socket);
  while(1) {
    zmsg_t *msg;
    int rc = zsock_recv(socket, "m", &msg);
    assert(rc == 0);

    char *header = zmsg_popstr(msg);
    zframe_t *zdata = zmsg_pop(msg);
    unsigned int *no = (unsigned int*)zmsg_popstr(msg);

    char *data = zframe_strhex(zdata);
    int len = zframe_size(zdata);
    printf("Size: %d\n", len);
```

```
    printf("Data: %s", data);
    printf("\nNo: %d\n", *no);

    free(header);
    free(data);
    free(no);
    free(zdata);
    zmsg_destroy(&msg);
    sleep(1);
  }
  zsock_destroy(&socket);
  return 0;
}
```

Our ZMQ client is based on several building blocks most ZMQ-focused applications reference. Inside the while loop, we define a pointer to a generic ZMQ message of type `zmsg_t`. This message object is then filled with data we receive from our socket in the next line. As every message in ZMQ is just a bunch of bytes with a length header prepended, it is our obligation to convert it into something meaningful. This means that we must know in advance what kind of data we're about to receive. ZMQ offers various functions for easy data type conversion which we use in our example. At the beginning we extract the header of the message first and then its contents. Here, the function call `zmsg_pop` is of importance as it returns a pointer to a *ZMQ frame*. A *frame* in ZMQ is the most basic structure for defining messages. It is a block of data with a header containing its length. Originally, ZMQ only had single-message frames, but later multipart messages got included so that a message now can contain arbitrary number of messages that the receiving side must "unpack". The difference between single-frame and multipart messages is that the latter have a special bit, called "more", set to 1 which indicates that there are more messages to be unpacked. In such case the receiving side would simply continue consuming further frames until it has reached a frame that has no "more" bit set. In our case, messages we will be receiving contain three frames: *command*, *data*, and a 4-byte-long *sequence number* in little-endian format.[9] The *command* is a string indicating the type of the message. This could be

- A block hash

- A transaction hash

- A raw block

- A raw transaction

This string is useful for filtering messages, for example. The *data* field contains the actual payload, like a serialized transaction or block hash. The *sequence number* indicates the position of a message within the sequence of all messages that were sent so far.

As we have a few very different types of frames to deal with, we need a proper mechanism to take care of them. For this the ZMQ API offers the option to define a "picture" of data, which is a string that defines each frame within a multipart message. For example, if our message contained a string and an integer, we would indicate them with "si". The ZMQ-API description of zsock[10] defines the following indicators that can be used to define message types:

```
i = int
u = uint
s = char *
b = byte *, size_t (2 arguments)
c = zchunk_t *
f = zframe_t *
h = zhash_t *
```

---

[9]https://github.com/bitcoin/bitcoin/blob/0.18/src/zmq/
zmqpublishnotifier.cpp#L147
[10]http://czmq.zeromq.org/manual:zsock

```
p = void * (sends the pointer value)
m = zmsg_t * (sends all frames in the zmsg)
z = sends zero-sized frame (0 arguments)
```

In our case, we expect a message of type "m", which means that all frames will be sent in a single message, so we can later unpack them with helper functions like zmsg_popstr and zframe_strhex. This way we convert raw data into meaningful structures like integers and strings. The rest of the program is printing those values and freeing up heap memory. When run in the console, the output looks like in Figure 6-9.

```
pi@raspberrypi:~/src/chainlistener $ ./chainlistener tcp://127.0.0.1:28333 rawtx
Size: 247
Data: 020000000001013C20055551C9FE7D7BD5E9E057FCBE5CEEA2FA1EEFB131D64629304D82DEEB41000000000171660
00000000017A914EFEF3E8751A5761C7F17A7D013736A55EB724E7187DEE232C90100000017A9145D480ED0F80D21AA49
C97ADB3EE9F3649FF82198C63BCD060ABB7AD54B02200E9C60BA948EAE8EBAF191B2A4A99A3E212C53FF44CA1288805A7
DC4CA002C3A7BA9496692342A1800
No: 524365
Size: 248
Data: 01000000000101451C668CD8C46C440075629E3946569A1F2C3A53D384C3F8E5FF093B7D47B06D0100000001716600
00000000017A914DBE4CF1636444B19ADB6AA7EF119B5DD70C0E38387C42F57000000000017A91451FE6A095EBB3FEF83
9970B83F5C4E60C40B8DA92350A37A79CDF536C58D0220016BD5BD046C90BAA1895F90B412337D4748A46F62A0DF31628
392A62CB0845615611B2FC800000000
No: 524366
```

Figure 6-9. *Listening to ZMQ transaction messages*

Summary

In this chapter we have learned how to configure and control Bitcoin's daemon application, bitcoind. We have learned to utilize the command line interface, bitcoin-cli, which is a powerful tool capable of executing even the most complex tasks. We have used it for sending funds and also for creating transactions from scratch. Another powerful feature of bitcoind is its capability of real-time, asynchronous messaging via ZMQ interfaces, which we have learned to configure and utilize. We have also written a client application in JavaScript C that consume messages sent from bitcoind's publish-subscribe interface.

CHAPTER 7

Bitcoin Script

In this chapter we will learn about the core element of Bitcoin, the language called Script. Script is an embedded programming language that runs inside every Bitcoin node and is responsible for processing transactions. Unlike most other programming languages, it wasn't designed upfront with formalized grammar and syntax. Instead of using a proper notation technique like Backus-Naur[1] to describe its syntax, Script was hard-coded in the very first version of Bitcoin.

Script, the Programming Language

Whenever we talk about sending or receiving funds in Bitcoin's network, what we really do is execute a series of commands that constitute Bitcoin scripts. Spoken from a very abstract level, we could say that all Bitcoin "sees" are scripts only. There are neither addresses nor bitcoins in Bitcoin's network. Everything that happens (or fails) in Bitcoin is based on some script execution. To learn "Script", which is its colloquial name, means to go much deeper into Bitcoin's code and touching things which are not even familiar to most programmers. Script is very different, both for technical and nontechnical audiences.

---

[1]https://en.wikipedia.org/wiki/Backus%E2%80%93Naur_form

© Harris Brakmić 2019
H. Brakmić, *Bitcoin and Lightning Network on Raspberry Pi*,
https://doi.org/10.1007/978-1-4842-5522-3_7

However, there is no reason to stay away from it, as Bitcoin could never exist without it. And the first step is to understand its base structures. The first among them is the Stack, a data structure used heavily in computer science.

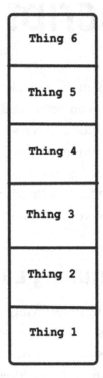

Figure 7-1. *Graphical representation computer's memory organized as stack structure*

A stack is a collection of "things" of any kind that are linearly ordered, where operations can only be done beginning with the top element. This constraint is also called LIFO (*last in, first out*), because any allowed operations have to begin with the top element. Bitcoin Script uses such a structure to manage and execute commands that come with transactions. As we have already seen in previous chapters, every Bitcoin transaction combines two script parts, a *locking* and an *unlocking* script, which then get executed as a single one. If the execution returns a TRUE value, a transaction will be accepted as valid.

Otherwise, the transaction will be rejected by the network. The reason for this seemingly complex behavior lies in the fact that without it no entity participating in the Bitcoin network could ever claim any *ownership of bitcoins*. There is no option to encode ownership of any funds in Bitcoin's blockchain as there is no way to define a "bank account" or any other kind of account in it. And because we don't have them at our disposal, there is no way for us to build relations like "X owns Y bitcoins". The only thing a party could own is *a proof* that gives *a right* to access certain elements, or funds, from the currently available UTXO set. To "own" bitcoins actually means to be in possession of a piece of code that solves the puzzle previously defined by the creator of the UTXO in question. This is mostly done by providing signatures created by using private keys. That's why wallets aren't "wallets" at all, but more like keychains as they never hold any bitcoins, but only private keys. Unlike physical ownership of metal coins or paper money, where we have direct access to them, the decentralized ownership relies on signatures as we always have to reference some previous transaction, before spending any bitcoins from them. To have a right to spend funds in real world, we only have to have *physical access* to them. The same right in decentralized world must be proven by *providing a signature* that unlocks funds from an unspent transaction that got created in the past.

Simply spoken, when you buy something in the real world, you don't have to track the past transactions of the coins in your purse. And nobody would ever ask you for such information. You just use coins to buy stuff with them. Not so in Bitcoin. There you must always have a reference to some previous UTXO and a valid proof of the right to change ownership of those funds.

To achieve such a goal, one basically must execute a small program that defines certain constraints and expects the claiming party to provide data that'll become integral part in the next Script execution. A *script* written in Bitcoin Script is a program that defines rules for releasing funds, which must be followed by the claimant. In most cases, such a script defines the amounts of bitcoins to be spent. This mostly includes *change*-transactions too, as well as the expected signatures that must be provided by the claimant. However, unlike most other programming languages, Bitcoin Script is not Turing-complete,[2] which means that it's incapable of executing *loops, jumps,* and complex control constructs. This was deliberately chosen and for a good reason: a Turing-complete programming language has no guarantee that it'll ever stop. For example, it is trivial to write a never-ending *for*-loop in a Turing-complete language, which basically means that the executing machine could never again be used for anything else. A simple example to show the power, and the potential for misuse, of Turing-completeness can be done directly in a browser. Open your browser's console, usually with F12, and type in this code.

```
for(;;) {
console.log("I will never end - " + new \ Date().
toTimeString());
}
```

After having started it with ENTER, the output will look rather boring and pretty harmless (Figure 7-2).

```
I will never end - 17:58:05 GMT+0200 (Central European Summer Time)     1972   debugger eval code:2:12
I will never end - 17:58:06 GMT+0200 (Central European Summer Time)     7120   debugger eval code:2:12
I will never end - 17:58:07 GMT+0200 (Central European Summer Time)     9835   debugger eval code:2:12
I will never end - 17:58:08 GMT+0200 (Central European Summer Time)     9117   debugger eval code:2:12
I will never end - 17:58:09 GMT+0200 (Central European Summer Time)     9728   debugger eval code:2:12
I will never end - 17:58:10 GMT+0200 (Central European Summer Time)     7927   debugger eval code:2:12
I will never end - 17:58:11 GMT+0200 (Central European Summer Time)     1927   debugger eval code:2:12
```

Figure 7-2. *Browser Console output*

---

[2]https://en.wikipedia.org/wiki/Turing_completeness

But only for some time, because soon your browser would start complaining about a web page that's consuming too many resources (Figure 7-3). The culprit here is of course the script we just started.

 A web page is slowing down your browser. What would you like to do?

Figure 7-3. *Browser warning*

Now imagine Bitcoin's network with nodes executing a script with similar logic. This would effectively cripple the network by exhausting all of its resources, regardless how powerful the participants are. That's also the reason why Turing-complete languages like *Solidity*, one of the scripting languages of Ethereum, which itself runs on top of EVM, the Ethereum Virtual Machine, have the costly "gas consumption" that has to be paid during execution of their programs. Every time a command gets executed, a certain amount of money must be paid or the script execution would stop. This is a strategy to stop malicious actors from exhausting their resources by exploiting the power of Turing-completeness.

Script Notation

We can define Bitcoin scripts as Stack-based programs written in *Reverse Polish Notation* that are guaranteed to stop at some point in time. Every Bitcoin transaction contains a script which must return a Boolean TRUE to be accepted as valid. To get to this value, one must solve all the puzzles given in the locking script and provide all the data needed via unlocking scripts. And just like any other programming language, Script too has its own set of commands, or as we call them "Op-Codes", which is short for Operation Codes. Every operation that Script can execute has a certain number assigned to it so that Bitcoin nodes can easily and quickly parse them when reading serialized scripts from the blockchain.

Due to the fact that Bitcoin Script is written in Reverse Polish Notation, the writing and execution of these OP-Codes looks very differently from most of the other programming languages. As we have already seen in the small example before, languages like JavaScript mostly write their *statements* or *object* names first (like `for` or `console`) and then, if needed, any number of parameters in parentheses. The logic there can be described as *command followed by parameters*. However, this is not the only way to represent an operation.

We all know the mathematical representation like *2 + 2*, where the operator stands between two operands. The Reverse Polish Notation changes the usual mathematical representation by moving the operator behind the operands so that **2 + 2** becomes **2 2 +**. At the first sight, the reader would maybe reject this way of writing, but RPN is actually more powerful and better suited for complex operations than the way we learned in school. This has to do with the way it treats operands and operators. When we write **2 2 +**, we actually mean put `2 and 2 into the stack` and the next operator you read will take as many operands as it needs to complete its operation successfully. In this case the + operator needs two operands, so that it would take both 2s and push back a 4 into the stack. Now imagine a more complex operation like $(2 + 3) * (4 - 2) + 10$. As we already see, we first need to use parentheses to make sure that $(2 + 3)$ and $(4 - 2)$ will be executed separately from other operations. This isn't needed in RPN as there we would simply write **2 3 + 4 2 - * 10 +**

If we combine this notation with our concept of the stack data structure, we can say that we do nothing else but putting operands into the stack first followed by operators that take out as much operands as they need to complete their respective operations. The operators we show here actually never go into the stack but instead execute operations by manipulating elements in the stack. We show them here only to demonstrate the order of operations being executed.

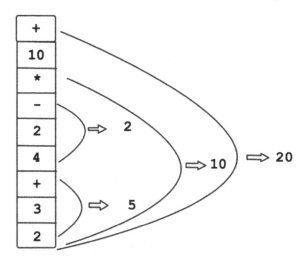

Figure 7-4. *Calculation with a stack*

In Figure 7-4 we start with the two innermost operations and forward their results to operators in higher layers until we have reached the topmost operation that also concludes the script execution.

The first two numbers 2 and 3 would be popped by + and its result, 5, pushed back into the stack. Then the next round of computation will be done, this time 4 and 2, and their result too would be pushed back. Then those two operands (5 and 2) would be multiplied, because * is the next operator that will be executed. Ultimately, their result 10 would be added to the other 10, which would return the final result, 20. As we can see, the RPN is not only ideal for stack-based languages, but it's also much more suitable for complex operations as it doesn't need any "supporting" infrastructure like parentheses.

Had this been a Bitcoin Script, the result would be TRUE, because our result is nonzero. In fact, it is allowed to create any kind of script and define any type of unlocking logic as long as we use the allowed OP-Codes and follow certain rules regarding script creation. Of course, a script that doesn't have any unlocking puzzles included is practically allowing anyone to pilfer the funds. Our following scripts would therefore look a bit more sophisticated than the last example from Figure 7-4.

The complete language of Script comprises of about 100 OP-Codes, but only a handful of them are responsible for the majority of transactions in the current blockchain. Over the next few pages, we will talk about some of them, create a few scripts, and also let them run in controlled environments.

OP-Codes

The OP-Codes[3] comprise of several types grouped as

- *Cryptographic functions*

- *Stack functions*

- *Flow control*

- *Bitwise operation*

- *Pseudo-words*

- *Arithmetic commands*

Regardless of type, every OP-Code is prefixed with OP, like OP_ADD, OP_DUP, etc. There are many older OP-Codes that can't be used, because they've been declared *disabled*, mostly because of security concerns. For example, several of string-operations have been marked as disabled (OP_CAT, OP_SUBSTR etc.). The adjective "disabled" in this case is actually a misnomer, because there is no valid way to re-enable them ever again, so it'd be better to call them "deleted".

Most of the allowed Op-Codes can be used in own scripts with the exception of pseudo-words that can never be part of any valid script.

---

[3]https://en.bitcoin.it/wiki/Script#Opcodes

Pseudo words are OP_PUBKEY, OP_PUBKEYHASH, and OP_INVALIDOPCODE. These can only be used internally for transaction matching.

The standard transaction script, which we already learned about in previous chapters, comprises of two parts, the locking script, also called scriptPubKey, and the unlocking script, called scriptSig:

scriptPubKey: OP_DUP OP_HASH160 <pubKeyHash> OP_EQUALVERIFY OP_CHECKSIG
scriptSig: <sig> <pubKey>

The scriptPubKey is being defined by the current owner of funds we want to get access to. The owner defines what's needed to unlock them, and we provide the solution by delivering our own script, scriptSig, that comprises of a signature and a public key that's related to the private key we just used to create the signature. This way we can prove that we indeed control the private key whose signature was expected in the locking script. The rest of the operation is already known to us. First, the unlocking script will be appended to scriptPubKey, and then the OP-Codes from scriptPubKey will be executed one by one, each time doing something with the signature and public key we provided, like duplicating the public key, hashing the public key, comparing data, and checking the signature. Here we can see the difference between those two scripts. The previous owner defined the *execution logic* while we have to provide *data* that will hopefully keep this logic running and ultimately deliver the needed TRUE value. We have no option to change the logic that comes with scriptPubKey. All we can do is to provide data and wait for the script to complete successfully.

But before we start our practical examples with different Op-Codes, let's look into some of the available commands and groups they belong to. The first group of Op-Codes are used for **pushing data** into the stack. These are commands like

- OP_0
- OP_1

- OP_2 through OP_16

- OP_FALSE

- OP_TRUE

- OP_PUSHDATA1

- OP_PUSHDATA2

- OP_PUSHDATA4

They serve to push data into the stack and can range from empty arrays like OP_0 to numbers like OP_16. An OP_6, for example, pushes number 6 into the stack, while OP_FALSE pushes a zero, which counts as Boolean FALSE in Bitcoin Script.

The second group of commands serves the purpose of **controlling the Script execution** (Table 7-1). These commands partially resemble the usual *if-else* constructs found in many other programming languages. However, the way they execute is different than "normal" *if-else* control structures.

Table 7-1. *Op-Codes for Script Execution Control*

Op-Code (Word)	Op-Code (Number)	Purpose
OP_NOP	97	**Do nothing**
OP_IF	99	**Execute statements if the topmost element in the stack is not False** (it also removes the element)
OP_NOTIF	100	**Execute statements if the topmost element in the stack is False** (it also removes the element)
OP_ELSE	103	**Execute statements if preceding IF, ELSE, or NOTIF wasn't executed**; otherwise ignore these statements
OP_ENDIF	104	**Mark the end of an IF/ELSE block.** All such blocks must end with an ENDIF; otherwise they'll be rejected as invalid

(continued)

Table 7-1. (*continued*)

Op-Code (Word)	Op-Code (Number)	Purpose
OP_VERIFY	105	**Check if topmost element is True**. If not, mark this transaction as invalid; otherwise do nothing. Removes the element
OP_RETURN	106	**Mark transaction as invalid**. This command always succeeds and is the default way of removing funds from the UTXO set. With this command one can "burn" coins

The third group of Op-Codes deals with management of the stack itself (Table 7-2). These commands can, for example, duplicate elements (OP_DUP), move them throughout the stack (OP_SWAP, OP_PICK, OP_ROLL), and similar operations. We will describe a few of them, but in general one will not very often deal with them. The most prominent of those commands is surely OP_DUP which we have already seen a few times, because it's the first command in many scriptPubKey locking scripts:

OP_DUP OP_HASH160 <pubKeyHash>

Table 7-2. *Stack Management*

Op-Code (Word)	Op-Code (Number)	Purpose
OP_DUP	118	Duplicate topmost item
OP_IFDUP	115	Duplicate topmost item if not zero
OP_DROP	117	Remove topmost item
OP_PICK	121	Copy *n*-th item to top of the stack
OP_ROLL	122	Move *n*-th item to top of the stack
OP_SWAP	124	Swap two topmost items in the stack
OP_TUCK	125	Copy the topmost item before the second-to-top item

The fourth group of commands are mostly declared as disabled and therefore can't be used anymore. They have been designed for **working with string values**, like concatenating or splitting them. The only available command as of now is OP_SIZE that calculates the string-length of the topmost stack and pushes this value to the stack. Other commands from this group are OP_CAT, OP_SUBSTR, OP_LEFT, and OP_RIGHT.

Another, also mostly disabled, group of commands deals with **bitwise logic**. It comprises of Op-Codes like

- OP_AND

- OP_OR

- OP_XOR

- OP_INVERT

- OP_EQUAL

- OP_EQUALVERIFY

Only the two last commands are available, and we have already used them in previous scripts. The difference between OP_EQUAL and OP_EQUALVERIFY is that OP_EQUAL only pushes a Boolean result into the stack, while OP_EQUALVERIFY internally runs an OP_VERIFY command that checks the returned value as well. If the result is TRUE, it will continue with script execution; otherwise it'd stop.

The next group of commands deals with **arithmetic** and is the largest of the groups. Most of its Op-Codes can be directly mapped to usual mathematical syntaxes found in other programming languages. For example:

- OP_MUL

- OP_SUB

- OP_ADD

- OP_DIV

- OP_NOT

- OP_MOD

and so on.

However, several of them are disabled and therefore can't be used in any scripts. It is also important to keep in mind that numerical inputs for these Op-Codes are constrained to 32-bit integers, whose return values also can overflow, which puts a great amount of responsibility on the programmer.

The last and the most important group of Op-Codes are **cryptographic operations** (Table 7-3). We have seen several of them, like OP_SHA256, OP_HASH160, OP_CHECKSIG, and others. These Op-Codes are the bread and butter of Bitcoin Script. Without them, no single locking script could ever be created, and there would be no way to produce any proofs of ownership.

Table 7-3. *Cryptographic Operations*

Op-Code (Word)	Op-Code (Number)	Purpose
OP_RIPEMD60	166	Get RIPEMD160 hash
OP_SHA1	167	Get SHA-1 hash
OP_SHA256	168	Get SHA-256 hash
OP_HASH160	169	Get a double-hash: first with SHA-256 then with RIPEMD160
OP_HASH256	170	Get a double-hash by using two times SHA-256
OP_CODESEPARATOR	171	Only match signatures to the data after the most recently executed OP_CODESEPARATOR

(*continued*)

Table 7-3. (*continued*)

Op-Code (Word)	Op-Code (Number)	Purpose
OP_CHECKSIG	172	Get a hash for all of the transaction inputs, outputs, and script, then compare it with the given signature
OP_CHECKSIGVERIFY	173	Same as OP_CHECKSIG, only with additional OP_VERIFY executed afterward
OP_CHECKMULTISIG	174	Compare given signatures against available public keys. It continues comparing until it has either found enough number of matches (*n-of-m*) or it stops if there are no more public keys left for comparison
OP_CHECKMULTISIGVERIFY	175	Same as OP_CHECKMUTISIG but with additional OP_VERIFY

Additionally, there are several Op-Codes that don't belong to any of the previous groups as they're either *reserved code-words* or pseudo-words, that can never be used in scripts directly (Table 7-4).

Table 7-4. *Reserved Words*

Op-Code (Word)	Op-Code (Number)	Purpose (Representation)
OP_PUBKEYHASH	253	Public key hash with OP_HASH160
OP_PUBKEY	254	Public key compatible with OP_CHECKSIG
OP_INVALIDOPCODE	255	Any unassigned Op-Code

Reserved words are following Op-Codes: OP_RESERVED, OP_VER, OP_VERIF, OP_VERNOTIF, OP_RESERVED1, OP_RESERVED2, OP_NOP1, and OP_NOP4 through OP_NOP10.

Testing Bitcoin Script with JavaScript

As there is no better way to learn anything than by doing practical examples, we will now build a small JavaScript/NodeJS environment for executing several of the previously mentioned Op-Codes. Being originally designed in C++ and running in an abstract machine, which only deals with raw bytes, learning Bitcoin Script inside Bitcoin's decentralized network itself is a rather hard task that demands deep knowledge about all of its intricacies, history, and also a good amount of C++ knowledge. To avoid such obstacles without losing practicality, which is always needed in Bitcoin, we will resort to a more welcoming and also easier to use environment based on NodeJS and JavaScript. However, we will still be using raw Script and it's Op-Codes as they are, so we will still be using Script.

Our setup is based on the same NodeJS environment we used previously during our experiments with ZeroMQ messaging. This time we just add another npm package by issuing this command:

```
npm install -S bitcoin-script
```

It will add bitcoin-script package to our `package.json` configuration. You can of course create a completely new package with `npm init` and then add `bitcoin-script,` or you can download the prepared environment that comes with this book, then install the packages with `npm install`, and run it with `npm start` in the console.

The package `bitcoin-script` allows us to write Bitcoin Script Op-Codes and execute them in the NodeJS environment. This of course makes the learning easier as we don't have to run our scripts inside a real wallet or node. This way it we can concentrate on the language itself without exposing us to everything around it, like networks, blockchain handling, and other nodes. Additionally, `bitcoin-script` package allows execution of previously mentioned "disabled" commands so that we can extend our experiments to parts of Bitcoin Script that aren't available in the "real environment" anymore. As a warm-up we will now write a very simple script that checks the current topmost value in the stack for Boolean "truthiness".

```
let evaluate = require('bitcoin-script').evaluate;
let parse = require('bitcoin-script').parse;
let myScript = "OP_TRUE OP_VERIFY";
console.log('Script result is: ' + evaluate(myScript));
```

In the above example, we used the Op-Code `OP_TRUE` to push a 1 into the stack. As we already know, `OP_VERIFY` pops the topmost value from the stack, and it marks the transaction as invalid if the value is not True. To execute this script, one can either type `node ./app.js` from within the directory where the script is located, or if running a NodeJS project with a `package.json`, execute the default start script with `npm start`. The result would be:

```
Script result is: true
```

There is another function available in `bitcoin-script` called "parse" that returns the *parsed structure* of the code.

```
let evaluate = require('bitcoin-script').evaluate;
let parse = require('bitcoin-script').parse;
let myScript = "OP_TRUE OP_VERIFY"
console.log('Script result is: ' + evaluate(myScript));
console.log('Parsed script is: ' + \ JSON.
stringify(parse(myScript), null, 3));
```

This is how the output now would look like

```
Parsed script is: {
   "value": true,
   "code": "stack.OP_TRUE();\nreturn stack.OP_VERIFY();"
}
```

We can now emulate the handling of locking and unlocking scripts by providing signatures and public key addresses. For this we can use any available data form "real world". Here is an example with OP_CHECKSIG, where we use another function from bitcoin-script called "unlock".

```
var unlock = require('bitcoin-script').unlock;

var scriptSig = '8459928119273117345498277881459870695761758288
32449159761054185418684773971871516179267582174550137845918758
09895616634049244428632442980789357056707969 0348726694288015a
15558ed9bebcf398684cb95988bb9fa1c59366415871e9ecc';
var scriptPubKey = 'OP_CHECKSIG OP_VERIFY';
console.log(unlock(scriptSig, scriptPubKey));
```

The result would be a Boolen value of TRUE, indicating that the signature corresponds to the given key.

As the whole purpose of Script in Bitcoin is to evaluate if a logic returns a *True* or *False*, everything we execute here will ultimately lead to a Boolean value. No matter how complex a script might be, the execution engine will in the end return one of these two possible values. This has to do with the nature of Script programs which are "predicates". In mathematics the term predicate means a function that can take any data but will always lead to either True or False. The range of input values for these functions is indefinite, while the possible output values are constrained to those two Boolean values.

To get a more visual representation on what's going on inside the scripting engine and also what its data structure looks like, there is a web site available for visual script execution (Figure 7-5):

```
https://siminchen.github.io/bitcoinIDE/build/editor.html
```

Here is the script from our JavaScript code in the web execution engine.

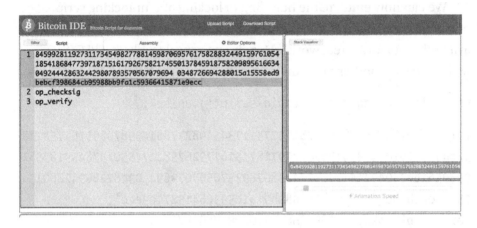

Figure 7-5. *Visual execution of Bitcoin Scripts*

As already mentioned, `bitcoin-script` allows us to execute disabled Op-Codes. All we need is to do is provide an additional parameter to the parsing engine. Here is an example of a script that uses the "disabled" `OP_MUL` command.

```
let evaluate = require('bitcoin-script').evaluate;
let script = 'OP_2 OP_2 OP_MUL OP_4 OP_EQUAL OP_VERIFY';
let useDisabledOpCodes = true;
console.log(evaluate(script, useDisabledOpCodes));
```

In this example we push two "2" and multiply them. Then we compare the result with 4 that of course leads to a True. The step-by-step execution would be like this:

- Push 2 into the stack.

- Push 2 into the stack.

- Take two values from the stack (the two "2"), and multiply them.

- Push the result of the multiplication into the stack (here, 4).

- Push 4 to the stack.

- Take two values (the two "4") from the stack, and compare them for equality.

- Push back the result of comparison into the stack. (here, "true")

- Check the topmost element from the stack for "truthiness".

The final result will be True, and therefore our script execution marked as successful.

Flow Control

If you have ever written code before, you will be able to understand the meaning of this short JavaScript code:

```
if (2 < 3) {
    console.log("Yes, this is true.");
} else {
  console.log("Nope, will never get executed!");
}
```

Just paste this code into your browser's console (*press F12 to open it*) and start it with ENTER. You should get a result like this:

```
> if (2 < 3) {
      console.log("Yes, this is true.");
  } else {
      console.log("Nope, will never get executed!");
  }
  Yes, this is true.
```

Figure 7-6. *Flow control example in JavaScript*

What we have done here (Figure 7-6) is a typical *if-then-else* branching logic, which lets the machine execute certain parts of the program depending on "truthiness" of some value. In our case we wrote the *condition* "2 < 3" and let the machine check in the if-statement, if it's true or not. Depending on the outcome, only one of the two possible *paths* could ever be executed. So far, so easy.

However, the IF-ELSE-ENDIF constructs in Bitcoin Script are a bit different. Or rather, *very* different. Let's try to understand them by analyzing this script:

```
IF
      AlicePubKey CHECKSIG
ELSE
      BobPubKey CHECKSIG
ENDIF
```

At the first sight, we recognize the usual keywords and different execution branches. The script itself seems to be a simple 1-of-2 *multisig*, where either of the parties can spend. However, as the IF statement has no visible conditions, the question is, how can any logic from this script be executed? Where does the condition come from?

The answer to this has to do with the stack data structure Script uses to operate. We already know that data can be pushed in or popped from the stack. Also, that operators can take one or more elements from the stack, do something with them, and push the results back. If this code is a *locking script*, then the missing conditions are part of the *unlocking script*, which the spending party must provide. What we see here is only one-half of the whole code. Now, let's imagine that we have the other half and want to execute the script as a whole. Where does the condition go? After the IF keyword, maybe? Like this:

```
IF condition
      AlicePubKey CHECKSIG
```

Sadly, this wouldn't work, because IF, like any other operator, must pop data from the stack first. There is no way that we could make IF, or any other operator, work on data that's coming after it. Therefore, the condition will always stay in front of IF, like this:

```
Condition IF
      AlicePubKey CHECKSIG
ELSE
      BobPubKey CHECKSIG
ENDIF
```

But how are we supposed to execute IF if there is no condition for it? The answer, again, lies in the way how IF. It always pops data from the stack first and depending on the result (TRUE or FALSE) executes the one or another code branch. This means that in our example, IF would pop one value from the stack and, if it qualifies as true (a non-zero value), execute the first branch. Otherwise, the script would continue with the branch under ELSE.

However, only having provided a condition alone isn't enough as the two branches contain CHECKSIG that would need two operands to execute properly: signature and public key. The public keys are given, but signatures are missing. Where do they come from? From the *unlocking script* of course. To execute either branch, the unlocking script must provide two elements: a value and a signature. And depending on the value, one of the two branches will be executed. In practice, this would mean that when Bob wants to spend funds locked by the script, he would have to provide FALSE + BobSignature, while Alice would need to push TRUE + AliceSignature into the stack. The condition in Script functions like a switch for the spending party to activate the "correct" code part. We also call the IF-ELSE-ENDIF constructs "guard clauses", because they isolate different code parts from each other.

In Figure 7-7 we see our locking script ordered horizontally, while the unlocking script that contains TRUE and AliceSignature is in the stack. The next Op-Code to be executed is IF, which pops the TRUE value from the stack.

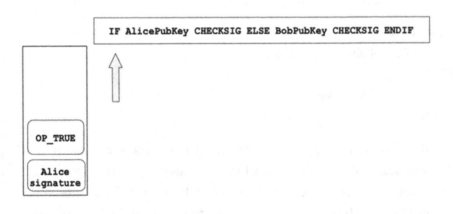

Figure 7-7. *Script execution with IF-ELSE*

The IF operator would now let the first branch execute. In the next step (Figure 7-8), AlicePubKey will be pushed into the stack, because it's not an operator. After it, CHECKSIG will be read, which pops two parameters from the stack: AlicePubKey and AliceSignature.

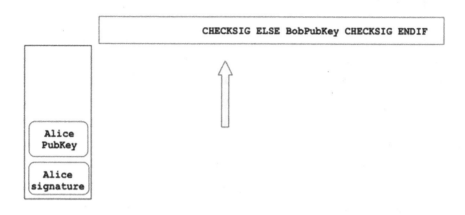

Figure 7-8. *CHECKSIG pops two elements from the stack*

And because CHECKSIG is the last command from the current branch (Figure 7-9), the other code after ELSE won't be read. CHECKSIG would check the signature of Alice and push a TRUE back, signaling that the transaction is valid.

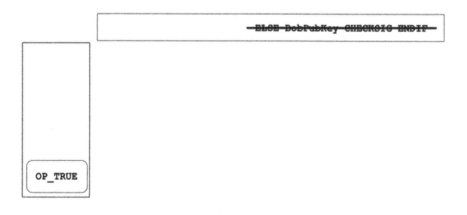

Figure 7-9. *CHECKSIG is the last command to be executed*

Summary

In this chapter we have learned about the very heart of Bitcoin, it's scripting language. Anything we do in Bitcoin is basically a script, or part of it. Every single transaction is based on some script that gets validated by every participating node. We have learned about its many commands and what their purposes are. We have also learned how to read Bitcoin Scripts and what constitutes them. We have learned how owners of funds create small locking scripts with puzzles that can only get unlocked by those who provide correct data like signatures and corresponding public keys. We have also learned how to test Op-Codes, the commands of Script, inside a controlled environment based on NodeJS.

CHAPTER 8

Bitcoin Practice

In this chapter we will learn how to automate Bitcoin's daemon with
systemd,[1] a software suite that provides service management facilities.
It will help us create Raspberry Nodes that are more resilient to failures.
We will also learn to communicate with Bitcoin nodes by utilizing packages
and libraries written in Python and JavaScript. Although Bitcoin offers
an easy-to-use graphical wallet, the real power lies in services that run
behind it. The knowledge about its interfaces and commands should be
part of every proper crypto-toolbelt. We will also learn to build our own
Bitcoin Explorer by using an inexpensive, database-independent tool
called btc-rpc-explorer. Following one of the golden rules in blockchains
"Don't trust. Verify.", we should always strive to utilize the information that
our own nodes provide. There is no need to rely on 3rd-party services, no
matter how convenient they might be, because validating Full Nodes, like
those we're building here, offer everything we need to be independent
actors in decentralized networks.

Automating Bitcoin with systemd

Like most of the other Linux distributions, Raspbian also provides the
systemd suite of tools, which are responsible for managing various services
(daemons). The systemd suite was designed to replace the two major

---

[1]https://en.wikipedia.org/wiki/Systemd

© Harris Brakmić 2019
H. Brakmić, *Bitcoin and Lightning Network on Raspberry Pi*,
https://doi.org/10.1007/978-1-4842-5522-3_8

Unix initialization systems, *BSD* and *UNIX System V*, which have existed since the early 1980s. As Bitcoin comes with its own daemon, `bitcoind`, we should look into `systemd`'s configuration scripts to set up own fully automatized Full Node. Especially when we are dealing with smaller Raspberry Pi devices like Zero Pi, the best solution should be a non-GUI variant that only runs the needed daemons. This way our Zero Pi would consume much less memory while still offering us all advantages we already know from "bigger" devices. In future chapters, when we approach the Lightning Network, the knowledge about `systemd` and its scripting mechanism will come in handy to create even more sophisticated nodes that utilize 2nd-layer solutions like web-based Lightning wallets and browser plugins.

Each time we start or reboot our Raspberry node, we face the `systemd` tools. The typical list with [`OK`] or [`WARNING`] messages during the boot process signals that our Linux is starting services. One of those services, or daemon as we call them in Linux, will be our `bitcoind` daemon. To configure it, we will need to provide certain arguments to the configuration script that will be located under `/etc/systemd/system`. We will name this script `bitcoin.service`. The content of this script comprises of several areas that describe

- When it should start and what its requirements are
- What the configuration parameters of `bitcoind` are
- What should be done in case of failure of `bitcoind`
- What hardening measures should be applied to `bitcoind`

Our script will look like this:

```
# Name and required services to start
[Unit]
Description=Bitcoin daemon
After=network.target
```

```
# start with these parameters
[Service]
ExecStart=/usr/local/bin/bitcoind -pid=/home/pi/.bitcoin/
bitcoin.pid \
                            -conf=/home/pi/.bitcoin/bitcoin.
                            conf \
                            -datadir=/home/pi/.bitcoin \
                            -daemon

# Process management
####################

Type=forking
PIDFile=/home/pi/.bitcoin/bitcoin.pid
Restart=on-failure

# Directory creation and permissions
###################################

# Run as pi:pi
User=pi
Group=pi
# Hardening measures
####################

# Provide a private /tmp and /var/tmp.
PrivateTmp=true

# Mount /usr, /boot/ and /etc read-only for the process.
ProtectSystem=full

# Disallow the process and all of its children to gain
# new privileges through execve().
NoNewPrivileges=true
```

```
# Use a new /dev namespace only populated with API pseudo
devices
# such as /dev/null, /dev/zero and /dev/random.
PrivateDevices=true

# Deny the creation of writable and executable memory mappings.
MemoryDenyWriteExecute=true

[Install]
WantedBy=multi-user.target
```

To be able to edit and save the script, we must use the sudo command.

```
sudo nano /etc/systemd/system/bitcoin.service
```

After we have completed the configuration script, we will need to register it with systemd and start it manually, or alternatively restart the node to let Linux start it among other scripts. As we have defined that our bitcoin.service script requires a working network connection, Raspbian will first wait for such a connection, before it attempts to start bitcoind. The installation of a script must be done once by invoking: *systemctl enable SCRIPT-NAME*. As always, here one should also use **sudo** to get administrative privileges.

```
sudo systemctl enable bitcoin
```

A system-controlled service can be started, stopped, or restarted anytime from the console. In our case we will have to start our new daemon first. However, we won't get anything back, neither a success information nor any error. To get such information, we have to use journalctl command.

```
journalctl -f -u bitcoin
```

We now have successfully started our systemd-controlled daemon. One additional command for getting detailed information, especially in case of errors or crashes, is `journalctl -xe` that will print any errors regarding running or failed daemons. But in our case, there are no visible errors, so all we'll get are harmless log-entries.

Now we can use the same remote control commands and also read from the standard logfile `debug.log` that's located in `.bitcoin` folder. If you ever change any of your `systemd` scripts, you must execute

```
systemctl daemon-reload
```

This command informs `systemd` about any changes done in its configuration scripts.

Using Bitcoin with Python

Our previous programming examples were based on JavaScript, but this of course isn't the only language that could be used to talk to Bitcoin nodes. Another easy-to-use and highly expressive language is Python, or more precisely Python v3. On the following page, we will be using a powerful python library called `python-bitcoinlib` that covers the standard Bitcoin interfaces and its protocol. Without much ceremonial code, as it often happens in other languages, one can relatively easy access most of the functionalities by issuing commands that almost directly map to original data structures from Bitcoin. But before we can use this library, we should make sure that we have installed `python3`, its package manager `pip3,` and also the bitcoin library itself. Usually, `python3` will be already installed as well as `pip3`, but if you happen to have removed it or otherwise missing, install it with

```
sudo apt install pyton3 python3-pip
```

The bitcoin library will be installed by using

```
pip3 install python-bitcoinlib.
```

Our first test with `python-bitcoinlib` will be to get a certain block from the current active chain. In our case this will be the `testnet` chain. As its standard under scripts that run in Linux, we will start our Python script with a special header that indicates its standard shell, which is the process that should open it by default. Maybe you have already seen similar scripts that contain such headers, very often with `/bin/bash` entries, that indicate shell scripts. The same way we will declare our Python script to "belong" to Python and give the default path of the binary that should open it by default.

```
#!/usr/bin/env python3
import bitcoin
bitcoin.SelectParams('regtest')
proxy = bitcoin.rpc.Proxy()
block = proxy.getblock(proxy.getblockhash(10))
print(block)
```

The first entry is the *import* command that binds the available `bitcoinlib` resources with our script so that we can access them later. In the next line, we select the `regtest` chain. The actual communication channel gets established in the following line by invoking `bitcoin.rpc.Proxy()` which automatically selects our `bitcoin.conf` configuration file.

Now, all that's left is to execute two functions combined together: `getblockhash` and `getblock`. As already mentioned, `bitcoinlib` closely follows the original Bitcoin API, and therefore many calls and functions are more or less directly mapping to their counterparts from C++-based code. The two commands could also be executed in the Debug console or indirectly by invoking `bitcoin-cli` command line interface. The result would be the same. To run this script, we switch to our shell and type

`python3 getblock.py.`

The result would look like this:

```
CBlock(536870912, lx(01beae916533845f25d170fb5b3f2745fb2cd42c
bf16c3293b148f9cc9451efe), lx(f6500dafb7f41d55c08ab521c2d241
1ce64a41a74a0ca5a1b225a8a3a7c979ae), 1564334164, 0x207fffff,
0x00000004)
```

As python-bitcoinlib implements various wallet functionalities, we can use them without having any connection to a running node. In the below example, we execute the script by that uses a private key from testnet and let it generate a new address.

```
import bitcoin
from bitcoin.wallet import CBitcoinSecret, P2PKHBitcoinAddress
bitcoin.SelectParams('testnet')
priv_key = \ 'cUHmPhwxCZN22yJP3orG1pgVSYrNcZtTB3KZMpPHXqyDnfFmzSF4'
secret = CBitcoinSecret(priv_key)
public_key = secret.pub
p2pkh_address = \ P2PKHBitcoinAddress.from_pubkey(public_key)
scriptPubKey = p2pkh_address.to_scriptPubKey()
p2pkh_address2 = \ P2PKHBitcoinAddress.from_scriptPubKey
(scriptPubKey)
print('P2PKH address based on public key: %s' % \ p2pkh_address)
print('P2PKH address based on scriptPubKey: %s' % \ p2pkh_address2)
```

This script demonstrates the capability of generating addresses from public keys of locking scripts.

```
P2PKH address based on public key: mmEj29nzqpQh8hGS6gChqCbhrWDP
UAjsSN
P2PKH address based on scriptPubKey: mmEj29nzqpQh8hGS6gChqCbhrW
DPUAjsSN
```

bitcoinlib can also create transactions. In the following example, we will be using regtest network instead of testnet, because this environment offers much easier generation of "test coins". Also, if your wallet is encrypted, don't forget to unlock it first.

```
import bitcoin
bitcoin.SelectParams('regtest')

from bitcoin.core import COIN, b2lx
import bitcoin.wallet
import bitcoin.rpc

rpc = bitcoin.rpc.Proxy()
addr = \ bitcoin.wallet.CBitcoinAddress('2NCbWGkCgntWxRJb3EKLiC
BTZrGUm1LyBt9')

txid = rpc.sendtoaddress(addr, 10 * COIN)
print('Transaction created: %s' % b2lx(txid))
```

To properly calculate amounts to be sent, we need the COIN constant. Also, we import the conversion function b2lx that converts the *Endianness*[2] to little-endian. This is because Bitcoin shows its transaction and block hashes in little-endian format.

We execute this script with python3 ./sendcoins.py and will get the ID of the transaction:

```
Transaction created: 7aea8ed620653526bb539af21bb02777c29aacbf8f
e2ffd2cb1584f4ee84a1e0
```

On your node the transaction ID will be different, but in any case, we can search for it with the standard command gettransaction.

```
Bitcoin-cli -regtest gettransaction \ 7aea8ed620653526bb539af21
bb02777c29aacbf8fe2ffd2cb1584f4ee84a1e0
```

---

[2]https://en.wikipedia.org/wiki/Endianness

Using Bitcoin with JavaScript

Another great programming language for communication and control of Bitcoin Nodes is of course JavaScript. And as we have already seen in previous chapters, JavaScript is not only easy to learn but also offers great environments for running its code, like NodeJS. Long gone are the times when JavaScript was merely a *glue language* for web developers. These days it powers some of the most complex backend services. In many projects it's not any longer the question "what should we write to achieve X" but rather "let's search for an npm[3]-package for X". JavaScript has definitely become *Google for software components*.

And because we in Bitcoin always strive to be independent from 3rd-party services by building our "home-grown" variants, we will now look into NodeJS ecosystem and what Bitcoin-oriented packages it offers. To be able to access those packages, one only has to have a working NodeJS environment that can be easily installed by following the instructions from `https://nodejs.org` web page. Many Linux distributions already have their own NodeJS packages available, but it's strongly recommended to install it from vendor's web page, because it's guaranteed that you will be using the latest stable version, which is not always the case with Linux distributions.

A typical NodeJS project comprises of a single directory with a `package.json` file in it. This file describes the project, it's package dependencies, and the available scripts which can be run with the `npm` command. Although this JSON file could be created manually, it's better to use the `npm init` command that would ask you a few questions about your project before generating a new `package.json`. After you have completed the short initialization routine, your new project directory would contain the `package.json` file that contains all the data you gave in plus every dependency and script you will include in future. Any change to the project also means changing the contents of `package.json`.

---

[3]NodeJS Package Manager, a tool for managing packages in the NodeJS environment

Using bitcoin-core to Communicate with Bitcoin Nodes

What we now want to use is a package that can help us communicate and control our full node. One of them is `bitcoin-core`, a package that maps Bitcoin functions to JavaScript very similar to `python-bitcoinlib`. To add this package, all we have to do is issue a command:

```
npm install -S bitcoin-core
```

This command not only installs this package, but it also adds it to `package.json`, because we have used the flag `-S`. In future, for example, when recreating the environment on another machine, all that is needed to get the same state is typing `npm install` again. This command would read all the dependencies from `package.json` and install the required packages.

Inside `package.json` a new entry regarding `bitcoin-core` is now visible.

```
"dependencies": {
    "bitcoin-core": "^2.2.0"
  }
```

Our next step will be to include this package in our source code. In JavaScript we have different options to load an external *module* into our own code, where each of the options depends on the environment we use. This could either be browsers or machines that aren't facing the web. In our case we are accessing a full node that certainly isn't facing the web directly, and we will surely want to keep it that way, not only because of security reasons. Also, our code will be running as "backend" JavaScript, that is NodeJS, where it doesn't have much to do with browser interactions, HTML, or DOM parsing. The standard way for loading modules in NodeJS is the `require`[4] statement which we have already approached in the last few JavaScript examples from previous chapters.

---

[4]`https://fredkschott.com/post/2014/06/require-and-the-module-system/`

After we have loaded the `bitcoin-core` that provides us with the needed Client mechanism, we will use it to create a new connection with our running Bitcoin node. In this example, our node runs on `regtest`. For other setups and blockchains, you will have to adapt the needed parameters accordingly.

```
const Client = require('bitcoin-core');

// setup client chain & access data
const client = new Client({
  network: 'regtest',
  username: 'raspiuser',
  password: 'mypassword',
});
```

The important fact here is that the statement **new** initializes a new object of type "Client", which is a term that comes from *object-oriented-programming* paradigm. This new object has certain capabilities, which have been defined in the package we just loaded. All we have to do now is to use them without thinking much of what the actual implementation inside `bitcoin-core` looks like. We concentrate on the visible interfaces only. This is the advantage we get from NodeJS and similar environments, because we don't have to think much about the implementation logic behind those modules. We only integrate them into our own environments. Our next step is to set up an area where we will be calling several asynchronous functions.

```
(async function() {

  // query wallet balance
  const balance = await client.getBalance();
  console.log(`Balance is: ${balance}`);
```

```
// create new address
const recipient = await client.getNewAddress();
console.log(`Got new address: ${recipient}`);

// optionally, unlock your wallet with a passphrase
// comment it out if wallet is not password enrypted
await client.walletPassphrase('mypassword', 10);

// sent 10BTC to previously created address
const txid = await client.sendToAddress(recipient, 10);
console.log(`Created transaction: ${txid}`)

// generate 10 more blocks to make transaction confirmed
const blocks = await client.generate(10);
console.log(`Generated blocks: ${JSON.stringify(blocks,
null, 3)}`);

// get detailed transaction information
const tx = await client.getTransaction(txid);

// copy certain transaction fields into a new object
const shorttx = {
                    confirmations: tx.confirmation,
                    blockhash: tx.blockhash,
                    txid: tx.txid,
                    details: tx.details
                };

// print out distilled transaction data
console.log(`Transaction data: ${JSON.stringify(shorttx,
null, 4)}`);

}());
```

Here we apply the logic that comes with our Client object. As previously mentioned, the Client *class*, which is another term from object-oriented-programming, maps closely to the original Bitcoin API (application programming interface). Therefore, we can easily try out some of the functions like getbalance and getnewaddress. And because the preferred way of naming things in JavaScript is the so-called Camel-Case, the Client offers its mapped functions as getBalance and getNewAddress.

Our application executes several tasks, that all rely upon a working full node and RPC. Therefore, certain options are needed to be active in bitcoin.conf like rpcuser, rpcpassword, rpcport, and rest. In the source code examples that come with this book, you can find predefined settings and adapt them to your environment. The goal of this application is to send 10BTC to another address it automatically created and then to generate a few more blocks to make the transaction confirmed.

```
Balance is: 14949.98412169
Got new address: 2MtZfNCPN7MYBnLGHFGb8AFAtA77u8KHFi1
Created transaction: c7500d43319935e5887fbbe4ae0cb0577b5fe04429
b00e0238f6e90b127cd386
```

Ultimately, the application would present a shortened version of the original transaction object.

```
Transaction data: {
    "blockhash": "31dddcbd358ed757aa488bb5ee4eed68e5cb4e266b422
    e3aff2c535cf390b8cd",
    "txid": "c7500d43319935e5887fbbe4ae0cb0577b5fe04429b00e0238
    f6e90b127cd386"
}
```

Using bitcoinlib-js with Multisig, SegWit, and P2SH

Another excellent package for NodeJS is `bitcoinlib-js` that we will be using here to generate addresses and *redeem* scripts. In most cases, the funds being sent through Bitcoin's network require only one signature. However, there are situations when funds must be controlled by several people.

For example, corporate funds whose access is shared by several executives. In such cases one would need a requirement of providing more than one signature before the funds in question can be spent. To solve this problem, the Bitcoin protocol offers *multisig*[5] or multiple signature-based transactions. Such transactions can only be spent when a predefined threshold is achieved, for example, when two of three possible signatures are provided. A concrete example would be a company with three managers, who have an agreement that for a successful transaction, at least two of them have to sign it off with their individual signatures.

To create such a transaction, we need to generate a new kind of redeem script that will contain multiple signatures. Until now, our redeem scripts have only contained a single signature and a public key. This time we want to create a more complex script that will also generate a new type of address which is called P2SH or *pay-to-script-hash*. Most of the previous addresses we have been using so far are called P2PKH or *pay-to-public-key-hash*, because they only contain a single public key hash.

When we send funds to a P2SH address, we're actually sending them to a script. However, as the sender has nothing to do with the logic behind the receiving entity, which must be provided by the receiver anyway, it's irrelevant if the receiving side provides a hash of a script or a hash of a public key. What counts is that the receiving side provides an unlocking script whose hash equals the hash expected in the `scriptPubKey` of the

---

[5]`https://en.bitcoin.it/wiki/Multisignature`

input transaction. However, the P2SH address format isn't a requirement for multisig addresses, as they could also be created in P2MS (*Pay to Multisig*) format without being "packed" into a P2SH address type.

Here are the two examples in P2MS and P2SH format:

Multisig Transaction in P2SH format (2-of-3)

scriptSig: OP_0 [sig1] [sig2] OP_2 [pk1][pk2][pk3] OP_3 OP_CHECKMULTISIG

scriptPubKey: OP_HASH160 <scriptHash> OP_EQUAL

The sender of funds expects the spender to provide a scriptSig whose hash value equals the scriptHash value defined in scriptPubKey.

Multisig Transaction in P2MS format (2-of-3)

scriptSig: OP_0 [sig1] [sig2]

scriptPubKey: OP_2 [pk1][pk2][pk3] OP_3 OP_CHECKMULTISIG

The sender of funds provides public keys together with the script logic to be executed upon signatures provided by the spender.

The difference between the two lies in the amount of information the locking script carries around. In the P2SH variant, the scriptPubKey only needs to know the hash of a future scriptSig, while the P2MS variant expects the scriptPubKey creator to know the minute details about public keys and script logic. This of course makes such locking scripts not only more complex but simply much bigger, which increases the transaction fees the sender has to pay.

The execution logic, however, is the same for both script types. What happens is that at the execution the two script parts will first be combined into one:

OP_0 [sig1] [sig2] OP_2 [pk1][pk2][pk3] OP_3 OP_CHECKMULTISIG

The scripting engine will be pushing the elements into the stack until it has reached CHECKMULTISIG. At the moment of its execution, the stack would look like this (Figure 8-1).

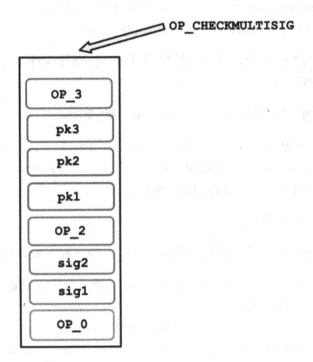

Figure 8-1. *Multisig Script*

CHECKMULTISIG would then take its arguments from the stack as follows:

- It'd query the number of Public Keys to pop from stack. Here: OP_3.

- It'd then take the Public Keys one by one.

- It'd then take the expected number of signatures that must map to either of those keys. Here we expect two. (OP_2)

- The signatures will be taken in the next step.

- At the end OP_0 will be popped, which is just a "bugfix", because the original implementation of CHECKMULTISIG had an off-by-one error. However, because we deal here with Consensus-critical code, it was decided to simply let it always take a 0, which has no effect on the operation itself. CHECKMULTISIG does nothing with it, but OP_0 must be there to prevent CHECKMULTISIG from failing.

- The last step is the execution of CHECKMULTISIG that now compares signatures to given keys and determines if the expectation can be satisfied. In this case it is 2-of-3, which means that the two signatures must correspond to at least two of three public keys.

Although it might seem complex at the beginning, the strategy behind Multisig is pretty straightforward. We create an address that internally "maps" to a certain number of public keys combined with logic that defines how many of them are needed to spend any funds associated with this address. Then we use this address for storing funds just like with any other. And to move those funds, we will have to provide the expected minimum number of signatures to unlock them.

Although it is certainly possible to create such addresses with bitcoin-cli or in the Debug console of the GUI wallet, we will try it later with bitcoinjs-lib that we install with npm install -S bitcoinjs-lib. The next step will be to load this module into our JavaScript file and learn a bit about the classes and interfaces this library offers.

SegWit Addresses

```
const bitcoin = require('bitcoinjs-lib');
const mainnet = bitcoin.networks.mainnet;

const keyPair = bitcoin.ECPair.makeRandom(
{ network: mainnet }
```

```
);
const result = bitcoin.payments.p2wpkh(
{ pubkey: keyPair.publicKey }
);
console.log(result.address);
```

The above script shows a minimal program that uses `bitcoinjs-lib` for creating a SegWit address. At the beginning we declare `mainnet` as our network and use the namespace "bitcoin" that comes from the `bitcoinjs-lib` module. This module provides functions we use to create keys and addresses. But before we continue discussing the code, we should explore this new address format and the reasons that led to its development. The format is called P2WPKH that we get by calling the `bitcoin.payments.p2wpkh` function.

P2WPKH stands for *pay-to-witness-public-key-hash* and came with the successful activation of the **SegWit soft-fork**[6] in August 2017. SegWit brings a new transaction format to Bitcoin that instead of relying on `scriptSig` for getting signatures uses a new feature called `witness`, where the unlocking data now resides. Unlike `scriptSig` the data in `witness` is no longer part of the transaction input, which saves lots of space as signatures usually consumes a considerable amount bytes. Often, we can see transactions losing more than 50% of space for signature data only.

This new free space SegWit provides us can now be used to include more transactions. As signatures are only needed when transactions are verified and later have no practical use, its relocation outside transaction inputs allows for optimization of transaction validation.

```
"in": [
{
  "prev_out":
    {
```

---

[6]https://bitcoincore.org/en/2016/01/26/segwit-benefits/

```
      "hash": "ab45ba34bb44545435394537…[shortened]",
      "n": 0
    },
  "scriptSig": "",
  "witness": "3044022079d553...[shortened]"
}
```

In the above snippet, we see that `scriptSig` is empty. As we have seen in previous examples, `scriptSig` would normally contain the unlocking script that is very often a data pair containing a signature and its corresponding public key. With SegWit transactions the data in `scriptSig` becomes irrelevant as all witness data, that is, the signatures, gets moved to a new property called `witness`. As shown in Figure 8-2, SegWit transaction inputs are separated from unlocking (witness) scripts that contain signatures.

Legacy, non-SegWit transactions   **SegWit transactions**

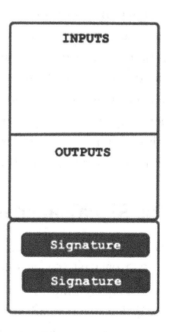
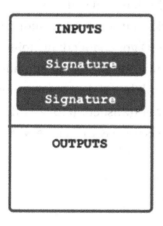

Figure 8-2. *Legacy and SegWit transactions*

However, to spend inputs by using witness data, one wouldn't need to apply a different method as the semantics remained the same. It's only the `position of witness data` that changed, which also solves the problem of *transaction malleability* as signatures are no longer included in transaction inputs.

Transaction Malleability Problem

The transaction malleability problem can be exploited by attackers who intercept transactions that aren't finalized yet and change their signature data. Because of this change, the transaction ID would change as well. Imagine a situation where sender A created a transaction that's spending 1BTC to address of recipient B. However, this transaction won't immediately get included into a block but will have to wait for some time in the mempool. Recipient B could now take this transaction and change the signature in `scriptSig` a bit. This would result in a completely new transaction ID. However, the transaction itself would still be valid and become part of one of the upcoming blocks, but sender A wouldn't be able to find it, because the original transaction ID got changed. Recipient B could now contact A saying that the original transaction never made it into a block. As sender A wouldn't be able to find the original transaction ID, he or she might be tricked into sending another transaction to B. With SegWit this problem is no longer existent as there is no way to change witness data that is now located outside of `scriptSig`.

The Significance of SegWit

Normally, we would expect `scriptPubKey` to contain some of the usual `OP_DUP`, `OP_HASH160`, `OP_CHECKSIG,` and similar Op-Codes. However, as `scriptSig` contains no data, there is no need to put any operations into `scriptPubKey`. Instead, `scriptPubKey` in SegWit transactions only contains two entries, a number (0) and a double hash (based on SHA-256 and

RIPEMD160), which can also be found in legacy transactions. Basically, all of the Op-Codes are gone, and only the hash and zero remained. The number 0 represents the **witness version**, because SegWit was designed to be extensible, which will be indicated with new version numbers in the future. Currently, its version is 0. And this is how a `scriptPubKey` in SegWit would look like:

```
0 0032c5570d75206aacc455c44bcc7cc8aa6c555a
```

By following this strategy of separation of transaction inputs from unlocking scripts (witnesses), blocks automatically gain more space for transactions. The default size of a Bitcoin block is 1MB, but with SegWit and its clever usage of available space, it could reach up to 4MB, if needed. This of course increases the overall throughput of Bitcoin transactions without sacrificing the ideal that even the smallest devices should be able to participate in the decentralized network.

Although other alternative strategies exist, which have been tested by several other cryptocurrency projects, none of them have provided any significant innovation. Mostly, their strategy was to copy Bitcoin's original source code and continuously increase the allowed maximum block size, hoping that with bigger blocks more transactions will come in, which of course failed completely. It's not only the block size that counts. The problem is that the bigger the blocks get, the greater the pressure on participating nodes will become. The increase in needed processing power, network bandwidth, and disk space would make operating nodes more expensive for individuals. This ultimately would lead to a decrease in the number of participating nodes, because it'd naturally shift toward powerful data centers, that can afford to deploy more resources.

And the less nodes participate in a decentralized network, the less decentralized it becomes. In fact, it becomes just as centralized as any other *centralized-by-design* network would be from the start. This directly affects the valuation of the currency it operates with, because fewer and fewer operators can decide on what the "correct transactions" are. The decentralization of Bitcoin is unmatched, and the innovation progress of this project is always striving to keep the balance between its constituents: validating nodes, miners, exchanges, users, and investors. Censorship resistance is one of the distinguishing features of Bitcoin that no other cryptocurrency can offer at the similar scale. Therefore, merely increasing the block size without providing true innovation is a dead end.

Bech32

In our current example, we will be using a new address type that comes with SegWit which is called *Bech32*. This address format is also called "native segwit" as it doesn't rely on the variant that still uses P2PSH address format to enclose SegWit data. In general, every SegWit transaction can be encoded in P2PSH format. This way non-SegWit processing nodes can still accept new transactions without any problems. All they see is the "old" P2SH address format without dealing with any of its details.

The native segwit format, however, is a completely new development and is also being used in the Lightning Network. In fact, Lightning Network wouldn't be possible without SegWit. This has to do with the previously mentioned *transaction malleability*[7] problem. The solution for it was the *Segregated Witness*[8] soft-fork that got activated in August 2017. Based on it was the development of Bech32 address type.

But to maintain compatibility with older clients that don't support Bech32 addresses, Bitcoin also offers alternative SegWit addresses that look just like older P2SH addresses. However, as only Bech32 offers certain advantages, like much lower transaction fees one has to pay, which can only be partially achieved by other addresses, we can expect that modern clients

---

[7]https://en.bitcoin.it/wiki/Transaction_Malleability
[8]https://en.bitcoin.it/wiki/Segregated_Witness

and services offered by the Bitcoin industry will gradually shift to Bech32, or at least offer it as an option for customers. In general, one should look for options that contain "send to SegWit address" or "native SegWit".

When we now start our initial JavaScript code with npm start, an address with prefix **bc1** will be returned.

```
bc1qt4c5zw0ag6vxe722uwfyvc07vmfr7p5snktrtq
```

All mainnet Bech32 addresses begin with **bc1,** and unlike older Bitcoin addresses, they are case-insensitive. This of course means a much greater safety for users when typing or telling them. The prefixes are **tb1** for testnet and **bcrt1** for regtest. In our examples we will be using mainnet only.

To change the network, simply select a different one from the namespace bitcoin.networks at the beginning of the script. We generate Bech32 addresses by using the function p2wpkh from bitcoinjs-lib. To get a SegWit address formatted as legacy P2SH, we would have to generate a redeem script, because P2SH addresses are based on *script hashes*. In our case, the script from which we will get the hash will contain a single address.

```
const result = bitcoin.payments.p2sh({
  redeem: bitcoin.payments.p2wpkh(
{ pubkey: keyPair.publicKey })
});
```

As the creation of P2SH-based addresses is more complex, we have to embed our address inside the "redeem" property. The data we provide there is the same: our *public key*. However, this time we won't be hashing the public key like we did with P2WPKH in the previous example but the script containing our public key. This is needed to wrap our new address type inside an older address type. The result is an address in the same format as any other P2SH address.

```
37Rvsssn7UmQdb5pwKANco9RwjoUTJwKUB
```

There is no way for non-SegWit nodes to distinguish between standard P2SH scripts and those who carry native SegWit addresses. We now have learned how to create redeem scripts. This will lead us directly to redeem scripts for *multisig* addresses we spoke about previously. In the example below, we create our multisig address as follows:

```
const keyPair1 = bitcoin.ECPair.makeRandom({ network: mainnet });
const keyPair2 = bitcoin.ECPair.makeRandom({ network: mainnet });
const keyPair3 = bitcoin.ECPair.makeRandom({ network: mainnet });

const pubkeys = [
  keyPair1.publicKey,
  keyPair2.publicKey,
  keyPair3.publicKey
];
const multisig = bitcoin.payments.p2sh({
  redeem: bitcoin.payments.p2ms({ m: 2, pubkeys })
});
```

We generate three addresses, and in the redeem script, we set the minimum number of acceptable signatures together with an array of corresponding public keys. This time we call the function **p2ms** that will generate a "pay to multisig" redeem script. The difference here is really only the number of addresses and our selection of "m". This comes from the shortcut "m-of-n" which is used to describe multisig options, like 2-of-3, 3-of-6, etc. Our array of public keys contained three addresses and is therefore the "n"-part. Therefore, the execution of the function **p2ms** could be read as generate a multisig redeem script that accepts *at least two valid signatures* which correspond to *the three keys* from this array.

Importing WIF Keys

Another useful feature is the import of **WIF**[9] keys. WIF stands for *Wallet Import Format* and is a way of formatting ECDSA[10] keys, which is the cryptographic algorithm for generating Bitcoin keys and signatures. The WIF format constitutes a standard for transferring keys between different applications. A private key generated in Bitcoin Core Wallet can be directly imported in another Bitcoin software like Electrum or hardware wallets like Trezor or Ledger.

```
const wif = \
'L12wE92KBbwS3RNFxeAnGLbmP5ibw8PRK2Lr1tfZrEvPqn1MP1MD';
const keyPair = bitcoin.ECPair.fromWIF(wif);
const { address } = bitcoin.payments.p2pkh(
{ pubkey: keyPair.publicKey });
```

Using Bitcoin with C++

Although we focus on the reference client that defines what Bitcoin is and how it operates, this isn't the only client that understands the Bitcoin protocol. One of the popular alternatives to Bitcoin Core is the libbitcoin[11] system, which is a highly modular set of libraries and applications that offer various functionalities for working with Bitcoin's blockchain, network, and consensus protocol. With libbitcoin one can develop applications that run on top of the Bitcoin protocol but also operate servers and clients that participate in the network. In the following

---

[9]https://en.bitcoin.it/wiki/Wallet_import_format
[10]https://en.bitcoin.it/wiki/Elliptic_Curve_Digital_Signature_Algorithm
[11]https://libbitcoin.org

examples, we will be using the `libbitcoin-system` development library. The installation can be done automatically by invoking the `install.sh` script, which we will download from project's GitHub pages:

```
wget \ https://raw.githubusercontent.com/libbitcoin/libbitcoin/
version3/install.sh
```

After the download, we will set the execute flag to the script:

```
chmod +x ./install.sh
```

We are now ready to kick off the download of needed libraries and the compilation of the system itself. The operation will take some time and will generate `lib`, `include`, and `share` directories in the path, which we will declare at script execution. It is recommended to use `/usr/local` as installation prefix to avoid problems with missing include files and libraries.

```
./install.sh --prefix=/usr/local/ --build-boost \
--disable-shared
```

As we have already compiled our Bitcoin Core wallet, there is no need for us to reinstall the libraries `libbitcoin` depends on. However, in case you are installing it on a new device, this is the `apt` installation command that you should execute before running the `install.sh` script.

```
sudo apt install build-essential autoconf automake libtool pkg-
config git
```

Generating Addresses

After the installation has completed, we open a new file called `genkey.cpp` and type in the following C++ code. This program will generate a new *testnet* (or *mainnet*) address each time we execute it.

```cpp
#include <bitcoin/bitcoin.hpp>
#include <string.h>
#include <iostream>

using namespace bc;
using namespace wallet;

int main()
{

// Generate random bytes for Secret Key
data_chunk seed(16);
pseudo_random_fill(seed);
ec_secret secretKey = bitcoin_hash(seed);

// Encode Secret Key and create uncompressed Private Key
std::string secretKeyHex = encode_base16(secretKey);
ec_secret privKeyEncoded;
decode_base16(privKeyEncoded, secretKeyHex);
// mainnet 0x8000, testnet 0xef00
wallet::ec_private privateKey(privKeyEncoded, 0xef00, false);

// Derive PubKey from PrivKey
ec_compressed pubKey;
secret_to_public(pubKey, privateKey);

// Generate PubKeyHash: first SHA256, then Hash160
auto pubKeyHash = bitcoin_short_hash(pubKey);

// Set address prefix (mainnet = 0x00, testnet = 0x6f)
one_byte prefix = { { 0x6f } };
```

```
// Setup address components
// Prefix + PubKey + Checksum (4-bytes)
data_chunk rawAddress(to_chunk(prefix));
extend_data(rawAddress, pubKeyHash);
append_checksum(rawAddress);

// Base58-encode to get Bitcoin Address
std::cout << encode_base58(rawAddress) << '\n';
return 0;
}
```

The execution starts with random data generation, which we will use to build our secret key. This key is then being used to create our uncompressed private key. Based on it, we derive the public key, which then will be hashed and combined with the components, which are part of any Bitcoin address: the prefix and the 4 bytes taken from the checksum value. Ultimately, we encode the raw key data with Base58. This C++ code is functionally similar to previous examples written in Python and JavaScript. To generate a *mainnet* address, we only have to change the encoding for the private key and the address prefix[12] of the public key.

To compile the code, we use the g++ compiler with the following flags:

```
g++ -std=c++11 -o genkey genkey.cpp $(pkg-config --cflags
libbitcoin --libs libbitcoin)
```

The resulting binary will be located in the current directory and should be executed with:

```
./genkey
n4FNLCnoPw6XidZfD3rAvkHrfevg4d7jTG
```

---

[12]https://en.bitcoin.it/wiki/List_of_address_prefixes

Generating Multisig Addresses

In this example, we will create a 2-of-3 multisig address and its locking script. The first function in the source code, gen_private_key, is responsible for private key generation and is functionally similar to the previous C++ example. However, the code for setting up the locking script will introduce some new functions.

```cpp
#include <bitcoin/bitcoin.hpp>
#include <boost/algorithm/string.hpp>

using namespace bc;
using namespace bc::wallet;
using namespace bc::machine;
using namespace bc::chain;

// for generating PrivKeys
ec_private get_private_key() {
// Generate random bytes for Secret Key
data_chunk seed(16);
pseudo_random_fill(seed);
ec_secret secretKey = bitcoin_hash(seed);

// Encode Secret Key and create uncompressed Private Key
std::string secretKeyHex = encode_base16(secretKey);
ec_secret privKeyEncoded;
decode_base16(privKeyEncoded, secretKeyHex);
wallet::ec_private privateKey(privKeyEncoded, 0x8000, false);
  return privateKey;
}
```

```
int main()
{

// Generate three different PrivKeys
auto privateKey1 = get_private_key();
auto privateKey2 = get_private_key();
auto privateKey3 = get_private_key();

// Derive three PubKeys from each PrivKey
ec_compressed pubKey1, pubKey2, pubKey3;
secret_to_public(pubKey1, privateKey1);
secret_to_public(pubKey2, privateKey2);
secret_to_public(pubKey3, privateKey3);

data_stack keys {to_chunk(pubKey1), to_chunk(pubKey2), to_
chunk(pubKey3)};

script multiSig = script(script().to_pay_multisig_pattern(2,
keys));

// print payment address
std::cout << "Address: " + payment_address(multiSig, 0x05).
encoded() << '\n';

// print multisig script
auto multiSigString = multiSig.to_string(1);
boost::to_upper(multiSigString);
std::cout << "Script: " + multiSigString << '\n';

}
```

After having generated three private keys, we derive three public keys from each of them. We then put them into a data stack and define the multisig-pattern our locking script should follow. In this case, we are creating a 2-of-3 multisig script. At the end, we select the type of the multisig address, which in our case will be P2SH (Pay-to-Script-Hash). The last few lines of the code will print this data on the console. The compilation follows the same rules as the last example:

```
g++ -std=c++11 -o multisig multisig.cpp $(pkg-config --cflags
libbitcoin --libs libbitcoin)
```

When we execute the program, an address and its accompanying locking script will be shown:

```
./multisig
```

Address: 345gUqhMuzLxbrVCSKGdQ7jGD1gF6xVQ4h
Script: 2
[0389E4F4428D92634C8FB010EE195E799D5CE65FBB4D6F1DAB3CD2FA68A62CF0AE]
[03890D2A945A76960C35A1D673F526E752715BDD6AE36181B1D2FF86490BBD4AAD]
[02ED60B8E1D8B7268C49B8B7E1F4FF1B5D71BAEB5C77E80DF82519C85D0AEE6AFE]
3 CHECKMULTISIG

Setting Up a Blockchain Explorer

Until now the only graphical interface we used was the standard Bitcoin Core wallet. However, there are many excellent applications and tools for easy access to blockchain data. One of them is the NodeJS-based blockchain explorer btc-rpc-explorer. As its name suggests, it uses the RPC API of Bitcoin to gather data and present it in a web page. In the following pages, we will learn how to configure it as a systemd service. Additionally, we will learn how to configure **UFW**, the easy-to-use firewall, to secure our Bitcoin Full Node.

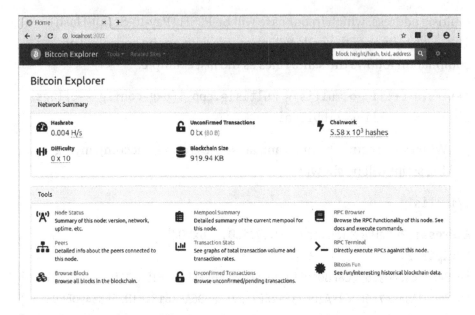

Figure 8-3. *Bitcoin Explorer based on bitcoin-rpc-explorer*

Our first task will be to install the btc-rpc-explorer as globally available NodeJS package. This is done by using the flag -g as show below.

```
sudo npm install -g btc-rpc-explorer
```

The binary of this package will be located in /usr/local/bin/btc-rpc-explorer. We will later use it in our systemd's daemon configuration script. But before we configure the daemon, we should take care of some initial settings needed by the explorer itself. We will have to provide correct authentication data, ports for the web interface, and other settings. By default, btc-rcp-explorer checks for the existence of .env file in its working directory. Our $HOME will contain this directory. Usually, the initial $HOME directory belongs to user pi, which is the standard Raspbian user that gets created at the operating system installation. Therefore, we will create a new directory in its $HOME and put .env file inside of it.

```
mkdir btc-explorer
cd btc-explorer
touch .env
```

We can now open this file with an editor like nano and enter these options.

```
BTCEXP_COIN=BTC
BTCEXP_HOST=127.0.0.1
BTCEXP_PORT=3002
BTCEXP_BITCOIND_HOST=localhost
BTCEXP_BITCOIND_PORT=18332
BTCEXP_BITCOIND_USER=raspiuser
BTCEXP_BITCOIND_PASS=mypassword
BTCEXP_BITCOIND_RPC_TIMEOUT=5000
BTCEXP_BASIC_AUTH_PASSWORD=mypassword
BTCEXP_RPC_ALLOWALL=true
BTCEXP_UI_SHOW_TOOLS_SUBHEADER=true
```

The above settings are not everything btc-rpc-explorer supports. For further examples check the .env-sample file provided by the project on their GitHub pages.[13] Also, for more detailed information about the options being used, check the companion source code.

We have now set up our authentication data, ports, and how the data should be presented in explorer's web pages. As we are running a "local-only" explorer without any public access, we've decided to activate all available RPC commands, which means that we can now do pretty much everything with our node by using a web browser only. This of course would be extremely dangerous if done with publicly available nodes. Therefore, take care of not activating the option BTCEXP_RPC_ALLOWALL when running a public-facing node.

---

[13]https://github.com/janoside/btc-rpc-explorer/blob/master/.env-sample

The next step will be to define a new systemd service that will start the btc-rpc-explorer binary at boot. Similar to previously defined bitcoin. service, we now open a new file /etc/systemd/system/btc-explorer. service to configure our Bitcoin Explorer daemon.

```
sudo nano /etc/systemd/system/btc-explorer.service
```

We will need to insert the following settings to run our btc-rpc-explorer daemon.

```
[Unit]
Description=Bitcoin Explorer
After=network.target

[Service]
WorkingDirectory=/home/pi/btc-explorer
User=pi
Group=pi
Type=simple
ExecStart=/usr/local/bin/btc-rpc-explorer
Restart=on-failure
RestartSec=5s
PrivateTmp=true

[Install]
WantedBy=multi-user.target
```

Similar to Bitcoin's daemon, we too will wait for a working network connection before starting bitcoin-rpc-explorer. Our working directory will be /home/pi/btc-explorer where our .env file is located. This will give btc-rpc-explorer direct access to its configuration. Our ExecStart option contains the full path to the binary that should be executed. After we have saved this file, we register the new daemon:

```
sudo systemctl enable btc-explorer.
```

We're now ready to start our explorer:

```
sudo systemctl start btc-explorer.
```

Then we check its status with

```
systemct status btc-explorer
```

We should get a result like this:

```
btc-explorer.service - Bitcoin Explorer
   Loaded: loaded (/etc/systemd/system/btc-explorer.service;
   enabled; vendor preset: enabled)
   Active: active (running) since Fri 2019-09-06 22:51:54 CEST;
   2 weeks 0 days ago
 Main PID: 444 (btc-rpc-explore)
```

Our daemon is running. Now we can open its web interface by visiting `http://localhost:3002` in our browser. Many interesting options will be available there.

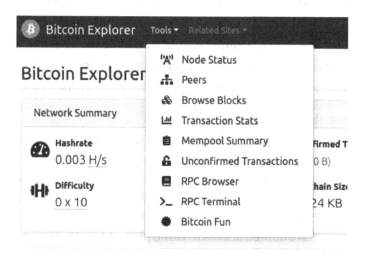

Figure 8-4. Bitcoin Explorer Window with several options shown

As our explorer is running without problems, we should now define a few firewall rules to constrain access to our Full Node. In general, firewall settings should be done for any node, regardless if it's being accessed via SSH only or web or any other combination of ports and services. Usually, the only ports that should be available for public access are

- 8333/TCP, which is the default port in Bitcoin's peer-to-peer network

- 22/TCP, the SSH port for secure shell logins

- Optionally 80+443/TCP for web interfaces (in our case it's 3002, which is the default `btc-rpc-explorer` port)

Unless you have other services running, there should be no other open ports available for public access. The easiest way to use firewall services is with `ufw` package:

```
sudo apt install ufw
```

The application UFW converts typed commands into proper `iptables` instructions. `iptables` is the default Linux packet filter[14] and is known to be rather complex and not very intuitive. Luckily, one doesn't need to learn all of its options to configure a reasonably secured operating system. All we need is to enable UFW itself and issue a few `allow` commands to open certain ports.

```
sudo ufw enable
sudo ufw allow from 192.168.0.0/24 to any port ssh proto tcp
sudo ufw allow from 192.168.0.0/24 to any port 3002 proto tcp
sudo ufw allow from 192.168.0.0/24 to any port 5900 proto tcp
```

Here we have enabled UFW itself, so it will be activated on any system start. We have then enabled access to three ports: SSH (22/tcp), our explorer (3002/tcp), and VNC server for remote desktop (5900/tcp).

---

[14]https://linux.die.net/man/8/iptables

In all examples I have used my local network, so you will have to change the network address. Additionally, we can also enable port 8333, which is the default Bitcoin *mainnet* port. For *testnet* you'd have to use 18333 instead.

```
sudo ufw allow from any to any port 8333 proto tcp
```

However, this depends on our preference, if we want to have a node that's serving the network with blockchain data. To participate in Bitcoin's p2p network is basically offering synchronization services to others, which is always a good thing as it helps strengthening the network. Another port that we should enable is 9735, which is the standard Lightning Network port.

```
sudo ufw allow from any to any port 9735 proto tcp
```

However, this too depends on what kind of node we are running. Normal Full Nodes that only participate in Bitcoin's network don't have to have that port opened.

Summary

This chapter was a practical one, and we have learned how to communicate and control our node by writing programs in JavaScript, Python, and C++. Working with wallets, addresses, and redeem scripts is much easier when done with powerful little NPM packages as we have learned by using `bitcoin-core` and `bitcoinlib-js`. We have also learned how to configure and register daemons with `systemd` service management tools. Now we are able to run our Bitcoin Full Nodes automatically without any user interaction as `systemd`'s facilities would take care of starting them at boot. We have also learned how to track daemons, modify their behavior, and publish changes by using console-based commands `systemctl` and `journalctl`. Ultimately, we have built a web-based Blockchain Explorer with `btc-rpc-explorer` and have also learned how to configure a firewall with UFW.

PART III

Using Lightning Network

CHAPTER 9

Introduction

In this chapter we will learn about the fundamentals of the Lightning Network: what it is, why it exists, what problems it solves, and how it's related to Bitcoin. The Lightning Network, as its name implies, brings its own network to the decentralization game started by Bitcoin, and this for a specific reason, which is based on a design property of Bitcoin: *it can't infinitely scale on the computational level.*

What Is the Lightning Network?

Bitcoin isn't designed to scale like most other computerized systems. Naturally, we would expect a network to offer solutions to various technological bottlenecks like throughput problems, transaction processing, or messaging. But Bitcoin explicitly follows a different strategy, by constraining the size of valid blocks to 1MB, by automatically adapting the block generation difficulty to the available hash power, and by keeping its message broadcasting protocol redundant.

However, this wasn't an "early design error", although they might be people arguing this way. Bitcoin's unusual design serves a purpose that is more important than computation scalability: Bitcoin is *socially scalable*.[1] This means that Bitcoin can be used by an indefinite number of actors without requiring them to resort to *trusted third parties* when doing

[1] https://unenumerated.blogspot.com/2017/02/money-blockchains-and-social-scalability.html

© Harris Brakmić 2019
H. Brakmić, *Bitcoin and Lightning Network on Raspberry Pi*,
https://doi.org/10.1007/978-1-4842-5522-3_9

business with others. When it comes to communication, people have only a very constrained capacity to do business with people they don't know personally. While we could easily discuss many contracts directly with our friends, no matter where they are physically, the same business would become too risky to us when done with people we don't know. To overcome this difficulty, we would have to resort to some trusted party, that would take care of keeping all participants "honest". The simplest example is buying goods on the web. Most of us would prefer buying them on a commercial platform that would take care of merchants delivering goods and customers paying for them. We wouldn't want to do the same business directly with anonymous people on the net no matter how nicely designed their web sites might be.

And even if we would buy something from a web site owned by a person, we would still want to do our payments via 3rd-party payment processors. When people do business with unknown entities or other people, they always strive *to minimize trust* in them by including impartial participants, which are able to enforce correct execution of contracts. However, as most of us know from various media outlets, there is seldom a day without a new security breach or data leak. In far too many cases, *the security holes are trusted third parties* themselves.[2] The trust we put in them is very often more dangerous than any potential risks that could arise from failed contracts.

Therefore, to be `socially scalable`, Bitcoin's protocol deliberately sacrifices its technological scalability by

- Consuming vast amounts of energy to incentivize mining[3]

- Having a very high and redundant transaction throughput via full broadcasting between all nodes

---

[2]`https://nakamotoinstitute.org/trusted-third-parties/`
[3]`https://bitcoin.stackexchange.com/questions/89972/why-is-proof-of-work-required-in-bitcoin`

These two factors make it possible for Bitcoin to achieve *automated integrity* that our old-style institutions can only get by employing literal armies of lawyers, managers, and other bureaucrats. One can rely on Bitcoin alone when setting up and executing contracts, because there is no way to cheat the whole system. The sheer wastefulness of Bitcoin's protocol *forces its participants to behave in their best interest*, which indirectly makes the whole network require only minimal trust to operate successfully. By substituting institutions and professionals with an army of robots (Bitcoin nodes), that control each other, Bitcoin's social scalability functions on a global level. Actors from different parts of the world can now participate in global business transactions without having to resort to any traditional, *trust-demanding* institutions, whose powers, and protection, usually end on national or legal borders.

The Lightning Network is the first implementation of a value-transfer layer, that runs on top of Bitcoin's Blockchain, because it relies on its social scalability and provides additional functionality that Bitcoin could never offer without sacrificing the social scalability itself. This network utilizes the blockchain as its settlement layer, where value transfers get finalized through execution of Smart Contracts, which are based on Bitcoin's Scripting Language. While Bitcoin's blockchain is known to have rather slow and energy-consuming block production times, which make small payments undesirable, the Lightning Network itself is focused on high-volume micropayments. The Lightning Network is also a set of specifications called **BOLT**[4] (Basis of Lightning Technology), which can be used to develop compatible clients and services by using any programming language and operating system. Currently, there exist three different but compatible implementations: *LND*, *c-lightning*, and *Eclair*.

Situations where a transaction would incur fees higher than the value being transmitted are impossible in the Lightning Network. And just like we have been used to it in Bitcoin, the Lightning Network itself requires no

---

[4]https://github.com/lightningnetwork/lightning-rfc

trusted third parties for its value transfers. Similar to Bitcoin, it uses strong cryptographic algorithms to lock and safely move money between nodes. Instead of being forced to sacrifice qualities we got from Bitcoin, we go a layer higher in the architecture without giving up what we have achieved so far. However, to enjoy faster payments and avoid expensive transaction fees, we have to rethink our node's role in this new network. Until now, we have been using it as a Full Node that contains all data about past transactions and validates new ones. This node was our sole point of truth. And we didn't care much about its networking neighborhood as long as we were getting valid data. Otherwise, our node would automatically ban any misbehaving participant. In the end, this is what a decentralized network promises to be.

But in Lightning Network, we have to adapt to a new way of thinking about finding other nodes, opening channels to them, calculating routes for value transfers, and taking care of our funds, which now must be kept directly available at all times, similar to running a "hot wallet". In Lightning Network our nodes are always online and must have certain amounts of money available for setting up own or routing other transactions. A node in this network is never alone and is either doing something for itself or helping others execute transactions. This is a completely new paradigm, which we have to get used to before jumping into it.

The Lightning Network indeed is freeing us from some of the constraints originating in Bitcoin, but it also brings new ones with it. Therefore, before we begin exploring it, we should see the Lightning Network as the first step toward many useful layers that will be built in future. Similar to the development of various TCP-/IP-based protocols like FTP, SMTP, HTTP, and others, the Lightning Network offers a possible solution to certain questions that arise in value-transmitting networks.

Payment Channels

Payment Channels constitute the backbone of the Lightning Network, because they make it possible to combine many off-chain transactions into only a few blockchain transactions. With off-chain transactions we mean transactions done on the Lightning Network without letting Bitcoin's blockchain know anything about them. When heard for the first time, this would of course provoke a question regarding the security of funds, because we are used to think about transactions as entries in the immutable ledger that must be present, in any blockchain copy on every full node, without exceptions.

How is it then possible to have a consistent chain of transactions when Lightning Network explicitly allows to "ignore" some of them? The solution of this paradox lies in the clever utilization of multi-signature addresses we spoke about in the previous chapter. Before any transaction is being made off-chain, the two parties willing to use the Lightning Network would first have to create a 2-of-2 multisig address to send their funds to. This initial or *funding transaction* would land on Bitcoin's blockchain just like any other (Figure 9-1).

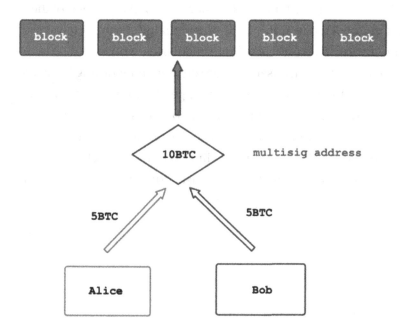

Figure 9-1. *Initial funding for a payment channel*

After having waited for the usual six blocks to confirm the funding transaction, the participants will become able to create new transactions to send funds back and forth, which would each time be changing the amounts of their respective funds. However, unlike the funding transaction, these **off-chain** or **commitment transactions** will never be finalized on the blockchain as they'd only exist in the Lightning Network, or more precisely, in the *channel* that the two participants created. What these transactions do is basically generating lots of "double spends", because each time participants update their funds by creating a new commitment transaction they'll point at the funding transaction again. However, they'd actually never try to double spend anything on the blockchain itself as they'll never touch it directly. And because they don't exist on the blockchain, they also don't have to follow its rigid rules like waiting for six blocks to confirm or to pay high fees to miners as there is no mining in Lightning Network at all.

Transactions of this type can transfer money at the speed of the Internet protocol while at the same time remaining completely trustless and without any need for trusted intermediaries, who would be taking care of funds. But if all transactions are created in Lightning Network's channels only, how can participants ever get their bitcoins back? Traveling at the speed of light is a nice property, but bitcoins only exist in Bitcoin's blockchain. And they never leave it. The answer lies in the **closing** or **settlement transaction** that must be finalized in the blockchain to make funds available to participants. This transaction informs the blockchain about the final state of funds (Figure 9-2).

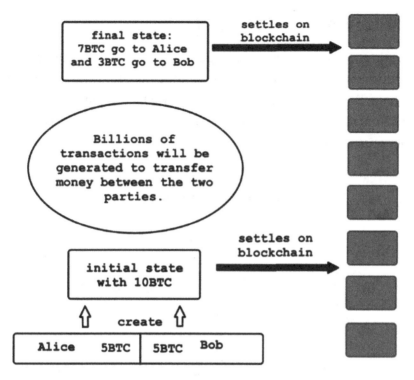

Figure 9-2. *Different states of a payment channel*

However, as there is no way for the blockchain to know that a certain transaction represents the "real" state of funds, we need a way to keep both parties honest. What if Bob decides to cheat and sends a closing transaction that gives him more bitcoins than he should own? How is Alice supposed to protect herself? As the blockchain is not here to help her out, because it doesn't know how many commitment transactions happened in between, we need a trustless mechanism that would prevent old commitment transactions to land on the blockchain. Indeed, such a mechanism exists and is embedded in the Lightning Network's protocol. It is called *Transaction Revocation,* and we will soon see it at work. But before we look at this security mechanism, actually a very weird trick, we should first describe in detail the actual mechanism of value transmission, the *commitment transactions.*

271

Commitment Transactions

After having opened a channel, each party can now alter the state of funds by creating commitment transactions without forwarding them to the blockchain. Every commitment transaction will be spending the original outputs from the funding transaction and indirectly invalidating previous transactions and states.

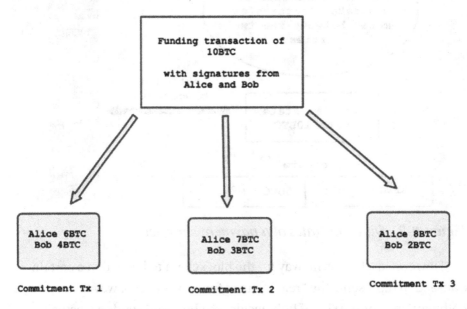

Figure 9-3. *Changing the state in payment channel through commitment transactions*

In Figure 9-3 we see three commitment transactions have been created and signed by Alice. Each time she changed the original state by assigning certain amounts to Bob and to herself. However, instead of forwarding any of those transactions to the blockchain, she is sending them to Bob, who could then use any of them to finalize it on the blockchain, if he wanted to close the payment channel. Bob too can create as many transactions as he wants and send them to Alice. It is also important to know that these transactions are only "half-valid", because neither party can include the recipient's signature in advance.

This can only be done by the recipient itself, if he or she decides to send a transaction to the blockchain. Therefore, the participants only declare themselves willing to spend the written amounts of bitcoins by providing their own signatures, which also have been used to create the multisig address, when the channel got opened. It is up to their counterparties to add their own signatures as well, thus making the transactions "completely valid" for the finalization in the blockchain.

Input	Output
Funding TxID **Alice Signature**	**Alice Address** **4BTC**
	Bob's Address + 144 blocks waiting time OR Alice revocation key + Bob's key 6BTC

Figure 9-4. *A "half-valid" commitment transaction from Alice*

As shown in Figure 9-4, transactions created in the Lightning Network contain two outputs that can be used for different purposes, depending on the use-case. Whenever a transaction is created in the channel, the two parties create *mirrored transactions* and exchange them. In the preceding example the transaction was created by Alice, which she signed and sent to Bob. There she declared,that Bob could get 6BTC sent to an address he previously communicated to her but only after having waited for 144 blocks, which is roughly a day. This *delay* is for a reason that we will discover shortly. Also, Alice assigned herself the remaining 4BTC in the first output above. The mirror transaction that Bob created at the same time and sent to Alice contains equal inputs and outputs, only differently organized (Figure 9-5).

273

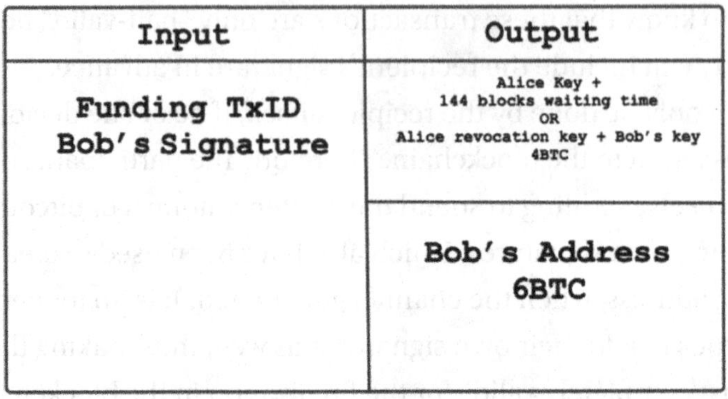

Input	Output
Funding TxID **Bob's Signature**	Alice Key + 144 blocks waiting time OR Alice revocation key + Bob's key 4BTC
	Bob's Address **6BTC**

Figure 9-5. *Mirror commitment transaction from Bob*

Here Bob declares in his second output that 6BTC belong to him, which corresponds to second output entry from Alice's transaction. However, he would get them immediately if Alice ever decided to send this transaction variant to the blockchain. As we already know, as long as neither party decides to close the channel, no transaction will ever be sent. But if either of them sends it, the counterparty would immediately get those bitcoins declared in it. This is how parties ensure that at the closing of the channel they will get their coins back as soon as possible, while those who have initiated the closure would have to wait for 144 blocks (or any other period that can be negotiated at the channel opening). This *waiting time*, of course, is for a reason that we will talk about shortly. If we recall the first transaction that Alice sent to Bob (Figure 9-4), we see in its second output some additional logic that's indicated with the Boolean **OR** (Figure 9-6).

```
          Bob's Address +
    144 blocks waiting time
               OR
     Alice revocation key +
             Bob's key
               6BTC
```

Figure 9-6. *The second output transaction from Alice's commitment transaction*

This part is an option that could be executed *immediately*, which also means *before* Bob could get those 6BTC after his waiting period of 144 blocks. But the catch is that this could only happen if the party using this option is in possession of Alice's *Revocation Key* and Bob's Key. In Bob's case this wouldn't be true, because Alice would not send her revocation key without a valid reason. When she created the above transaction and declared that Bob should own 6BTC, she also created a new key pair. Her **revocation key** is this **private key**.

This step in the whole transaction sequence is of crucial importance, because each time parties create a new "half-valid" transaction, they also generate new key pairs. Now the question is, why do they need them? To answer it, we have first to describe their purpose by looking at how a transaction invalidates a previous one. When Alice creates a new commitment transaction, she not only creates new inputs, outputs, and addresses. She also sends to Bob the revocation key that was used in the previous commitment transaction.

The second transaction in Figure 9-7 creates a new state in the payment channel which also invalidates the previous transaction.

Input	Output
Funding TxID˜ **Alice Signature**	**Alice Address** **3BTC**
	Bob's Address + 144 blocks waiting time OR Alice Revocation Key + Bob's Address 7BTC

Figure 9-7. *New commitment transaction that changes the state*

Alice has created a new key pair a new address. Here she sends 3BTC to herself, that is, 1BTC less than in the previous, now invalidated, commitment transaction. Bob should now get 7BTC, which is 1BTC more. The rules regarding channel closure and blockchain finalization are the same; only the monetary values have changed. Bob can either close the channel (any party could do this anytime), but he would, again, have to wait for 144 blocks, before he can take those 7BTC. Or he can simply keep the channel open, because there is no need for either party to immediately send a transaction for finalization. And of course, there is still the option to immediately sweep those 7BTC if Bob somehow gets Alice current revocation key. But this, again, wouldn't be possible, because Alice only revealed her last revocation key to Bob so he could only immediately get 6BTC from previous transactions, if he ever wanted.

This of course is something Bob wouldn't want. He'd rather finalize the current transaction that gives him 7BTC after 144 blocks. The previous revocation key seems to be of no real use to Bob. However, what would happen when Alice suddenly decided to send the previous commitment transaction to the blockchain? This transaction would bring her back 1BTC, effectively taking it back from Bob, who's still hoping to get his 7BTC as declared in the current transaction. What could Bob now do to prevent Alice from executing the invalidated transaction on the blockchain? For the blockchain itself, all transactions are valid. Commitment transactions can only be invalid in their respective payment channels.

In such a situation, the revocation key of the previous transaction would come in handy, because Bob can now immediately execute the second option from the old transaction (Figure 9-4) and get all of the bitcoins. The second half of its output script demands possession of Alice's Private Key and Bob's Key, which Bob now can provide. Ultimately, Alice would lose all of her bitcoins she initially used to fund the channel. This is the reason revocation keys exist and have to be shared between parties each time they update the channel state by creating new transactions.

As long as both parties are honest, the only reasonable way to close the channel and get the bitcoins out is by executing the first part of the script. If a party is honest, then there should be no problems for he or she to wait for a predefined number of blocks. Otherwise, the cheater should be punished by waiting, while the cheated party would immediately grab all of the remaining bitcoins. All the cheater would get is an input transaction with a spent output.

The punishment in Lightning Network is a severe one, because it leaves the cheating side without any funds. This way both parties are incentivized to behave honestly at all times as there is no way to prevent the automatic revocation, when one party tries to cheat on the other. As Alice has already signed every transaction, all Bob would have to do is provide his own signature and send it to the blockchain. And it's obvious that Bob would have an interest in forwarding the last transaction to the blockchain as it promises him the greatest payment. Although there wouldn't be anything preventing him from finalizing any of the older transactions, we can assume that a party would be interested in maximizing own profits.

Multihop Payments

But Lightning Network doesn't end at bidirectional payments. In fact, such payments are not happening very often as we mostly buy products and services from people or entities, we know nothing about, or simply don't care who they are. Although very promising, the whole setup process is still cumbersome, because it requires that somehow two parties find each other, agree upon a certain amount of initial funds, and then be sending funds back and forth. This would work for payments among friends maybe, but it's not very helpful when acting on a more global scale. Did we lose our social scalability by onboarding the Lightning Network? The answer is "no", and it has to do with a more complex payment channel setups called *Multihop Payments.*

Lightning Network wouldn't be a network if it didn't provide a way to transfer money over multiple "hops". Just like the Internet would be of no use as information network if there was no way to forward packets over multiple computers, the same applies to Lightning Network, with the difference that it's a *network of value* as it transfers scarce digital assets that can't be replicated. The capability of forwarding the payments throughout the whole network without having to trust any node along the way is what makes the Lightning Network a true network of value. Indeed, we keep the social scalability from Bitcoin without sacrificing the speed we get from our new network.

Additionally, we also win in terms of anonymity, because when nodes don't have to trust their neighbors, they also don't need to know who they really are. While Bitcoin, due to its transparency, merely offers *pseudonymity* with addresses, the Lightning Network is a completely opaque place, where nodes operate in total anonymity. This is achieved by utilizing the Onion routing we know from networks like Tor. In Lightning Network a node only knows about its predecessor and successor. It has no option to assemble more detailed information about the nodes surrounding it except by doing it by itself, also called

Source Routing.[5] Nodes can also act as routers for forwarding of payments between nodes that don't know each other and also don't care where a payment is coming from or is going to. Given enough liquidity, a node could participate is such a network and also earn fees for offering routing services to other nodes. One can even operate a node that itself isn't executing any direct business operations (buying or selling) but instead acting solely as "money transmitter" for other nodes. Imagine a following scenario involving three nodes, Alice, Bob, and Reginald.

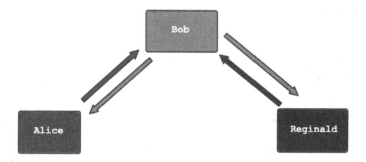

Figure 9-8. *Money transmission between multiple nodes*

In Figure 9-8 we see that Alice has no knowledge of Reginald as only two payment channels are open, one between Alice and Bob and the other between Bob and Reginald. How is Reginald supposed to receive money from Alice, when there is no open payment channel between them? The solution is the creation of forwarding networks of point to point channels with *Hash Time-Lock Contracts*.

Hash Time-Lock Contracts

The HTLC's are a new type of smart contracts based on Bitcoin Script but with special Op-Codes that got activated in a soft-fork. More precisely,

---

[5]https://github.com/lightningnetwork/lightning-rfc/blob/master/04-onion-routing.md

there are two new Op-Codes[6] that were created specifically for the
Lightning Network: CHECKSEQUENCEVERIFY and CHECKLOCKTIMEVERIFY.
We have already used the former in our previous scripts, because
CHECKSEQUENCEVERIFY is the Op-Code behind the delay in output scripts
we saw before. The waiting time of 144 blocks we used in our examples
(Figures 9-4 and 9-5) is being enforced by this Op-Code. This is how a
simplified syntax of output scripts from previous examples would look like:

Output 0:
<Alice Key> **CHECKSIG**
Output 1:
<144 blocks>
CHECKSEQUENCEVERIFY
DROP
<Bob's Key> **CHECKSIG**

The first output is easy to understand as we simply check if Alice's key
corresponds to her signature. The second output, however, is a bit more
complicated. There we have first to check if the number of blocks after
this transaction got into the blockchain has crossed the threshold of 144
blocks, before we then **DROP** this number and then check Bob's key for
correspondence with his public key.

Why are we doing it that way? The reason for this small confusion lies
in the fact that nodes running older versions of Bitcoin, that is, those that
know nothing about the two new opcodes, CSV and CLTV,[7] will see one of
the unused No-OP-Codes instead. In this case it's the NOP3. And because
NOP-Codes never pop any data from the stack, we have to issue an extra
DROP command to remove the checked delay of 144 blocks, because this
value is irrelevant to older nodes. Therefore, *soft-forked* nodes would read
the script as 144 + CSV + DROP, while older nodes would still be seeing

---

[6]https://en.bitcoin.it/wiki/Timelock
[7]Abbrev. for CHECKSEQUENCEVERIFY and CHECKLOCKTIMEVERIFY

`144 + NOP + DROP`. This is a small trick that helps updating the Bitcoin network without forcing a hard fork, which is always an extremely risky and potentially value-damaging operation. By executing soft forks, we make sure that older nodes can still participate in the updated network without being forced to update immediately.

However, we have two new Op-Codes, and the second one hasn't been used so far. This will change shortly, when we try to send money not to our counterparty in the payment channel but to someone unrelated to us. In such cases we have to expand transactions with additional scripts that would have the CLTV Op-Code included.

If Alice wanted to send money to Reginald, she would need something that only Reginald knows to prevent any other party from stealing funds being sent from her to Reginald. Indeed, such a value exists and must be generated by Reginald. It is basically a long string of bytes that he keeps for himself and gives Alice a hash of it.

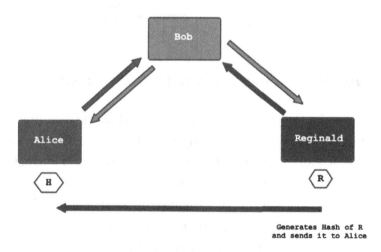

Figure 9-9. *Generating hash H from preimage R*

After Alice has received the hash, *H*, of Reginald's *preimage*, *R*, as it's usually being called, she can create a new type of script that uses the CTLV Op-Code to execute multihop payments (Figure 9-9).

In our case, Alice wants to send 1BTC to Reginald by using Bob's node to forward her payment. Of course, she doesn't want to put her trust in Bob to be honest and forward 1BTC to Reginald and therefore creates an output that would give 1BTC to Bob only if he can provide R, which nobody knows except Reginald. However, she also puts an additional constraint into it. If Bob can't provide R until block height 600,000, the funds will go back to Alice.

Input	Output
Funding TxID Alice Signature	Alice Address 2BTC
	Bob's Key + 144 blocks OR Alice Key + Bob's revocation key 7BTC
	HLTC Bob + R OR CLTV Alice 600,000 block height 1BTC

Figure 9-10. Alice's transaction with HTLC Smart Contract

With this script (Figure 9-10), Alice creates an incentive for Bob to try to find R. But because she tells Bob only about H, there is only one way for Bob to learn about R: he must forward the transaction to Reginald. The HTLC scripts are more dynamic, but also more rigid, because they use the CLTV Op-Code that isn't using relative block heights as CSV does. Instead, it compares the current block height with the predefined (and unchangeable) height included in their script code. In previous transactions, the block heights were calculated by using the height of the block the transaction got included at. In HTLCs we don't have such a luxury and must also expect that sometimes a script might fail, if it got included in a block that was "too late".

After Alice has sent this new "half-signed" transaction, and Bob also generated the mirror variant of it, our Lightning Network would now look like in Figure 9-11.

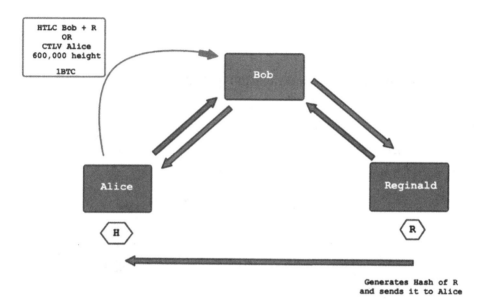

Figure 9-11. *Alice has sent her HTLC to Bob*

As Bob has no other option to learn about R but to ask Reginald, he then creates his own transaction that includes an HTLC script. However, this transaction is unknown to Alice, and she also doesn't care. All she cares about is that Bob can't get R and steal 1BTC she is sending to Reginald. Bob's transaction would include Reginald and a decreased block height, because he doesn't want to be too late with the other script he got from Alice. Therefore, he chooses 599,856 block height that is 144 blocks less (Figure 9-12).

```
        HLTC Reginald + R
              OR
CLTV  Bob  599,856 block height

              1BTC
```

Figure 9-12. *Bob's own HTLC*

The network state looks now like in Figure 9-13.

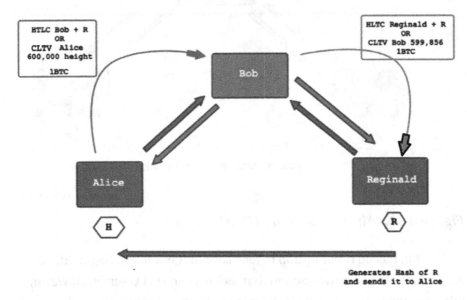

Figure 9-13. *Bob has forwarded Alice's HTLC to Reginald*

Reginald of course can provide R and therefore fulfill the requirement imposed by Alice's HTLC script that got forwarded by Bob. At the same time, Bob learns about R, because Reginald must publish it to the blockchain to finalize the transaction. Bob then uses R in its own HTLC script he previously got from Alice. And he also hopes of not being too late, because block times are rigid. He solves his own HTLC and informs everyone about it in the blockchain.

But the 1BTC has been already spent by Reginald, and therefore Bob can't access them anymore. Alice learns about R as well and would also try to get back her 1BTC, but again, Reginald has already spent them. And this was also her goal, actually. The advantage of this approach is not only the technique done with HTLC Smart Contracts but also the fact that there is no limit regarding available connections. In our example, Alice could also have received her HTLC from someone else, and Reginald could also be forwarding it to someone else. The only requirement for participation in multi-hop payments is the liquidity of a node. For example, if a node has funded a channel with 1BTC, then future payments it can forward can be up to 1BTC. If a node operator wishes to earn more fees, he should then think about opening more channels and especially more liquid ones. The more liquid channels a node operates, the greater the chance that it will be selected in future multi-hop payment transactions.

Pathfinding

As channels can be opened and closed anytime, the Lightning Network behaves differently from the usual networks we know. When we surf the Internet, our computer automatically *takes* one of the available routes (Figure 9-14).

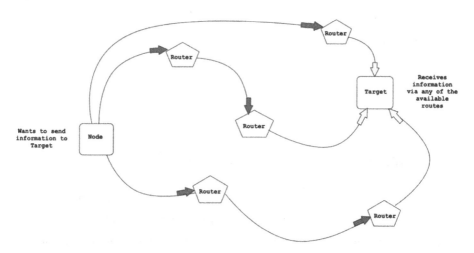

Figure 9-14. *Internet routing with multiple possible routes*

Not so with the Lightning Network. Here a node has first to get enough information about the liquidity of other payment channels, which could forward the value it wants to send to its target. We say that a node has *to find a path*. And because payment channel balances can change anytime, the pathfinding process becomes a very dynamic task (Figure 9-15). This of course is exactly the opposite of what happens in the Internet, where routes are much more stable. The importance of Payment Channels for Pathfinding lies in their liquidity. In Lightning Network, the Payment Channels constitute the edges of this network, while nodes are continuously searching for the best possible path between them. In Figure 9-15 a node wants to send 1BTC, and the payment channels with lower balances cannot participate.

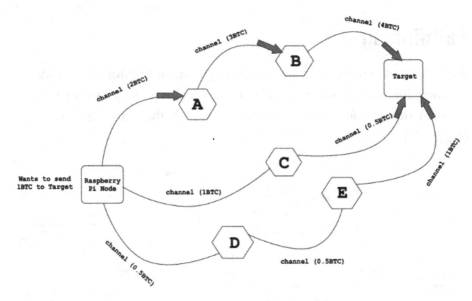

Figure 9-15. *Finding a path with enough liquidity*

Also, the Internet transfers information that can be replicated easily, while Lightning Network always transfers money that must not (and cannot) be replicated. When a route in the Internet goes down, our data packets get rerouted automatically over alternative ones (Figure 9-14).

Would this happen to us in the Lightning Network, there would be no way for us to "restore" our money. And because liquidities of nodes can change without warning, the routes in Lightning Network are not guaranteed to be long-lived. Nodes can come and go anytime, as we have already seen in our scripts, where parties can decide to take their funds at will.

Fees

However, one important factor is still missing from our example with Alice, Bob, and Reginald (Figure 9-13): the monetary *incentive* for Bob to forward any transactions is missing. It is true that he got incentivized by Alice to learn about R, but so far there was no *reward* for money transmission service he provided to Alice and Reginald. If this was always the case, the Lightning Network would very much depend on the altruism of other people.

Therefore, the multi-hop operations we described in our example would always include fees to be paid for services offered by other onodes. Alice would first learn about fees Bob is expecting to get from others and increase the amounts she's sending so that it would include those fees. Instead of sending 1BTC to Reginald, she would be sending 1.00000001BTC, for example, so that Bob can chip away 0.00000001BTC. However, when we say *fees in Lightning Network*, we don't mean the ones from the mining business. As here is no mining activity at all and electricity costs are more or less negligible, nodes can only charge extremely small values, usually sub-satoshi values. This also affects the values being forwarded. Mostly, multi-hop payments are very small and actually never contain whole bitcoins.

In general, the Lightning Network should be used for micropayments or when payments should be done on demand and very quickly, for example, when the consumption of services depends on a continuous incoming stream of money. A popular example is watching a channel that is streaming videos as long as money is coming in. In such cases the customer running a Lightning Node would open a channel and continuously be creating new transactions that are sending sub-satoshi denominated values to recipient's address.

Summary

In this chapter we have learned about the fundamentals of the Lightning Network. We have learned how to set up a payment channel between two nodes and create transactions that never hit the blockchain. We have also learned about Lightning Network's embedded security features, that help in preventing theft. Based on our knowledge about bi-directional payment channels, we have learned how to create multi-hop payments to forward money between nodes that don't know each other. As Lightning Network needs special Op-Codes, we have also learned what they are and how they work.

CHAPTER 10

c-lightning

In this chapter we will learn how to set up a Lightning Node based on
c-lightning, one of the three implementations of the BOLT specification.
Using our previously configured Full Node, we will join the Lightning
Network by opening and funding new channels to other nodes. We will
also learn how to pay invoices and create own payment requests.

Compilation

Our first step will be to clone `c-lightning` project's sources.

```
git clone https://github.com/ElementsProject/lightning.git
```

Then we will have to install certain libraries that are needed to
successfully compile our `c-lightning` binaries.

```
sudo apt install -y autoconf automake asciidoc build-essential
git libtool libgmp-dev libsqlite3-dev python python3 python3-
mako python3-pip net-tools sqlite3 zlib1g-dev libsodium-dev
```

However, as we have already learned how to compile Bitcoin Core
Wallet, a few of these libraries will be already available and mentioned
during installation. In any case, we simply let the process finish.

© Harris Brakmić 2019
H. Brakmić, *Bitcoin and Lightning Network on Raspberry Pi*,
https://doi.org/10.1007/978-1-4842-5522-3_10

Afterward, we will install the Python3 libraries from test and doc directories. For this we change the directory with cd lightning and execute the following commands.

```
sudo pip3 install -r tests/requirements.txt
sudo pip3 install -r doc/requirements.txt
```

Now we are ready to compile the c-lightning suite. In the cloned directory lightning we enter ./configure to start generation of *Makefiles*.

After the configuration process has completed successfully, we should get the command prompt back. We are now ready to enter the make command to kick off the compilation. If there were no errors, we would simply get the command prompt back as the final result. The last step is to install the binaries with sudo make install.

Configuration

Before we start the daemon lightningd, we have to provide a proper configuration that is by default located in .lightning/config. We first create the directory in our own $HOME and open the file config with an editor of our choice.

```
mkdir .lightning
touch .lightning/config
nano .lightning/config
```

The daemon reads the configuration entries when it starts up. They can be overridden by the flags given to the daemon on the console. If we prefer another location or configuration file, for example, we could change them by adding flags --lightning-dir and --conf. Our default configuration settings would contain following entries:

```
alias=LIGHTNING_NODE_NAME_HERE
rgb=CA1F7B
```

```
addr=:9735
network=testnet
bitcoin-cli=/usr/local/bin/bitcoin-cli
bitcoin-datadir=/home/pi/.bitcoin
bitcoin-rpcuser=raspiuser
bitcoin-rpcpassword=mypassword
bitcoin-rpcport=18332
bitcoin-rpcconnect=127.0.0.1
log-prefix=raspi-lightning
ignore-fee-limits=true
fee-base=10
daemon
```

Our configuration file contains settings for

- The name of our node.

- The color, which is an RGB value, that should be used to show our node in available Lightning Network explorers.

- The IP address and port lightningd will listen on. Here we accept any IP address, and our port will be 9735, which is the default port according to BOLT specification. *Unicode character 9735 is the symbol for lightning.*

- The network variant.

- The connection settings for accessing our local Bitcoin RPC API.

- The prefix for entries in lightning.log file.

- Two additional settings regarding fee calculations, to make lightningd less strict (this should only be used in *testnet*).

- The option *daemon* to run lightningd and other daemons in the background.

291

After we have saved this file, we can start the daemon on the console with

```
lightningd --testnet
```

The output returned by `lightningd` would look like this:

```
2019-09-21T18:48:11.751Z INFO raspi-lightning
2019-09-21T18:48:11.751Z INFO raspi-lightning Server started
with public key 0370e894fa6e8ff735dc3278543ea2718c632ce380aaf30c
e35fa261e8c0c7611e, alias BTC-TEST-RASPI-LIGHTNING-NODE (color
#ca1f7b) and lightningd v0.7.2.1-56-g49496ab-modded
```

We have successfully configured and started our `c-lightning` daemon.
Now it is time to learn how to control it with `lightning-cli`, its command
line interface. Our first step will be to get basic information about our own
node by issuing this command:

```
lightning-cli getinfo.
```

It will give us a picture about our network connection, blockchain type,
and the current state of our wallet.

```
{
    "id": "0370e894fa6e8ff735dc3278543ea2718c632ce380aaf30ce35fa2
    61e8c0c7611e",
    "alias": "BTC-TEST-RASPI-LIGHTNING-NODE",
    "color": "ca1f7b",
    "num_peers": 35,
    "num_pending_channels": 0,
    "num_active_channels": 35,
    "num_inactive_channels": 0,
    "address": [
        {
            "type": "ipv4",
            "address": "37.201.115.117",
```

```
        "port": 9735
      }
    ],
    "binding": [
      {
          "type": "ipv4",
          "address": "0.0.0.0",
          "port": 9735
      }
    ],
    "version": "v0.7.2.1-56-g49496ab-modded",
    "blockheight": 1579246,
    "network": "testnet",
    "msatoshi_fees_collected": 5582,
    "fees_collected_msat": "5582msat"
}
```

As we can see, my node is already connected to several other lightning nodes. In the Lightning Network, nodes remember their channels and can easily reopen them as long as their peers are online as well. A channel can also be declared *pending*, which is always the case when a new channel opens, because the initial funding will take some time to settle on the blockchain. The same applies to closing a channel as we have learned in the previous chapter. A node can issue a close command, but the finalization will always take a certain number of blocks both of the nodes agreed upon when they created the channel in the first place.

Setting Up a Lightning Node

When a completely new node is started, the first step we'd have to take care of is to properly fund its wallet, because in Lightning Network channels can only be opened by nodes who have money at their disposal. Of course, it could be possible that some other node would connect ours, but as nobody "out there" knows about it, the chances are extremely low.

The first command we execute is creating a new address for our node, where we will send our tBTC to:

```
lightning-cli newaddr
```

If you don't have any, you can visit web-based "testnet faucets" listed below. There are many faucets on the net, but some of them are full of ads and sometimes even spyware. In general, one should be careful when visiting faucets, especially those who promise "real bitcoins". In our case, however, we are only searching for monetary useless but technologically very useful tBTC coins.

Figure 10-1. *A website of a testnet faucet showing the tBTC that got sent to our node*

- https://testnet-faucet.mempool.co

- https://coinfaucet.eu/en/btc-testnet/

The address we got is in Bech32 format, because this is the default address format in the Lightning Network. It looks like this:

```
{
    "address": "tb1qg085r8xmfs2yxapsykjmnprvv4lqx9fnql7nnh",
    "bech32": "tb1qg085r8xmfs2yxapsykjmnprvv4lqx9fnql7nnh"
}
```

Our lightning node maintains its own, separate wallet, that is not visible to our Bitcoin node and vice-versa. If you happen to be using a faucet that doesn't support Bech32 addresses, you can create a P2SH formatted address with:

```
lightning-cli newaddr p2sh-segwit
```

However, the bitcoins we're sending to our lightning node aren't "lost forever" and can be later taken out and sent back to our Bitcoin node's wallet. But to properly function, our lightning node must have direct access to its own bitcoins, because lightning nodes are "hot wallets" that must always be online for their payment channels to work. A lightning node that's offline isn't capable of receiving and sending anything, which is contrary to what we have learned about Bitcoin.

In Bitcoin, you can send funds to any address, regardless if the node's owner is running it right now or not, because the blockchain is copied over many other nodes that will take care of this particular transaction to settle. In the Lightning Network, nobody cares about your transactions and channels. Therefore, a node that wants to receive money must also be there to take it.

After we have received some tBTC from one of the faucets, we are ready to fund our node. For proper funding we don't need full tBTC coins, because even small amounts like 0.0001 tBTC would be perfectly sufficient. We will now check the current balance of our node by executing:

```
lightning-cli listfunds
```

The data returned would vary from node to node, but they'd all contain two areas: channels and outputs. Those represent funds that have been locked in channels and unspent outputs that could be later used for funding new channels. Here I am showing only a few entries from the complete list.

```
"outputs": [
    {
        "txid": "08271bd9ad24dbef72b224882210f51aefa49c5578ff
        1f56a1efc71c17d769a7",
        "output": 0,
        "value": 999501,
        "amount_msat": "999501000msat",
],
"channels": [
    {
        "peer_id": "02d6c7db1df781d53b1b9a96eb269d4316353dc4a
        939f0d7363fa50439c1ba0a9c",
        "short_channel_id": "1576603x120x0",
        "channel_sat": 500000,
        "our_amount_msat": "500000000msat",
```

As Lightning Network's primary use is for micropayments, the units we know from Bitcoin are simply too large. One bitcoin contains 100,000,000 *satoshis,* and in Lightning Network we count in *milli-satoshis,* which are 1000 times smaller than a single *satoshi.*

Our next step is to open a payment channel. Currently, we have no peers at all. The next command would return only an empty list:

```
lightning-cli listpeers
```

The easiest way to find peers on *testnet* is by using one of the publicly available lightning explorers. However, take care of not accidentally using *mainnet* explorers. If you try to open a channel with one of their nodes, you will get weird blockchain errors, indicating that your node is trying to send funds from a chain they don't recognize. A good *testnet* explorer with search functionality is located at `https://1ml.com/testnet` (Figure 10-2).

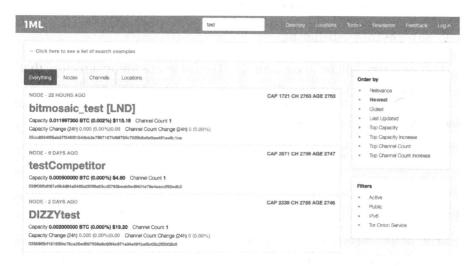

Figure 10-2. *A Lightning Network testnet explorer*

To connect with another node, we need its ID, IP-address, and port (if not using the default one). Some of the nodes you might find show no IP addresses and ports, which means that they're running as *private nodes* that nobody can connect to. This is nothing unusual as there is no rule that a Lightning Node must be available to anyone in the wider network. It always depends on the use-case if a node should be public or not. Merchants might surely want to operate public nodes, because customers should be able to send payments to stores anytime. Someone paying monthly bills only would rather prefer to remain private.

Port Forwarding with upnpc

If your node is running within a private network, where the only routable IP address is located on the router configured by your provider, chances are that you will either have to configure port forwarding or activate it via UPnP (Universal Plug and Play). With UPnP one can let the node automatically configure and update port forwarding. The package MiniUPnPc is available in Raspbian's apt package repository.

```
sudo apt install miniupnpc
```

Our next step will be to create a small script in our home directory that will execute upnpc. Later we will insert them into crontab's list.

```
nano ~/update_port_fwd.sh
```

Then enter this script:

```
#!/bin/sh
upnpc -e "lightning network" -a 192.168.0.87 9735 9735 TCP
```

The script will be executed by the shell to call the upnpc binary, which will establish the port forwarding for port 9735 for the given IP address. The IP address shown in the previous picture should be changed to your machine's address that you can get by executing ifconfig on your node's terminal.

After having saved the script, we change its flags by making it executable.

```
chmod + x ~/update_port_fwd.sh
```

You should also check that your router supports and has currently activated UPnP. As there are many different router-types, the location will vary greatly. Usually, it's a single option that can be activated and deactivated. Here's one example of such an option in a router (Figure 10-3).

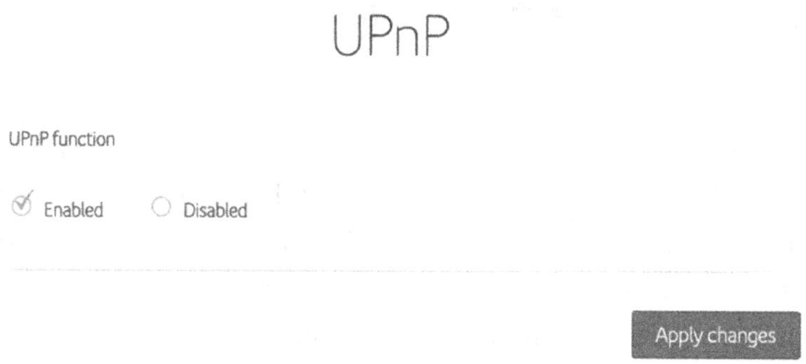

UPnP

UPnP function

☑ Enabled   ○ Disabled

Apply changes

Figure 10-3. *Activating UPnP on router*

We can execute our script once to test its functionality. Afterward, we will insert it into crontab to avoid manual typing in future.

```
./update_port_fwd.sh
```

If we get an answer containing the port 9735 and the external IP address from which the incoming packets will be forwarded to our node, we are ready to set up two entries in our crontab's list. We open crontab in edit mode:

```
crontab -e
```

We then add these two lines:

```
@reboot    /home/pi/update_port_fwd.sh
*/10 * * * * /home/pi/update_port_fwd.sh
```

The first entry will execute our script at each reboot, while the second would do it every 10 minutes. This way we keep our port forwarding intact without having to manually take care of script execution and port checking.

Creating Payment Channels

When searching for nodes in the test explorer, we should prefer the newest ones, because the older the entry, the greater the chance that a node isn't online anymore. Also, we should look for the capacity they offer. If the capacity, that is, the number of coins, is too low, we might later have problems with routing our payments. The bigger the payments we want to send, the greater the capacity of our "neighborhood" should be. Also, we too should provide enough liquidity for other nodes to consider us as worthy of connecting and opening new payment channels. The more liquidity we offer, the greater the chance to become a routing node for others, who would then pay for our payment forwarding services.

After we have selected a node with good characteristics, we will issue two commands, one for creating the channel and the other for funding it. The command

```
lightning-cli connect NodeID@IP:Port
```

expects a node ID, IP, and port which we get from the explorer. The format I am using here is *NodeID@IP:Port,* but they can also be given as separate arguments.

If the connection was successful, the result we get will be a new ID that points at the new payment channel. Our next step is to properly fund it. However, this task can sometimes be very tricky, for example, when the counterparty expects an initial payment that's higher as we would like to pay for it. In such cases we can either accept the parameters given by the node or close the connection and search for a more suitable counterparty. To close a connection, we need to use:

```
lightning-cli disconnect ChannelID
```

In our case, however, the other node's expectations were acceptable to us so that we agreed upon investing 500,000,000msat, that is, 500,000 satoshis.

The command for funding a new payment channel is

```
lightning-cli fundchannel ChannelID amount_of_satoshis
```

Immediately, we would get back the raw transaction and its ID, which will be published on the blockchain. We will now have to wait for three confirmations before we can use the channel. In the meantime, we can explore it by issuing the command:

```
lightning-cli listpeers
```

Previously, it showed us only an empty list as no other node was connected with us. Now we get a large JSON object containing many details about our peer node, the channel, the funding amounts, and various other rules both nodes agreed upon.

The information about the current state of the channel is also there.

```
"status": [
"CHANNELD_AWAITING_LOCKING: Funding needs 3 more confirmations
to lockin."
]
```

The more peers we get, the larger the output of listpeers will become. Also, our wallet balance has changed as we can see it by executing

```
lightning-cli listfunds
```

Previously, the channels property of the returned JSON object was empty. This time it contains information about funds that were used to fund our payment channel. We also can use our private Bitcoin *testnet* explorer to search for our funding transaction. But as the Bitcoin *testnet* is globally available, any other *testnet* explorer could be used as well.

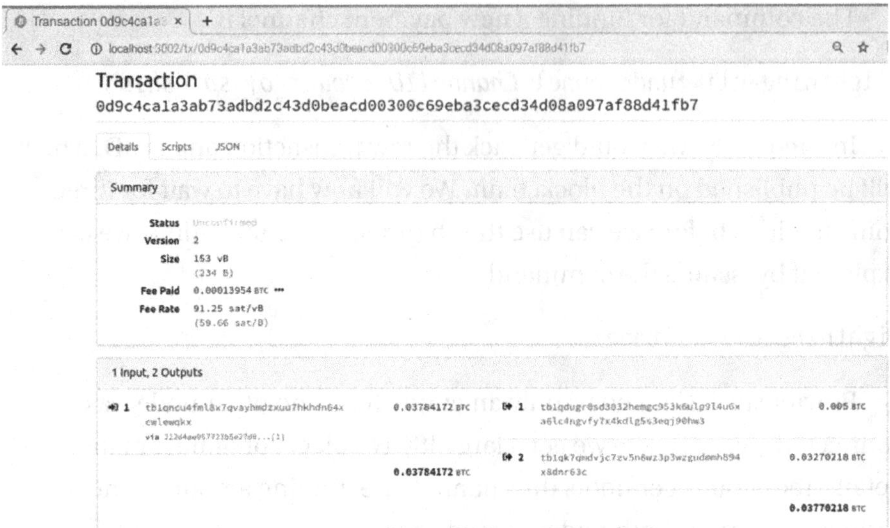

Figure 10-4. *Searching for funding transaction in testnet explorer*

One must take into account that block generation in Bitcoin's *testnet* is not as predictable as in *mainnet*. Therefore, it could take a considerable amount of time until the three blocks get generated.

Ultimately, the funding transaction will get confirmed which will be indicated by a changed entry in peer information JSON.

```
"status": [
"CHANNEL_NORMAL: Funding transaction locked."
]
```

The output of getinfo has changed as well.

```
"num_peers": 1,
"num_pending_channels": 0,
"num_active_channels": 1,
"num_inactive_channels": 0,
```

We have successfully funded our first payment channel. Both nodes can now send payments and generate invoices. However, to increase our networking capability, we should connect more nodes. For example, the node that belongs to operators of the search engine we used can be found here (Figure 10-5).

```
https://1ml.com/testnet/node/02312627fdf07fbdd7e5ddb136611bdde9
b00d26821d14d94891395452f67af248
```

Figure 10-5. *Searching for peer nodes*

To create a payment channel with it, we repeat the commands and only replace the NodeID and IP:

```
lightning-cli connect \ 02312627fdf07fbdd7e5ddb136611bdde9b00d2
6821d14d94891395452f67af248@23.237.77.12:9735
```

After the connection got established, we fund the new channel with

```
lightning-cli fundchannel \ 02312627fdf07fbdd7e5ddb136611bdde9b
00d26821d14d94891395452f67af248 100000
```

Here I have funded the channel with 100,000 satoshis.

Similarly, we will have to wait for three blocks for our funding transaction to get confirmed. After a while, we will be able to find our node by entering its ID in the search engine.

Figure 10-6. *Searching for own Lightning Node*

There is also an option to claim ownership of a node. A user would be asked to open a channel to search engine's public node with a certain amount of satoshis defined by the search engine, which will only be shown to the user. For this, obviously, one has to register there first.

Running c-lightning on Regtest

An alternative way of learning how to use c-lightning would be to run our Bitcoin Core node in *regtest* mode and with multiple lightningd processes. They would access the same *regtest datadir* of the Bitcoin daemon. In our case the default *datadir* is $HOME/.bitcoin. We'd also need a separate *regtest* lightning directories for each lightningd, because the current one we use was created under *testnet,* and its sqlite3 database wouldn't be compatible with the *regtest* network.

As c-lightning uses the sqlite3[1] database internally, each network needs a separate one. One can't switch from one network to another without having created a new sqlite3 database for it. Therefore, we

---

[1]https://sqlite.org

create two separate directories, .lightningd_regtest1 and .lightningd_ regtest2, and initialize two separate lightningd processes with following parameters:

```
lightningd --network regtest --lightning-dir \ $HOME/.
lightning_regtest1 --bitcoin-datadir \ $HOME/.bitcoin    --addr
127.0.0.1:20000 --daemon
```

```
lightningd --network regtest --lightning-dir \ $HOME/.
lightning_regtest2 --bitcoin-datadir \ $HOME/.bitcoin --addr
127.0.0.1:20001 --daemon
```

Then we can generate a few bitcoins by using the RPC calls generate or generatetoaddress from the console with the bitcoin-cli tool. And just like with *testnet* nodes, we would have to fund our two *regtest* variants by using the same set of commands as already done in *testnet*. The last step will be to connect those nodes with each other by using their lightning IDs, which we can get with the command lightning-cli getinfo. Of course, our single Bitcoin node must already be running in *regtest* mode, which we declare by activating the option regtest=1 in bitcoin.conf. However, this setup wouldn't be as "realistic" as the one with testnet.

Using c-lightning

With our configured *testnet* node, we should now try to use our payment channels for buying something. One good opportunity to test the machinery is the website https://starblocks.acinq.co where we can buy cappuccino from a demo coffee shop (Figure 10-7).

Figure 10-7. *A Lightning coffee shop*

After we have selected our favorite coffee variant, we click "*checkout*" and copy the given payment request. A payment request is a long alphanumeric string that always begins with *ln* and the network prefix, which in our case is *tb1* (Figure 10-8).

Figure 10-8. *A Lightning payment request with QR code*

Alternatively, we could have paid our coffee with an application that supports QR codes. And in the following chapters, we will install such an application. Our next console command is `lightning-cli pay`, which we use to pay the invoice. We simply copy the given `bolt11` string from the payment request when executing this command.

The returned result contains information about the payment status, its destination, and the amount paid in milli-satoshis. Simultaneously, the coffee shop will inform us about the successful payment as well (Figure 10-9). This is the power of the Lightning Network. *Instant payments* without trusted intermediaries and waiting times like block confirmations.

Figure 10-9. *Payment successful*

We can also decode the payment request with

```
lightning-cli decodepay BOLT11
```

Replace BOLT11 with the bolt11 string from your payment. You should get a JSON object containing data like this:

```
{
    "currency": "tb",
    "created_at": 1567804722,
    "expiry": 3600,
    "payee": "03933884aaf1d6b108397e5efe5c86bcf2d8ca8d2f700eda99
    db9214fc2712b134",
    "msatoshi": 1900000,
    "amount_msat": "1900000msat",
    "description": "1 Scala Chip Frappuccino",
    "min_final_cltv_expiry": 20,
    "payment_hash": "0085fac18d88cc622ba9fdbd8567ff47f0083efd94e
    254a2c9684f09ea0f616b",
    "signature": "30440220020e2bcc88f6996714056557164467640731 8e
    3b15578ff9076cc68779a6638e02204afe1dd6eabddac6bfd3fa5c010c13
    e834dfc9e058a1e4003f0a267b57abe8a1"
}
```

Indeed, it is always a good idea to check the contents of payment requests before paying them, especially when dealing with unknown services. The same functionality is also available in various mobile applications that can read QR codes. To list all previous payments the command listpayments can be used.

Currently, there is only one payment, so the list in this node is rather short. To issue a payment request on our own, we have the command invoice that needs a few parameters:

- Requested amount in milli-satoshis

- Payment name

- Payment description

There are another parameters, like *expiry time* and *fallback addresses*, which we don't need right now.

```
lightning-cli invoice 100 "PaymentRequest1" \
"my fist payment request"
```

The resulting JSON object contains the payment hashes, the default expiration time and the most important entry: the bolt11 string. This is our own payment request similar to the one we just paid. The warning in the last line is informing us that our node isn't well-connected, which is currently the case as we only have one payment channel open. Therefore, we should open more and especially open more channels with nodes that offer sufficient liquidity. We could also decode our payment request with decodepay.

We would now have to forward this request to the paying side. This can be done via any other transport medium, as long as the original *bolt11* string remains unchanged and paid within the given expiry time, which is 1 week by default. And of course, there is a command to list them all:

```
lightning-cli listinvoices
```

Activating Experimental Features

The functionalities we used so far are part of every c-lightning
distribution. However, there is a way to activate special features, which
are useful for people who want to try out different scenarios, especially
when working on c-lightning's source code. It is needless to say that such
features could be very dangerous and provoke various problems ranging
from "normal" ones like daemon crashes up to losing assets. But as long
as the binaries are being executed in *testnet* or *regtest* mode, the risks are
acceptable. To activate them, the following flags must be added when
executing the configure script.

- --enable-developer

- --enable-experimental-features

- --disable-valgrind

- --enable-static

The first two options activate the compilation of developer and
experimental features, while the other two remove extra checks and
activate static builds, which create single binary bundles that don't load
external libraries. After having recompiled the binaries, we get a new group
of commands.

```
=== developer ===

dev subcommand=crash|rhash|slowcmd
    Developer command test multiplexer

dev-compact-gossip-store
    Ask gossipd to rewrite the gossip store.

dev-fail id
    Fail with peer {id}

dev-forget-channel id [short_channel_id] [force]
    Forget the channel with peer {id}, ignore UTXO check with {force}='true'.

dev-ignore-htlcs id ignore
    Set ignoring incoming HTLCs for peer {id} to {ignore}

dev-listaddrs [bip32_max_index]
    Show addresses list up to derivation {index} (default is the last bip32 index)

dev-memdump
    Show memory objects currently in use

dev-memleak
    Show unreferenced memory objects
```

Figure 10-10. *New commands for lightning-cli*

Using Plugins

c-lightning is very modular and capable of loading of plugins, which can be written in any programming language that can process streams from stdin (standard input) and stdout (standard output). A plugin is a separate piece software that lightningd will load at start. A plugin can be as simple as a logger or very complex with several commands, which can be activated with lightning-cli. The capability of introducing new commands, which can then be used via the standard interface, lightning-cli, is a powerful feature of c-lightning. A new command would basically become part of the standard interface with its own help information and error handling.

To load a plugin, one must provide its full path by using the --plugin flag. There exists a GitHub repository with many interesting community-provided plugins. https://github.com/lightningd/plugins. We will clone it to our device by using the standard git clone command. A good start into c-lightning's plugin system will be the summary plugin from this repository. The plugin itself is written in Python, which we have already installed during our previous compilation tasks. Our first step will be to install the needed requirements for this plugin. For this we use the standard package manager pip3. We go into the subdirectory with cd summary and execute the following command from there:

```
sudo pip3 install -r requirements.txt
```

The pylightning package that got installed by pip3 is the client library for lightningd. It implements the mechanics needed for communication with the Unix socket offered by lightningd. Every lightningd plugin must communicate over this socket. However, as dealing with Unix sockets is not very intuitive and error prone, libraries like pylightning are here to take away a lot of burden regarding "ceremonial code" so that plugin developers can concentrate on more important tasks.

To load test the plugin, we will have to stop our current lightningd instance with:

```
lightning-cli stop.
```

Then we will start it again, but this time with the plugin flag added to it:

```
lightningd --plugin=/home/pi/ln-plugins/summary/summary.py
```

The daemon will start, and it would look like nothing else happened. However, the plugin is there and running. It even got integrated into lightning-cli. If we execute lightning-cli help, the following entry would be shown among the usual commands.

```
summary
        Gets summary information about this node.
```

And it also provides its own help information when we execute this:

```
lightning-cli help summary
```

To use the plugin, we won't have to deal with new binaries or interfaces as all communication would still go over the standard lightning-cli interface.

To execute the plugin, one has to type in this command:

```
lightning-cli -H summary
```

How the Plugin System Works

Essentially, for a plugin to be considered valid by lightnignd, it has to understand at least these two methods: init and getmanifest[2]. The init method must be available in the plugin so that lightningd can establish a communication channel with it. After the init method has been called by lightningd, the plugin must respond. The response itself can be any data as the current version of lightningd is simply discarding them. The important part is the *signal given by the plugin* that it's ready to process commands which will be sent to it later.

The second method, getmanifest, is more complex and is being used to describe the plugin so that lightningd knows what the plugin can do. The information in getmanifest is organized as a JSON object and comprises of following parts:

- options
- rpcmethods
- subscriptions
- hooks
- dynamic

Except dynamic, all others are data arrays. A plugin can declare itself "dynamic", which means that it can be managed later, while lightningd

---

[2]https://lightning.readthedocs.io/PLUGINS.html#a-day-in-the-life-of-a-plugin

is running. For plugins that should never be stopped, this entry must be set to "false". Plugins can provide their own methods, which then will be shown among the standard commands in `lightning-cli`. The `summary` plugin we used is providing such a command that is declared by its `getmanifest` entry. In such cases, a plugin is acting as an extension to the standard machinery provided by the `c-lightning` suite.

But a plugin doesn't have to provide a command to be accepted. It can also be just a passive consumer of events generated by `lightnignd`. For this the subscription part in the `getmanifest` definition should be used to define, which events the plugin is interested in. The following is an example with two event subscriptions.

```
"subscriptions": [
            "connect",
            "disconnect"
    ],
```

Although being rather small, plugins are powerful entities that can be combined with other environments running outside `c-lightning`. For example, a plugin could take data from `lightningd` and forward it to a web-API, which then would be used by a web server to generate reports on the current state of `lightningd`. `c-lightning` and other BOLT implementations provide backend services that take care of connecting and managing the Lightning Network without dictating what else should be done with them. It's up to users and application developers to provide meaningful and user-friendly applications that run on top of the raw machinery.

Writing a Plugin

We will create a JavaScript plugin that listens to events[3] from `lightningd` and writes them to a logfile in `/tmp` directory. In particular, we are interested in these events which we define in `config.json` file:

```
{
    "subscriptions": [
        "connect",
        "disconnect",
        "channel_opened",
        "invoice_payment",
        "warning",
        "forward_event",
        "sendpay_success",
        "sendpay_failure"
    ]
}
```

The configuration file gets loaded by `plugin.js` script source, where the whole logic of the plugin resides. To start the plugin script, we have to activate the daemon with the `--plugin` flag that gives the full path of the plugin source file.

```
lightningd --plugin=$HOME/ln-plugin-js/plugin.js
```

The output in the console would contain basic information about your `lightnind` instance.

---

[3]https://github.com/ElementsProject/lightning/blob/master/doc/PLUGINS.md

315

```
2019-09-28T11:51:32.795Z INFO raspi-lightning -----------------
2019-09-28T11:51:32.795Z INFO raspi-lightning Server started
with public key 0370e894fa6e8ff735dc3278543ea2718c632ce380aaf30
ce35fa261e8c0c7611e, alias BTC-TEST-RASPI-LIGHTNING-NODE (color
#ca1f7b) and lightningd v0.7.2.1-307-g12da10c
```

But before trying to start the plugin, we must take care of marking it executable so that `lightningd` can start it. This is done with

```
chmod +x plugin.js
```

When we open `plugin.js` in an editor, we see that it begins with the usual header, or *shebang*,[4] that declares its loader mechanism. Then come a few lines of `require` imports, because our plugin relies on several external packages that we have previously installed by executing npm `install` from within plugin's directory.

```
#!/usr/bin/env node
const fs = require('fs');
const split = require('split');
const config = require('./config.json');
const logfile = '/tmp/clightning.log';

const logger = require('tracer').console({
  transport : (data) => {
      fs.createWriteStream(logfile, {
          flags: 'a',
          encoding: 'utf8',
          mode: 0666
      }).write(`${data.rawoutput}\n`);
  }
});
```

---

[4]https://en.wikipedia.org/wiki/Shebang_(Unix)

```
let inputLine = '';
const manifestJson = {
  "jsonrpc": "2.0",
  "id": 1,
  "result": {
    "options": [],
    "rpcmethods": [],
    "subscriptions": config.subscriptions
  }
};

function log(severity, message) {
  logger.info(`${severity} | ${message}`);
}

function processLine (line) {
  inputLine += line;
  try
  {
    const json = JSON.parse(inputLine);
    inputLine = "";

    if (json["method"] == 'init') {
      process.stdout.write(JSON.parse('{}'));
      log('info', 'init call answered');
    } else if (json["method"] == 'getmanifest') {
      manifestJson.id = json.id;
      process.stdout.write(JSON.stringify(manifestJson));
      log('info', JSON.stringify(manifestJson));
```

```
    } else {
      log('info', JSON.stringify(json));
    }
  }
  catch(e){
  }
}
function initPlugin() {
  log('info', 'starting plugin');
  process.stdin.pipe(split()).on('data', processLine);
};

module.exports = initPlugin();
```

The logging mechanism of our plugin is based on an external npm package called tracer.[5] After having declared the transport logic that should be used by tracer, we define the expected manifestJson variable. This structure describes our plugin. In our case, we're only interested in listening to events so that rpcmethods and options property in manifestJson will remain empty. If we were instead declaring own functions and options, we would be using them. The third property, subscriptions, is where we use the data gathered from config.json to declare all the events our plugin wants to hear about. This way we can simply change the contents of config.json without touching the script itself. All it needs is a restart of the plugin.

The most important function is processLine, where the communication between plugin and lightningd happens. More precisely, lightningd is sending chunks of data via stdin (standard input). It then expects the plugin to combine and parse those chunks into meaningful JSON objects and eventually answer with new JSON objects by using

---

[5]www.npmjs.com/package/tracer

stdout (standard output). Therefore, our plugin is not allowed to use stdin/stdout for anything else, like console outputs for example. If we want to output something on our console, we can use stderr instead. An example of an entry in /tmp/clightning.log that informs about a successful payment would look like this:

```
2019-09-28T13:44:43+0200 <info> plugin.js:40 (log) info |
{"jsonrpc":"2.0","method":"sendpay_success","params":{"sendpay_
success":{"id":7,"payment_hash":"3c4e92dad907428653cb6b9e4cf795
57912625d843180237f5892b4889b27c6e","destination":"03933884aaf1
d6b108397e5efe5c86bcf2d8ca8d2f700eda99db9214fc2712b134",
"msatoshi":1900000,"amount_msat":"1900000msat","msatoshi_sent":
1900002,"amount_sent_msat":"1900002msat","created_at":1569671081,
"status":"complete","payment_preimage":"3f78998a26f96305a44e891
a4c52122f4d685be76da9c7c267d7a3a82c187561","bolt11":"lntb19u1pw
c73uepp5838f9kkeqapgv57tdw0yeau427gjvfwcgvvqydl43y453zdj03hqdp8
xys9xcmpd3sjqsmgd9czq3njv9c8qatrvd5kumccqp5lvqz4au3vpge8lx70948
3ecxfkwvnzrvgmzh7x54xw0l3jfts558xh7p3jxm6sk7eulm4c5gg00w8rkk508
tvacwh4mtf2my6ezprwcqnx4muq"}}}
```

Here we have bought some coffee from our shop, and the corresponding event sendpay_success was generated by lightningd.

The plugin.js code itself is being executed at the end of the source file by using the module.exports statement that maps to initPlugin() function call. As we aren't interested in "exporting" any function to lightningd, which wouldn't be able to understand it anyway, we instead call the function initPlugin() and forward its results to lightningd. In this case the result is a working plugin that immediately starts reading data from stdin and registers itself by replying to init and getmanifest methods sent by lightningd. From this point on, the whole communication is basically a continuous exchange of JSON data.

Running c-lightning with systemd

Being a daemon itself, it is obvious that the best way to run lightningd is by writing a separate systemd script which would start it at each boot. We will create a new file called clightning.service in the standard systemd directory under /etc/systemd/system.

```
[Unit]
Description=c-lightning network daemon
Requires=bitcoin.service
After=bitcoin.service

[Service]
ExecStart=/usr/local/bin/lightningd --daemon --testnet \
        --lightning-dir=/home/pi/.lightning \
        --conf=/home/pi/.lightning/config \
        --log-file=/home/pi/.lightning/lightning.log
PIDFile=/home/pi/.lightning/lightningd-testnet.pid
User=pi
Group=pi
Type=forking
Restart=always
RestartSec=10
PrivateTmp=true
ProtectSystem=full
NoNewPrivileges=true
PrivateDevices=true
MemoryDenyWriteExecute=true
```

To make sure that it will start only after bitcoin.service has started, we add a starting requirement in the [Unit] part of its configuration. The [Service] part describes the execution of lightningd and the configuration options it needs to select the correct network. The PIDFile entry is important, because for every network type we use, its `pidfile` should reflect the name of the network. The hardening measures at the end are for protecting the operating system from attacks, for example, in cases when the service got compromised.

To activate it, we use the standard `systemctl` command `enable`.

```
sudo systemctl enable clightning
```

Now we can either reboot our device and wait for Bitcoin and c-lightning services to boot or start it immediately with

```
sudo systemctl start clightning.
```

To trace its execution, we can use the `journalctl` with

```
journalctl -f -u clightning
```

Summary

In this chapter we have learned to build, use, and extend the c-lightning implementation of the BOLT protocol. We have learned how to find other nodes and open payment channels with them. Also, we have learned how to buy coffee by using the Lightning Network and experience fast payments without any intermediaries and long block generation times. We have learned about the extensibility of c-lightning and how to use its plugin system. And to make our Lightning Node as automatic as possible, we have written a `systemd` script that starts the Lightning Network machinery at boot.

CHAPTER 11

LND

In this chapter we will learn how to use LND,[1] an implementation of the BOLT specification written in Go.[2] LND is compatible to `c-lightning,` and everything we have learned so far can be applied on it as well.

Compilation

To compile LND we will have first to download and set up our Go development environment. As LND needs a version of Go that's not available in the official Raspbian apt packages, we will download a precompiled binary package and extract it manually. The package should be downloaded in the $HOME directory of the current user. Although this book can't teach you much about Go, let's just give a short description of it. Go is a relatively new programming language developed by Google. Its primary purpose is development of backend services that should run for a long time without being interrupted. Go has a C-like syntax, but unlike C it uses a garbage collector that takes care of memory management, thus relieving the programmer from all the problematic `malloc/free` function calls and unsafe pointer operations, that very often sit at the root of so many software vulnerabilities and sudden crashes.

```
wget https://dl.google.com/go/go1.13.linux-armv6l.tar.gz
tar xvf go1.13.linux-armv6l.tar.gz
```

---

[1]https://github.com/lightningnetwork/lnd
[2]https://golang.org/

© Harris Brakmić 2019
H. Brakmić, *Bitcoin and Lightning Network on Raspberry Pi,*
https://doi.org/10.1007/978-1-4842-5522-3_11

A new directory named go will be created. The executables are located under $HOME/go/bin which we want to declare as globally available. For this we open the $HOME/.bashrc file with an editor. This file is where our *bash shell* settings and other properties are located.

We will then add this line to the end of .bashrc.

```
export PATH=$PATH:$HOME/go/bin
```

We save the file and type source .bashrc in the console. Don't forget the dot before the file. This is the Unix/Linux convention for naming hidden files. To check that our go compiler is now available system-wide, we type this:

```
go version
```

It should return: go version go1.13 linux/arm

The next step will be to prepare the source directories for golang's artifacts and binaries. We will create a directory named gocode in the current $HOME directory and later add two new paths to .bashrc. The first one is $HOME/gocode itself, that will serve as GOPATH, which must always be present, because golang demands it. This directory is where all cloned sources, artifacts, and binaries will be located. The second path points to where our future LND binaries will be, so we want them to be globally available as well.

```
export GOPATH=$HOME/gocode
export PATH=$PATH:$GOPATH/bin
```

We are now ready to get LND sources. We only need a single command that will kick off everything and download not only LND but also all of its dependencies.

```
go get -d github.com/lightningnetwork/lnd
```

The sources will be located in the GOPATH directory which comprises of three subdirectories: bin, pkg, and src. After the sources have been downloaded, we go into LND's source path inside GOPATH.

```
cd $GOPATH/src/github.com/lightningnetwork/lnd
```

There we execute our well-known tandem:

```
make && make install
```

This will kick off various compilations, not only of LND but also of every other dependency it needs to run.

This is one of the advantages of golang's environment as it offers transparent dependency management. Unlike other environments, where users have to take care of manually downloading and installing every single dependency, golang keeps the compilation and versioning invisible.

The compilation process we just started will need a few moments to complete, because LND references many other packages. Like c-lightning LND is a very modular package that comprises of several binaries. The two we will be dealing with are lnd, the daemon, and lncli, the command line interface. However, there are many other packages, for example, Neutrino, an alternative lightweight Bitcoin client software designed for mobile devices.

After the compilation process has ended, we will have new binaries in $GOPATH/bin.

On the next few pages, we will learn how to set up an lnd configuration file and how to create a separate wallet with lncli. We will see a few differences between c-lightning and LND regarding the configuration structure, but this won't be reflected on the public interface as both implementations are compatible to each other. It is very easy to connect different types of nodes together, which we will try out later in this chapter.

Configuration

The LND daemon uses a configuration file called lnd.conf that's by default located in a hidden directory named .lnd. After we have compiled LND sources, we manually create such a directory and put this file into it.

```
mkdir $HOME/.lnd
touch $HOME/.lnd/lnd.conf
```

We will then open lnd.conf with a text editor to enter configuration settings that will define the name of the node, the used ports, and the location of the *macaroon* files, which are decentralized bearer credentials, that can be issued for various tasks and with different access rights.

```
[Application Options]
debuglevel = info
maxpendingchannels=5
no-macaroons = false
alias = LND_NODE_NAME_HERE
color = #BBA142
datadir = "~/.lnd/data"
listen=:9736
adminmacaroonpath = \ "~/.lnd/data/chain/bitcoin/testnet/admin.
macaroon"
readonlymacaroonpath = \ "~/.lnd/data/chain/bitcoin/testnet/
readonly.macaroon"
invoicemacaroonpath = \ "~/.lnd/data/chain/bitcoin/testnet/
invoice.macaroon"
```

At the first start, LND will create two of them: admin.macaroon and read_only.macaroon. Also, it will generate a macaroons.db file. For every network being used (*mainnet, testnet*), there will be a separate set of macaroons that can be found in separate chain-directories inside .lnd. In general, the admin.macaroon file should be treated as a private key, because those who have access to it have also access to all funds that are locked in LND-based nodes. In *testnet* scenarios this might be a less important issue, but when running on *mainnet,* one simply can't be paranoid enough. One should take great care of those files.

lnd.conf comprises of five parts:

- Node settings

- RPC/API settings

- Network/blockchain settings

- Autopilot settings

- Bitcoin daemon settings

Not all of them are mandatory, like autopilot, but it's always a good strategy to try them out. Apart from macaroon settings, the others are more or less the same as in c-lightning's configuration. The important difference here is the selected port number that is not the default 9735 to prevent port blocking when c-lightning is running at the same time. Indeed, it is possible to run different daemons as the same time on a single hardware platform, as long as their identities and ports are different. Additionally, LND offers the option of using NAT (network address translation) for scenarios where nodes are running in local non-routable networks.

Similar to Bitcoin's daemon, LND can listen to API queries via RPC and REST.

```
rpclisten=localhost:10009
rpclisten=[::1]:10010
restlisten=localhost:8080
restlisten=localhost:8443
```

The network and blockchain settings define the network and Bitcoin daemon that should be used. In our case this will be *testnet* and bitcoind daemon.

```
[Bitcoin]
bitcoin.mainnet = 0
bitcoin.testnet = 1
bitcoin.active = 1
bitcoin.node = bitcoind
```

The autopilot is an interesting feature of LND as it allows automatic creation of payment channels. In the autopilot settings, we can declare how much of the available funds should be reserved for this functionality and also the number of allowed nodes. In our case, however, the autopilot is deactivated.

```
[autopilot]
autopilot.active = 0
autopilot.maxchannels = 5
autopilot.allocation = 0.6
```

The last entry describes the connection settings for bitcoind's RPC API and the ZMQ messaging interface that we have met in Chapter 6.

```
[bitcoind]
bitcoind.rpchost = localhost:18332
bitcoind.rpcuser = raspiuser
bitcoind.rpcpass = mypassword
bitcoind.zmqpubrawblock=tcp://127.0.0.1:28332
bitcoind.zmqpubrawtx=tcp://127.0.0.1:28333
```

After we have saved this file, we can execute lnd in the console and observe its log messages. After a few promising messages, the daemon stops and expects us to unlock its wallet.

```
LTND: Waiting for wallet encryption password. Use `lncli
create` to create a wallet, `lncli unlock` to unlock an
existing wallet, or `lncli changepassword` to change the
password of an existing wallet and unlock it.
```

Unlike with `c-lightning`, where a wallet got created automatically, here we have to manually set up a wallet and also secure the 24-word seed mnemonic, which can be used to recreate this wallet. Therefore, before we continue our journey with LND, we have to use the other binary that got compiled at the beginning: `lncli`, the command line interface. We type `lncli create` in the console. A dialog will appear asking us for a password and an optional seed mnemonic. For now, we simply say "no" and let the tool generate a new wallet and mnemonic for us. This mnemonic should be safely stored so we can later restore the wallet.

After we have set up our wallet and secured the mnemonic, we are ready to start LND. We type another command with `lncli`, but this time to unlock the wallet:

`lncli unlock.`

For this operation to succeed, the LND should be already running and waiting for the unlock command to complete. This is how the daemon would react after the wallet got unlocked.

```
LNWL: Opened wallet
Sep 21 22:14:47 lnd lnd[13253]: 2019-09-21 22:14:47.974 [INF]
LTND: Primary chain is set to: bitcoin
Sep 21 22:14:47 lnd lnd[13253]: 2019-09-21 22:14:47.986 [INF]
LTND: Initializing bitcoind backed fee estimator
Sep 21 22:14:47 lnd lnd[13253]: 2019-09-21 22:14:47.987 [INF]
LNWL: Started listening for bitcoind block notifications via
ZMQ on 127.0.0.1:28332
Sep 21 22:14:47 lnd lnd[13253]: 2019-09-21 22:14:47.987 [INF]
LNWL: Started listening for bitcoind transaction notifications
via ZMQ on 127.0.0.1:28333
```

The daemon is now capable of reading its wallet and communicating with `bitcoind` process.

It will now take a few moments to synchronize with the current blockchain. For the current setup to work, it is needed to let LND daemon run in a separate window (tab) or shell. Apart from unlocking the wallet, there will be no other interaction with LND so that lncli will serve as the gateway to the daemon and its functionalities, very similar to lightning-cli.

On the next few pages, we will be creating new channels by using similar commands. Most of the time, the commands will even have the same semantic meaning, which is expectable as both daemons implement the same specification, BOLT.

Using LND

Our first step toward a working LND node is to load up some tBTC. Here we can use the previously mentioned tBTC faucets. The command for creating a new address in LND is

```
lncli -n testnet newaddress p2wkh
```

The option -n testnet is important to inform lncli about the network currently being used. By default, lncli refers to *mainnet* which is not the case in this example.

To get information about our current balance, we use:

```
lncli walletbalance.
```

It will return a JSON object containing the general balance and the information of how much of it is confirmed.

```
{
    "total_balance": "9504751",
    "confirmed_balance": "9504751",
    "unconfirmed_balance": "0"
}
```

To open a new payment channel, we need to find a public node, which we can easily find via https://ml1.com/testnet. Our first step will be to open a connection to another node:

```
lncli -n testnet connect NodeID
```

The result returned will be an empty JSON file, which is a good indicator. When an error happens, this object contains a description of the error. Now we can try to open a payment channel with this node by using its NodeID with the command openchannel. The parameter --local_amt indicates the amount of satoshis we are going to use to fund the channel.

```
Lncli -n testnet openchannel NodeID --local_amt SATOSHIS
```

If the opening was successful, the result would contain the funding transaction ID. The status can be queried with pendingchannels command. After a while the needed confirmation level will be reached, and the returned value from pendingchannels will become empty. We now get our new payment channel shown in the list returned by listchannels.

Payments and Invoices with LNCLI

To pay with LND, we use the lncli's command payinvoice, which we give the bolt11 string we already approached in the last chapter. The difference between c-lightning and LND is that LND asks for confirmation before the payment is being sent. Apart from the required flag --pay_req for the bolt11 string, the rest of the process is the same.

To create an invoice, we use the addinvoice with parameters --amt for the expected amount in satoshis and --memo which is a short description of the invoice being created.

```
lncli -n testnet addinvoice --amt 1 --memo\
"and invoice with LND"
```

The property pay_req in the returned JSON contains the bolt11 string that the paying side should use.

```
{
    "r_hash": "76b9aad1bce2cb3bd76dfe2b6c67e5a9985568cf2f0c0
    587170a4899c5876b50",
    "pay_req": "lntb10n1pwcdpsupp5w6u645duut9nh4mdlc4kcel94x
    v926x09uxqtpchpfyfn3v8ddgqdqlv9hzq6twwehkjcm9ypmkjargypx
    yu3qcqzpgflspyjqv5jamc05w7738k3w5hz8kh7ahe3p04jkf0x95271
    zms4jm87ncnefh5q4k6ukvu49m6nd8vkeqrjrmcamk48mphjp72e0p4c
    qeglj7r",
    "add_index": 1
}
```

Running LND with systemd

LND is a daemon and therefore perfect for running under systemd. Just like we did with bitcoind and c-lightning, LND too will get its configuration file that will start it on each boot. But unlike c-lightning we will have to provide the password with lncli manually. The content of LND's configuration file will comprise of settings for its name and requirements, its configuration paths and flags, as well as hardening settings to isolate it from the rest of the operating system.

```
[Unit]
Description=LND Lightning Daemon

[Service]
ExecStart=/home/pi/gocode/bin/lnd
ExecStop=/home/pi/gocode/bin/lncli stop
PIDFile=/home/pi/.lnd/lnd.pid
```

```
User=pi
Group=pi
Type=simple
KillMode=process
TimeoutStartSec=60
TimeoutStopSec=60
Restart=always
RestartSec=60

PrivateTmp=true
ProtectSystem=full
NoNewPrivileges=true
PrivateDevices=true
MemoryDenyWriteExecute=true
 [Install]
WantedBy=multi-user.target
```

We will activate our new service with `sudo systemd enable lnd`. We start the daemon with

```
sudo systemctl start lnd
```

We will query its status afterward with

```
systemctl status lnd
```

One more step is needed to unlock the wallet. `lncli unlock` will do this for us.

Signing and Verifying Messages

The `lncli` tool offers an easy-to-use message signature and verification functionality. With it one can generate messages that will be signed with the node's private key and can be verified on other nodes. To sign a message, one only needs to use the signmessage command together with the message that should be signed. The returned value would be the signature that will be later used to verify the message.

```
lncli -n testnet signmessage "hello, world"
{
    "signature": "d6rp9ba383k4xbhiwc3zw5q75wtd5aezrd8kxbm65t969
    9x848xsw8hrjycqxrtiohy94xqrtyitqfbpoj4k8fxa3ufnrenz1ji7gewz"
}
```

To verify the message, we need the signature created previously. In the command line, the signature follows the --sig flag.

```
lncli verifymessage --msg "hello, world" --sig \
d6rp9ba383k4xbhiwc3zw5q75wtd5aezrd8kxbm65t9699x848x
sw8hrjycqxrtiohy94xqrtyitqfbpoj4k8fxa3ufnrenz1ji7gewz
{
    "valid": true,
    "pubkey": "03052ae5c77d75264a13ab0d34520bd8260de9542e7d930
    cbe6bc5137485f065f3"
}
```

The returned result will then indicate if the given message and signature fit together.

Summary

In this chapter we have learned how to compile, install, and use the second BOLT implementation, LND. We have learned how to set up a Go programming language environment to compile LND's sources. We have also created a systemd configuration to start LND at each boot. We have also learned how to open and fund payment channels with LND.

CHAPTER 12

Web Apps

In this chapter we will learn how to set up user-friendly mobile apps for Lightning Network users. Undoubtedly, Lightning Network is a powerful platform, but like any other technology, it can only be of use to others if applications exist, that are user-friendly, intuitive, and abstracting away all the minute details only specialists should know.

Installing Spark Wallet

Spark Wallet[1] is a web-based wallet GUI that can run on desktop and mobile browsers. It runs on top of c-lightning and offers an intuitive UI and supports scanning of QR codes. It is available in the NPM package repository. It should be installed as globally available NodeJS package.

```
sudo npm install -g spark-wallet
```

By default, it listens on port 9737 where it can be accessed via any web browser. To start the wallet, type spark-wallet in the console. It will subsequently start its internal web server that will take care of forwarding data between the web browser and c-lightning daemon. It expects the c-lightning configuration to be located in .lightning directory, but this can be changed by giving it an alternative path with --ln-path parameter at start. By default, Spark Wallet generates a new administrator user and its

---

[1]https://github.com/shesek/spark-wallet

© Harris Brakmić 2019
H. Brakmić, *Bitcoin and Lightning Network on Raspberry Pi*,
https://doi.org/10.1007/978-1-4842-5522-3_12

password, if there is no existing cookie file in its `.spark-wallet` directory. To prevent this, use `--login` option to set up your own administrator account.

As long as the application is running, the console will be blocked. Later, we will learn how to configure a `systemd` service for Spark Wallet to have it running in the background. When we now open our browser at port 9737, we will be asked for username and password (Figure 12-1).

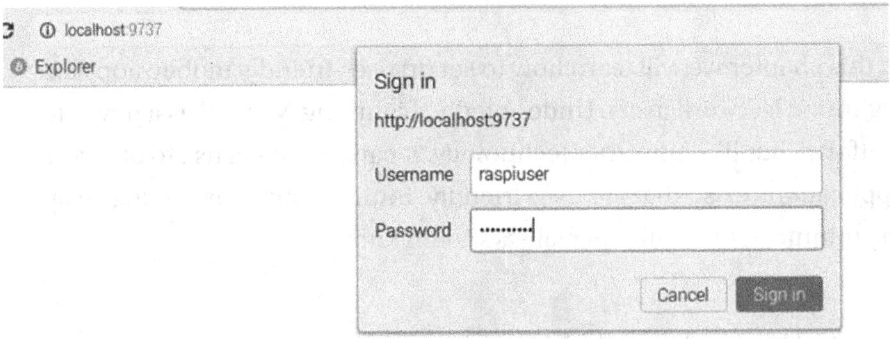

Figure 12-1. *Spark Wallet Administrator login*

This will happen only once at the initial start.

After we have entered our user data, a web page containing information about our device and funds will open. You also will be asked if the current web app is allowed to send you notifications (Figure 12-2). You should give it the needed permissions. This is especially useful when running it in a mobile browser.

Figure 12-2. *Show Spark Notifications in browser*

Ultimately, we will be presented a web page as shown in Figure 12-3.

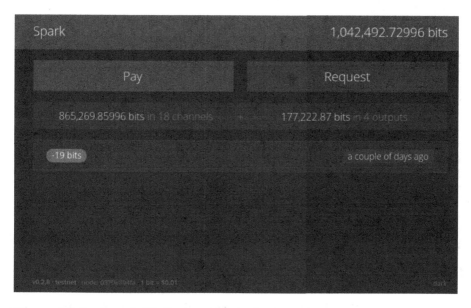

Figure 12-3. *Spark Wallet main window*

Although it might look minimalistic at the beginning, this web page contains everything a user-friendly wallet should have.

Using Spark Wallet

We can pay invoices, create our own payment requests, and browse through a list of our past payments, which are shown below the two buttons. There is also a short, green link visible in the footer of the page that leads to node management features (Figure 12-4).

Figure 12-4. *Link at the bottom of Spark's main window*

The channel list shows their activity, available funds, and peer information (Figure 12-5).

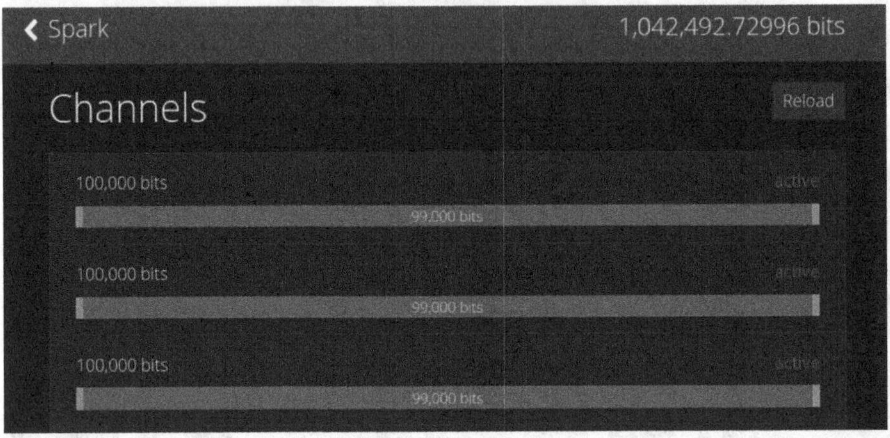

Figure 12-5. *Channel list*

Apart from listing data regarding current channels, Spark Wallet allows us to create new ones. At the end of the channel list is a button that leads to a web form for creating new channels (Figure 12-6).

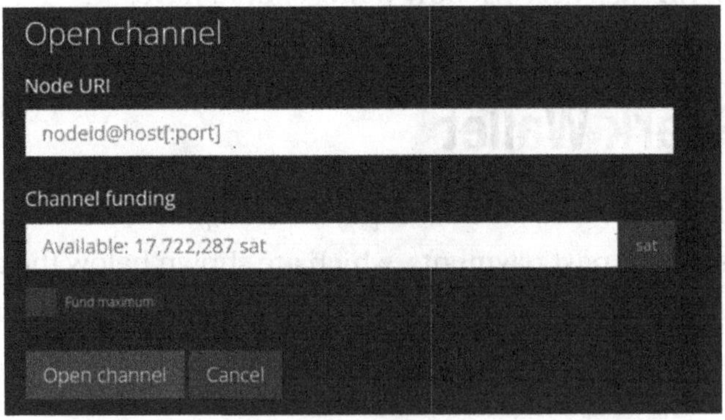

Figure 12-6. *Opening a new payment channel in Spark*

The two most important functions of course are paying invoices and generating requests. It only takes a few clicks to execute everything without much typing (Figure 12-7).

Figure 12-7. *Creating new payment requests*

To pay an invoice, we can either use QR Codes, for example, when running in a mobile browser, or via `bolt11` string as previously done with console-based tools (Figure 12-8).

Figure 12-8. *Decoding a payment request*

We can then confirm payment or reject it (Figure 12-9).

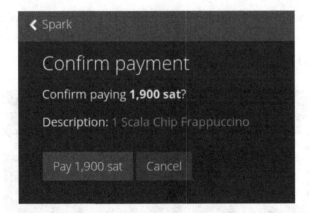

Figure 12-9. *Confirming a payment request*

A successful payment will be indicated both in the page header and in the list below (Figure 12-10).

Figure 12-10. *Header information about a successful payment*

Running Spark Wallet with systemd

Software like Spark Wallet, which is running its own server in the background, should usually run automatically and be ready as soon as possible. Therefore, we will set up a `systemd` service that will start Spark Wallet after `c-lightning` daemon it depends on. And as `c-lightning` itself depends on Bitcoin daemon, our Lightning Network node will become a well-designed little machine with all the tools needed to serve as a decentralized, user-friendly tool box.

We will open a new service file under /etc/system/system.

```
sudo nano /etc/systemd/system/spark-wallet.service
```

```
[Unit]
Description=Spark Wallet
Requires=clightning.service
After=network.target

[Service]
WorkingDirectory=/home/pi
User=pi
Group=pi
Type=simple
Restart=on-failure
RestartSec=5s
PrivateTmp=true
ExecStart=/usr/local/bin/node \
/usr/local/bin/spark-wallet --login raspiuser:mypassword

[Install]
WantedBy=multi-user.target
```

We will activate our new service with:

```
sudo system enable spark-wallet.
```

Ultimately, we start it with sudo systemctl start spark-wallet. Its outputs can be traced with sudo journalctl -f -u spark-wallet.

From now on, systemd will start Spark Wallet on every system start.

Installing Joule Browser Extension

Joule Browser extension is another user-friendly solution that abstracts away all the complexities of the Lightning Network without losing its most powerful features. Joule Browser depends on LND and can be installed with a few clicks. It supports Chrome, Firefox, Opera, and Brave browsers. In our case we will be using Chromium, the open-source variant of Google's Chrome. To begin with the installation of this browser add-on, we visit the vendor's page at `https://lightningjoule.com/` and click the button that says "Install for Google Chrome" (Figure 12-11).

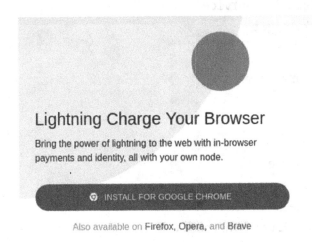

Figure 12-11. Joule home page

We will be redirected to Chrome Web Store where we start the installation by clicking the option "add to Chrome" (Figure 12-12).

Figure 12-12. Joule browser plugin from Chrome Web Store

342

After the installation has completed, our browser will inform us about a new plugin that's been added to it (Figure 12-13).

Figure 12-13. *Joule was installed successfully*

A new tab will be open automatically asking us what kind of node we are running. We select the first option "Local Node" (Figure 12-14).

Joule will request for additional permissions which we must allow, because it needs to communicate with the node via browser (Figure 12-15).

Figure 12-14. *Selecting a node type*

Figure 12-15. *Joule needs certain permissions to communicate with nodes*

The next step will ask us about the REST interface our LND daemon must operate for Joule to be able to communicate with it. By default, LND uses port 8443 for HTTPS and 8080 for HTTP. However, it could happen that a certificate warning like this would appear (Figure 12-16).

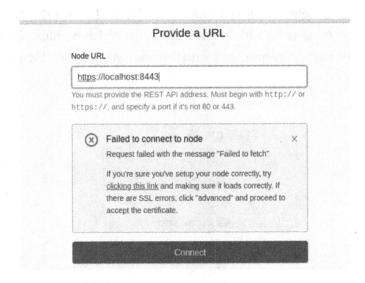

Figure 12-16. *Accessing the REST interface*

We can get rid of it by by opening a new tab and pointing the browser to https://127.0.0.1 that will lead to a similar certificate warning.

This has to do with the fact that LND generates its own, self-signed TLS certificates at the first start. They are located in its root directory .lnd.

The certificate warning we see in the new tab offers the option to "proceed to 127.0.0.1 (unsafe)" which of course isn't unsafe for us as this is our own daemon's TLS certificate. By clicking this link, Chromium would accept the certificate and stop throwing warnings about it in the future. We can now close this tab and try again to add the REST API (Figure 12-17).

This server could not prove that it is **127.0.0.1**; its security certificate is not trusted by your computer's operating system. This may be caused by a misconfiguration or an attacker intercepting your connection.

Proceed to 127.0.0.1 (unsafe)

Figure 12-17. *Accepting the self-signed certificate*

However, we should use https://127.0.0.1:8433 instead of the offered URL https://localhost:8443. The Joule add-on would now accept the URL and show us the next window for uploading macaroon files. These are located under .lnd/data/chain/bitcoin/testnet (Figure 12-18).

Figure 12-18. *Uploading macaroons*

If you can't see this directory, activate the option "show hidden files" in your file manager. After having uploaded the two macaroons, a node-confirmation window will appear (Figure 12-19). We are ready to use Joule with our node.

Figure 12-19. Confirm node settings

After we have confirmed it, a window with our node's data and available channels and peers will appear (Figure 12-20).

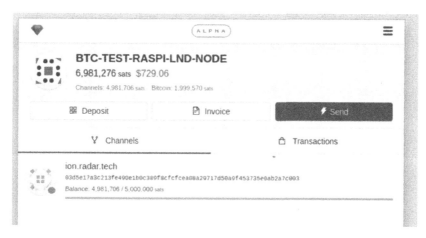

***Figure 12-20.** Node information window*

However, we don't have to use this window anymore as the same functionalities are from now on available via the small diamond logo in the upper right corner in the browser's window. The Joule browser plugin is a very user-friendly alternative to console tools from the LND suite we used before.

Summary

In this chapter we have learned how to install and configure web-based, user-friendly Lightning Network tools. Everything we learned in the previous chapters was hopefully interesting to tech-savvy users, but it wasn't that much user-friendly. For Lightning Network and Bitcoin to succeed, user-friendly tools that abstract away the complexities are of crucial importance. Spark Wallet and Joule that we used in this chapter are only two of many other examples being currently developed. The world of Lightning Network is still at the beginning, but we don't have to wait for too long as useful tools are available already.

APPENDIX A

Books and Papers

Books

Economics

Economics in One Lesson, *Henry Hazlitt*, ISBN-13: 978-0517548233

Basic Economics, *Thomas Sowell*, ISBN-13: 978-0465060733

Crashed: How a Decade of Financial Crises Changed the World, *Adam Tooze*, ISBN-13: 978-0670024933

The Ascent of Money, *Niall Ferguson*, ISBN-13: 978-0143116172

The Ethics of Money Production, *Jörg Guido Hülsmann*, ASIN: B003NX6Z3W

Denationalisation of Money, *F. A. Hayek*, ASIN: B005DTKORM

Society

The Sovereign Individual, *James Dale Davidson and Lord William Rees-Mogg*, ISBN-13: 978-0684832722

Exit, Voice, and Loyalty, *Albert O. Hirschman*, ASIN: 0674276604

© Harris Brakmić 2019
H. Brakmić, *Bitcoin and Lightning Network on Raspberry Pi*,
https://doi.org/10.1007/978-1-4842-5522-3

Technology

Mastering Bitcoin 2nd Edition, *Andreas Antonopoulos*, ASIN: B071K7FCD4

Programming Bitcoin, *Jimmy Song*, ISBN-13: 978-1492031499

A Dissection of Bitcoin, *Paul Huang*, ASIN: B0198LXI5K

Bitcoin Internals, *Chris Clark*, ASIN: B00DG8EPT0

Applied Cryptography, *Bruce Schneier*, ISBN-13: 978-1119096726

Essays and Papers

Bitcoin: A Peer-to-Peer Electronic Cash System, *Satoshi Nakamoto*, https://bitcoin.org/en/bitcoin-paper

Bitcoin's Academic Pedigree, *Arvind Narayanan and Jeremy Clark*, https://queue.acm.org/detail.cfm?id=3136559

Blockchain Proof-of-Work is a Decentralized Clock, *Gregory Trubetskoy*, https://grisha.org/blog/2018/01/23/explaining-proof-of-work/

Shelling Out: The Origins of Money, *Nick Szabo*, https://nakamoto institute.org/shelling-out/

Money, Blockchains, and social scalability, *Nick Szabo*, https://unenumerated.blogspot.com/2017/02/money-blockchains-and-social-scalability.html

The many traditions of non-governmental money (part I), *Nick Szabo*, https://unenumerated.blogspot.com/2018/03/the-many-traditions-of-non-governmental.html

Smart Contracts: Building Blocks for Digital Markets, *Nick Szabo*, https://web.archive.org/web/20151222144315/szabo.best.vwh.net/smart_contracts_2.html

APPENDIX B

Problems and Solutions

Bitcoin Core Wallet

Problem: The configuration script could throw the error: Configure could not find version of library.

Solution: Append flag --with-boost-libdir=/usr/lib/x86_64-linux-gnu to the configure script, for example:

```
./configure --with-boost-libdir=/usr/lib/x86_64-linux-gnu [...
other flags follow..]
```

On 32-bit Raspbian you should use */usr/lib/arm-linux-gnueabihf* instead.

LND

Problem: At start, LND throws the error: cannot unmarshal object into Go struct field GetBlockChainInfoResult.softforks

Solution: Check out one of the **v0.18.x** branches from bitcoin's repository (e.g., git checkout v0.18.1) and recompile and reinstall your local Bitcoin version. As of now (September 2019), LND only supports **v0.18.x** versions of Bitcoin Core reference client.

© Harris Brakmić 2019
H. Brakmić, *Bitcoin and Lightning Network on Raspberry Pi*,
https://doi.org/10.1007/978-1-4842-5522-3

Problem: How to create backups of channels and funds located in them?

Solution: Since v0.6 LND offers the *static channel backups* scheme.

There is a file in `.lnd/data/chain/bitcoin/testnet` (`mainnet`), called `channel.backup`, that is used to restore the channels. This file is encrypted with your wallet seed.

The official guide can be found here: `https://github.com/lightningnetwork/lnd/blob/master/docs/recovery.md`

However, take into account that by default *channel.backup* is located on the same dis*k* where LND runs, so it's always a good strategy to copy it to another disk. Here is a script that automatizes this task:

`https://gist.github.com/alexbosworth/2c5e185aedbdac45a03655b709e255a3`

More info on Static Channel Backups: `https://github.com/lightningnetwork/lnd/releases/tag/v0.6-beta`

c-lightning

Problem: How to create backups of channels and funds located in them?

Solution: Copy `hsm_secret` from `.lightning` to a safe place first. Later, in case your node has crashed, you should follow these instructions to get your funds back:

- Start `lightningd --port=0` (this disables any communication)

- Run `lightning-cli newaddr` a few times

- Stop lightning daemon with `lightning-cli stop`

- Run `sqlite3` with these options

  ```
  sqlite3 .lightning/lightningd.sqlite3 "UPDATE vars SET
  val= 500000 WHERE name='last_processed_block';"
  ```

- Start lightningd --port=0 again

- Initiate fund recovery with lightning-cli withdraw all

It will now depend on your peers how long it will take, until all channels are closed and your funds available again. Meanwhile *you will have to use another c-lightning instance* as this node wouldn't be available for any new channels or any other operations.

Important   Take care of not reusing or copying the `lightnind.sqlite3` database file. Publishing an old state in Lightning Network will provoke revocations of transactions, which ultimately lead to loss of funds.

Networking Problems

Problem: The UFW (firewall) is blocking UPnPC port mapping.
Solution: You should allow UDP packets for UPnPC inside your local network. Add this rule to your node's UFW filter rules (replace the **IP** range with your own):

> sudo ufw allow from **192.168.0.0/24** port 1900 to
> any proto udp

Index

A

Addresses
  Base58, 51, 56
  Bech32-type, 55
  Bitcoin address, generation, 53
  command getnewaddress, 54
  command line tool bitcoin-cli, 54
  double-SHA256 function, 52
  dumpwallet, 55
  key types, 54
  P2SH-type, 54
  public key, 52
  testnet and regtest types, 56
  walletpassphrase, 55
Asymmetric cryptography, 60, 74

B

Back-linked list of blocks, 17
Base58Check format, 52
Basis of lightning technology
        (BOLT), 267
Bech32-type address, 55
Bitcoin
  access, 169
  bitcoin-rpc-explorer, 256, 258
  blockchain (*see* Blockchain)

blockchain explorer, 255
compilation, 120–122
configuration file, 165–169
consensus rules, 7, 8
JavaScript language, 233
  asynchronous
      functions, 235, 236
  Bech32, 246–248
  bitcoin-core, 234
  bitcoinlib-js package, 238
  multisig script, 238, 240
  P2PKH, 238
  P2SH, 238
  package.json file, 233
  scriptPubKey, 244
  SegWit address, 241–244
  transaction data, 237
  transaction malleability
      problem, 244
  WIF keys, 249
JSON format, 168
monetary systems, 9
money, 3–6
public blockchain, 11–13
raw transaction
  createrawtransaction
      command, 179
  getblock command, 185

© Harris Brakmić 2019
H. Brakmić, *Bitcoin and Lightning Network on Raspberry Pi*,
https://doi.org/10.1007/978-1-4842-5522-3

M

U, V

UTXO set, 62

W, X, Y, Z

Wallet data, 129

Wallet encryption

    console window, 145

    menu entry, 141

    new password, 142

    private key, 146

    transactions tab, 143, 144

    walletpassphrase command execution, 145

warning message, 142

window menu, 144

Wallets

    keeping and managing key pairs, 78

    master private and public keys, 84

    nondeterministic and deterministic, 78

    password, 84

    private key, 83

    software and hardware tools, 79

    type-1 deterministic, 80

    type-2 deterministic, 81

    variants, 84

Web-based wallet, 335

Printed in the United States
By Bookmasters